Geo. N. McLean

The Rise and fall of Anarchy in America

From its Incipient Stage to the first Bomb Thrown in Chicago.

Geo. N. McLean

The Rise and fall of Anarchy in America
From its Incipient Stage to the first Bomb Thrown in Chicago.

ISBN/EAN: 9783743418943

Manufactured in Europe, USA, Canada, Australia, Japa

Cover: Foto ©ninafisch / pixelio.de

Manufactured and distributed by brebook publishing software (www.brebook.com)

Geo. N. McLean

The Rise and fall of Anarchy in America

LIBERTY ENLIGHTENING THE WORLD.

THE RISE AND FALL
—OF—
Anarchy in America.

FROM ITS INCIPIENT STAGE TO THE

FIRST BOMB THROWN IN CHICAGO.

A COMPREHENSIVE ACCOUNT OF THE GREAT CONSPIRACY
CULMINATING IN THE

Haymarket Massacre,

MAY 4th, 1886.

A MINUTE ACCOUNT OF THE APPREHENSION, TRIAL, CON-
VICTION AND EXECUTION OF THE LEADING
CONSPIRATORS.

——BY——

GEO. N. McLEAN.

"ORDER IS HEAVEN'S FIRST LAW."

PROFUSELY ILLUSTRATED.

SOLD BY SUBSCRIPTION ONLY.

R. G. BADOUX & Co.
CHICAGO & PHILADELPHIA.
1888.

CHAPTER I.

INTRODUCTION.

"Order is Heaven's First Law"—Liberty Enlightening the World—The Red Flag—The Price of Liberty—Our National Institutions—When Judgment and Justice is Abroad in the Land the People will Learn Righteousness ... 9

CHAPTER II.

ANARCHISTS.

Their Nationality — First Agitation—Leader of Anarchy — Revenge Circular— The Haymarket Meeting — The Lehr und Wehr Verein — The Massacre — Dispersing the Mob.. 12

CHAPTER III.

THE GREAT CONSPIRACY.

Bravery of the Police—The Occupation of the Conspirators—The Trial—Securing a Jury — Bombs in Court — Evidence of Detective Johnson—Parsons Swears He "Wont Eat Snow-Balls Next Winter"—Drilling Anarchists— Pinkerton Detectives—Cross-Examination—Bombs and Dynamite—Parsons' View of the Board of Trade—Guns, Dynamite and Prussic Acid Advocated by Spies—Prosecution Rests Its Case.. 20

CHAPTER IV.

THE DEFENSE.

Under a Cloud—A Struggle For Life—Contesting Every Point by Shrewd Counsel—Braving It Out — Throttling the Law — Fielden on the Stand —

CONTENTS.

Laughable Testimony by Henry Schultz, Who Said He was a Tourist—Schwab's Evidence—Spies Testifies—Postal Card From Herr Most—Close of the Defense... 64

CHAPTER V.
ARGUMENTS FOR THE PROSECUTION AND DEFENSE.

Opening Speech by Frank Walker—"We Stand in the Temple of Justice"—Zeisler for the Defense, Ingham for the Prosecution—Messrs. Foster and Black for the Defense — Julius S. Grinnell Makes Closing Speech for the State 100

CHAPTER VI.
INSTRUCTIONS OF THE COURT.

The Verdict—Blanched Faces—The Court to the Jury—Biography, Age and Residence of the Jurors.. 119

CHAPTER VII.
THE CONSPIRACY AND MASSACRE.

Names and Number of Killed and Wounded—Unearthing the Plot—Officers at Work—Crowned With Success—Report of Grand Jury—The Number of Widows and Orphans Resulting From One Explosion..................... 119

CHAPTER VIII.
COST OF TRIAL.

Extracts from *Zeitung*—Motion for New Trial—Motion Overruled............. 139

CHAPTER IX.
SPIES ADDRESSES THE COURT.

Three Days' Speeches by the Doomed Men—Their Reason Why the Law Should Not be Executed.. 150

CHAPTER X.
MISCELLANEOUS MATTER.

Arbeiter Zeitung— Mrs. Parsons — Her Arrest in Ohio—Her Arrest in Chicago—

CONTENTS.

Herr Most Endorsing the Bomb-Throwing—The Panic He Could Create in a Big City in Thirty Minutes With 3,000 Bombs in the Hands of 500 Revolutionists.. 181

CHAPTER XI.

SUPERSEDEAS GRANTED.

United States Supreme Court Sustain Original Verdict—Parsons' Letter to Governor Oglesby—Lingg Defiant—Refusing to Sign a Petition for Executive Clemency—Their Impertinent Letters to the Governor..................... 184

CHAPTER XII.

FIELDEN PENITENT.

His Letter to the Governor—Spies' Last Letter to His Excellency—Willing to Die for His Comrades.. 219

CHAPTER XIII.

LINGG SUICIDES.

Dr. Bolton With the Prisoners—They Decline Spiritual Comfort—The Last Night of the Doomed Men—Parsons Sings in His Cell—Telegrams for Parsons—His Last Letter.. 223

CHAPTER XIV.

DESCRIPTION OF THE EXECUTION.

Threatening Letters — Pitying Justice -- Outraged Law Vindicated — Mercy to the Guilty is Cruelty to the Innocent--The Unchanged, Everlasting Will to Give Each Man His Right—Abuse of Free Speech—"The Mills of God Grind Slow, But Exceedingly Fine"—Captain Black at the Anarchists' Funeral... 231

CHAPTER XV.

A DESCRIPTION OF HERR MOST'S SANCTUM.

A Den Where Anarchy Was Begotten—The Anarchist Chief's Museum of Weapons and Infernal Machines—Easy Lessons in the Art of Assassination... 240

CHAPTER XVI.

BIOGRAPHY OF HERR MOST.

His Past Career and Early Training—His Imprisonment in the Bastile and Red

CONTENTS.

Tower for Preaching His Gospel of Blood—Extracts From His Inflammatory Utterances—"Whet Your Daggers"—"Let Every Prince Find a Brutus by His Throne."... 246

CHAPTER XVII.
BIOGRAPHY OF SPIES,
And the Other Seven Condemned Men—Their Birthplace, Education, and Private Life—Parsons' Letter to the *Daily News*, After the Explosion, While a Fugitive From Justice.. 251

CHAPTER XVIII.
BIOGRAPHICAL RECORD OF JOHN BONFIELD,
Inspector and Secretary of Police Department—Biographies of Sheriff Matson, Judge Gary, Judge Grinnell—Tribute to Captain Schaack................ 259

CHAPTER XIX.
EULOGY TO THE POLICE.
Boldly They Fought and Well — Contrast Between Capital and Labor — The Anarchists' Fatal Delusion—The United States National Anthem 264

PREFACE.

In view of the many phases and complications involved in the labor question, along with the cosmopolitan element engaged in forcing, as it were, measures intended to revolutionize labor, trade and commerce, this subject becomes of extreme delicacy to treat, the intricacy of which affect all classes and conditions of men, and threatens to convulse society from the outer crust of uppertendom to the inner sub-strata of human interest, affecting largely the social, civil, and political interests of the ever-enlarging generations of mankind.

The dark cloud standing out in bold relief outlined against the political horizon of this great republic seems to be gathering in intensity. Just now the lull in matters pertaining to this great question of CAPITAL and LABOR, seem like the "calm that precedes the hurricane." Animosities and antagonisms are widening the gulf between these conflicting interests of society, and anarchy and socialism, assuming a belligerent attitude, threaten a disruption of good and wholesome government.

We bid a hearty God-speed to any innovation upon the stereotyped and superannuated system, or dogmatic usage in the interests of absolute and overwhelming monopolies, which has for its object the general well-being of our common humanity, the elevation of the universal brotherhood of mankind, and the perpetuity of American institutions.

We do not believe in monopoly and oppression : but the final triumph of right over wrong by honest, earnest and persevering endeavor.

SOCIALISM.

A theory of society which advocates a more precise, orderly and harmonious arrangement of the social relations of mankind than that which has hitherto prevailed,—*Webster.*

COMMUNISM.

The reorganizing of society, or the doctrine that it should be reorganized, by regulating property, industry and the means of livelihood, and also the domestic relations and social morals of mankind; socialism; especially the doctrine of a community of property, or the negative of individual right in property.— *J. H. Burton.*

ANARCHY.

Want of government, the state of society where there is no law or supreme power, or where the laws are not efficient, and individuals do what they please with impunity.— *Webster.*

INTRODUCTION.

"ORDER, HEAVEN'S FIRST LAW."

Never before, perhaps, in the history of any great nation, was there a time when wise, honest and unswerving men were necessary at the helm of the great social and political ship of American freedom than at the present time, in order that she may weather the blasts, pass in safety the dangerous reefs and shoals of any *party politics*, maintain the majesty of her laws, grow strong in truth, making aggressive warfare upon error and superstition, "and having done all to stand entire at last," "with her lamps trimmed and burning," her liberty enlightening the world.

One of our great minds has said: "Our country, though rich in men of faithfulness and power, and having escaped from the difficulties of earlier times, perceives new questions which demand whatever of counsel the wise and thoughtful can give," for an era so active in thought and impulse is always perilous to the nation and need strong men, wise and calm in the midst of her greatest storms. Many of our nation's noblest sons within a short space of time have bowed in obedience to the behest of that monarch whose summons all must obey. In our minds we go back to that period when our country was young, and behold manly forms, marked by intellectual dignity, and bearing in their countenance the unmistakable insignia of true and noble manhood. They, too, have passed away, and home and sanctuary know them no more; but the light found in such characters assist in solving the difficult problems of today. Our nation's God can make of a poor and humble craftsman a mighty statesman. Many such lives are poured full of honors, and their graves are fresh and green in our memories. Nothing can equal in grandeur the interminable extent of our vast prairies, covered with blossoming buds. Every lover of nature, and home and country can daily hear a grand anthem of praise ascend to God for the munificence of his unspeakable gifts.

"From that cathedral boundless as our wonder
  Whose quenchless lamps the sun and moon supply."

These pastoral symphonies are dear to all our hearts. We love our country, and gazing upon our glorious flag, we feel it means to

"*Friends a starry sky,*"
But to foes
"*A storm in every fold.*"

Untarnished its honor, and the undimmed radiance streaming down from every star upon our glorious banner for over one hundred years, what usurper dare insult her national prowess and trail her honors in the dust, or flaunt the red flag of anarchy and socialism in the face of our national greatness?

Anarchy cannot prevail, as "order is heaven's first law," and "eternal vigilance the price of liberty."

Our measureless prosperity as a nation have caused to seek employment, protection and a home beneath the ample folds of our grand old flag, many representatives from almost every nation under the sun, to whom have been extended all the rights, social, civil, religious and political, of free-born American citizenship, while obedient to its laws. We who seek this country as our home, because of its advantages and the superior facilities for obtaining a livelihood or of amassing wealth, can be guilty of no baser act than to endeavor to sow the seeds of discord and confusion among the peaceful and well-organized brotherhood in this land of freedom and prosperity; and all violations of good and wholesome law, endangering the peace and prosperity of citizens, or the overthrow of our national institutions, are deserving of the nation's frown.

What greater insult can be offered to the children of freedom than for people of foreign birth to usurp the birthrights and trample upon the institutions for which their fathers bled and died?

Never before were citizens of any country placed on trial for so grave and flagrant a transgression, who received such consideration and fairness at the hands of the administrators of law and justice as did the participants in the Haymarket tragedy.

In view of the deep turpitude of their crime great credit is due to all the standard papers of the city of Chicago, and the Press of the United States, for the fair and impartial manner in which they represented the Anarchists' case during the trial and pending the execution. The articles appearing from time to time in their columns seemed ever tempered with mercy. Yet firmness characterized all their expressed opinions. The institutions of our country are dear to every true and loyal American.

The outrage perpetrated upon our high order of civilization called for life in exchange for the lives sacrificed by the tragic events of the night of May the 4th, 1886. Every right-thinking journalist acknowledged the justice of the sentence and said, so let it be; believing that when "judgment and justice are abroad in the land the people will learn righteousness."

CHAPTER II.

ANARCHISTS—THEIR NATIONALITY—THE FIRST AGITATION—
LEADERS—ANARCHY—THE "REVENGE" CIRCULAR—THE
HAYMARKET MEETING—THE MASSACRE.

Scarcely has the chronicler of time recorded fifty years in the eventful history of Chicago since it was known only as a little trading post for the Indians of the west and northwest, but being the central and distributing point for the interminable fertile territories stretching away toward the land of the setting sun, its progress in wealth and population has been unprecedented. The superior facilities for obtaining supplies, and the demand for implements for agricultural purposes, have conspired to render Chicago one of the most important commercial cities on the globe. And to-day it stands the grainery of the American Continent, the great repository and commercial reservoir of continental America, with a cosmopolitan population of over seven hundred thousand. Capitalists engaged in mammoth manufacturing enterprises like McCormick and others, in order to secure cheap labor to the exclusion of native skilled workmen, have imported to this country thousands of foreigners who, after gaining a foothold in the land, have turned upon their employers in organized bands with measures intended to be revolutionary.

The troublesome element consisted largely of the ignorant lower classes of Bavarians, Bohemians, Hungarians, Germans, Austrians, and others who held secret meetings in organized groups armed and equipped like the nihilists of Russia, and the communists of France.

THE HAYMARKET MASSACRE.

They called themselves socialists. Their emblem was *red*. They paraded the streets of Chicago without let or hindrance in 1878, carrying a red flag and making insulting and incendiary speeches at Lake front park, and at several of the public halls of the city.

This free country accorded to them without regard to birth or nationality the rights of freedom of speech, and we shall see how that indulgence beyond the bounds of propriety has been abused. In 1877 they held secret meetings to organize their forces, and during the same year there were several labor riots.

• In 1879 anarchists and socialists united to endeavor to secure by their votes and influence as mayor DR. ERNST SCHMIDT, and as city treasurer F. STAUBER. Polling nearly 10,000 votes they secured several representatives in the city council.

On the evening of the 2d of July, 1879, Captain Bielfeld, with ten of the gang known as the Lehr and Werh Verein, left Turner Hall, marching from Twelfth to Union, then returning, Lieut. Callahan secured their arrest. As a test case for a violation of the law relative to the militia, Bielfeld alone was booked to appear before the police court on the 3d of July, 1879. Rubens, his attorney, gave bonds for his appearance. The defendant then took a change of venue to Morrison, becoming his own bail to appear at that place in the afternoon. Bielfeld, with his attorney, and prosecuting attorney Cameron, were present. The case was continued for one week. The following day being the Fourth of July, was looked forward to with solicitude as a day when Chicago might expect riot and carnage. Bielfeld had been bound in $300 bonds but was released on habeas corpus the same day on an application to Judge Barnum, who pronounced the majority of the clauses in the militia law as unconstitutional.

In November, 1879, a similar case was argued before the supreme court which in its rulings sustained the constitutionality of the militia law in direct opposition to Judge Barnum's rulings and opinions. This opinion was a reversing of Judge Barnum's decision restricting armed bodies of socialists, anarchists, or communists from parading the streets, deciding that in matters pertaining to the peace and safety of citizens the police powers are plenary.

In the autumn of 1879 the Bohemian anarchistic agitators held a picnic at Silver Leaf Grove, in the vicinity of Douglas Park, and being annoyed by uninvited guests, at the command of their captain, Prokop Hudek, they fired a round of ball cartridge into the promiscuous crowd, seriously wounding quite a large number of citizens. Their captain, and the entire company of would-be assassins, were arrested and brought to the corner of Madison and Union streets, where the police were compelled to use their utmost efforts to prevent the enraged and outraged citizens from lynching the leaders of the gang of outlaws. The peace-loving and law-abiding citizens were so exasperated at the audacity and cupidity of the uncivilized horde that it was with difficulty the police induced them to disperse without wreaking a summary vengeance upon these organized bandits, who were beginning to operate with impunity in the very midst of the highest order of civilization and refinement.

The United States Supreme Court acknowledge and defend the right of citizens to assemble, *without arms*, when the object is to make known, in proper language, any grievance. But they must in all cases be under the control, direction and protection of the police force. But all meetings to organize, or any organized gatherings for the purpose of subverting law and order, all armed mobs making incendiary speeches or advocating violence are subject to military law, and under the control of the police, as the guardians of the public peace.

From the time of the arrest of *Herman Presser*, on the affirmation of the militia law, by the Federal Court, in 1886, all armed demonstrations of the socialistic element from this time ceased, but in secret they matured their fiendish plottings against the law-abiding citizens and safety of American institutions, becoming skilled in the manufacture and use of dynamite bombs as a weapon for the purpose of destroying life and property, and the intimidation of the officers of law and justice.

The leaders of anarchy and socialism with whom we have to do, more particularly in this volume, are viz.: August Spies, Samuel Fielden and A. R. Parsons, Spies being the editor of the *Arbeiter Zeitung*, and A. R. Parsons editor of the paper known as the *Alarm*.

The eight hour system of labor had been agitated for some time, and the first of May, 1886, was the time set for it to go into effect by all the trade and labor unions. It was suspected by many that the insubordinate element of socialists and anarchists would take advantage of the already fermented state of the working classes, to make a bold stand to revolutionize and demoralize, by their treasonable and inflammatory speeches, the otherwise peaceful and respectable citizens of Chicago. The McCormick reaper works, with over one thousand employes, mostly foreigners, had been out on a strike for several weeks, and being at fever heat the anarchists sought to produce a riot among these turbulent men, who only needed a leader and some encouragement, which they were soon to receive from Spies. On May 2d a large force collected at or near the junction of Eighteenth street and Centre avenue. Here they reversed the American flag, carrying it top side down, symbolic of the revolution they intended to work in American institutions. They marched down the Black Road to the prairie in front of McCormick's works, where August Spies addressed them in extravagant language, exciting the mob by a seditious and inflammatory speech, at the close of which the effect was plainly visible, as the mob at once attacked the works of McCormick, demolishing a portion of it, and seriously injuring several non-union men who were employed there. The six police there on duty bravely tried to hold the fort, but were forced to give way before nearly three thousand infuriated men, when they turned in a call for assistance, and were reinforced by the arrival of thirty more officers, who bravely beat back their assailants, killing one of the mob by a shot from a revolver, and wounding several others, The repulsed mob then retreated, and their leaders repaired to office of the *Zeitung* to prepare a circular, and printed it in German and English, which was headed *Revenge*, and the English copy read as follows, which they circulated throughout the city:

REVENGE.

"Revenge, working men! to arms! Your masters sent out their bloodhounds—the police. They killed six of your brothers at McCormick's this afternoon. They killed the poor wretches, because they, like you, had the courage to disobey the supreme will of your bosses. They killed them because they dared ask for the shortening of the hours of toil. They killed them to show you, 'free American citizens,' that you *must* be satisfied and contented with whatever your bosses condescend to allow you, or you'll get killed. You have for years endured the most abject humiliation; you have for years suffered immeasurable iniquities; you have worked yourselves to death; you have endured the pangs of want and hunger; your children you have sacrificed to the factory lords—in short, you have been miserable, obedient slaves all these years. Why? To satisfy the insatiable greed to fill the coffers of your lazy, thieving master. When you ask them now to lessen your burden he sends his blood-hounds out to shoot you, kill you. If you are men, if you are the sons of your grandsires who have shed their blood to free you, then you will rise in your might, Hercules, and destroy the hideous monster that seeks to destroy you. To arms we call you! To arms! YOUR BROTHERS."

The German portion differed from the above mainly in the following passage: "*Why? Because* you dared ask for the shortening of the hours of labor." In the German copy it ran: "Because you dared ask for all that you believed to be your rights." Instead of being addressed, as in the English, to American citizens, it was directed to the followers of anarchy and socialism.

Another circular was distributed calling a meeting at the Haymarket for the night of May 4, and urging workingmen to arm and go in full force. In the *Arbeiter Zeitung* appeared the letter "Y," meaning Ypsilon, which was the signal for the armed anarchists to turn out, and in the department of the paper known as the "Letter-Box" the word "Ruhe," signifying that the time for revolution was at hand.

There were about three hundred and fifty anarchists carrying concealed weapons at the Haymarkst massacre on the 4th of May, 1886, and probably about fifteen hundred present in all at the time of the explosion. A. R. Parsons had delivered his speech and Samuel Fielden was portraying to the sympathizing crowd, with all the eloquence he could command, the wide and yawning unbridged gulf between capital and labor, when seven companies of police, numbering nearly two hundred men, under command of their superior officers, swooped down upon the lawless mob. Captain Ward, in clear and ringing tones, commanded these land pirates to quietly disperse, when from an alley contiguous was seen in the darkness a little line of fire passing directly over the heads of the motly crowd. The hissing fiend, hurled by some practiced hand to perform its hellish mission, fell directly between two of the ranks of our brave and noble officers, and exploded with a detonation which seemed to shake the city from center to circumference, dealing death to several brave and noble officers, while the wounded and dying numbered over sixty, who a moment before were in the best of spirits and in the discharge of their duty as protectors of public peace, were stricken down without a moment's warning. But was there a man dismayed, although the groans of the wounded and mangled victims could be heard in every direction, not knowing but the next instant another explosion would strew the ground with fresh victims from their ranks? Scarcely had the sound of the explosion died away in the echoing distance, or the smoke from the fatal bomb rose up to be lost in the dark and murky clouds, ere the spirit of patriotism rose up in their hearts, inspiring them to deeds of noble daring, when they boldly charged in a solid column this band of treacherous outlaws. Captain *Bonfield* seized a revolver from the hand of a fallen officer, at the same time drawing his own revolver, and from both hands he rained a shower of lead into the ranks of the enemy. Under this aggressive movement the anarchists began beating a hasty retreat.

The wounded officers were removed to the *County Hospital*, while a large detachment were kept busy during the night caring for the dead and dying. The exact number of killed and wounded among the anarchists could not be ascertained, as they were removed from the ensanguined field immediately by their friends to places of safety, and medical assistance secured for them from among the socialistic fraternity.

On the 5th of May, Rudolph Schnaubelt was arrested on suspicion that he was an important factor in the conspiracy. On an investigation which followed, he very adroitly managed to impress the authorities of his innocence, when he was discharged, and he at once disappeared from the city; but during the progress of the trial, evidence was obtained which proves almost conclusively that Rudolph Schnaubelt was the arch fiend who hurled the deadly bomb causing so many brave officers to bite the dust without a moment's warning.

CHAPTER III.

This great and unprecedented anarchistic conspiracy of May 4th will doubtless result in a blessing to America. First, it will teach the administrators of law and justice the necessity of being watchful of this treacherous element in society which would thus ruthlessly violate every sacred principle of right and honor.

The bravery of the police on that eventful night of May 4th is worthy of note in the history of Chicago, and those who fell in the defence of our birthrights as American citizens have builded a monument in the hearts of a grateful people that shall endure while the star-spangled banner shall continue to wave "O'er the land of the free and the home of the brave." Were we to disturb, disquiet, and bring up from their tombs the most hideous monsters from the dead of the dark and superstitious ages of the gloomy past, their hands deep purple with the blood of their murdered fellow men, we should fail to find a parallel that would compare with this unscrupulous cold-blooded massacre, along with the bold attempt at the subversion of law.

On the fifth of the month eight of the leaders of anarchy were arrested and indicted for murder and conspiracy. The police raided the office of the *Arbeiter Zeitung*, the organ of the socialistic and anarchistic labor agitators, obtaining quantities of dynamite bombs, flags, and inflamatory literature which was offered in the trial as corroborative evidence. AUGUST SPIES, a German, was the editor of the *Zeitung* and a ringleader of the anarchists. A. R. PARSONS, an American, was editor of the *Alarm*. SAMUEL FIELDEN, of English nationality, laborer. OSCAR NEEBE, German. ADOLPH FISCHER, a German. LOUIS

Ling, a German, carpenter. George Engle, German, and Michal Schwab. These are the ones who were indicted for murder and anarchy. A. R. Parsons fled the night of the riot and consequently was not arrested, but he subsequently came in and gave himself up to the officials in the criminal court, doubtless thinking by this semblance of honor to impress the court of his innocence and thereby secure acquittal.

The attorneys for the State in the prosecution were as follows: Julius S. Grinnell; and assistants State, George Ingham and Frank Walker.

Col. W. P. Black, Solomon Zeisler, and Mr. Foster, of Iowa, were for the defence, who availed themselves of every technicality in the interests of their clients. Four long and tedious weeks were consumed in obtaining a jury, exhausting fourteen panels of jurors in securing twelve competent men to try this case. His Honor, Judge J. E. Gary, presiding.

The names of the jury accepted by the State and the defence were Major J. H. Cole, F. E. Osborne, S. G. Randall, A. H. Reed, J. H. Bruyton, A. Hamilton, G. W. Adams, J. B. Greiner, C. B. Todd, C. A. Ludwig, T. E. Denker, and H. T. Sanford.

An application was filed with State's Attorney Grinnell for a separate trial in the case of Neebe, Spies, Schwab, and Fielden, but was overruled by his Honor, Judge Gary, as they had been jointly indicted for conspiracy and murder.

On Friday, July 10th, 1886, the case of the anarchists was opened by the prosecution in the taking of evidence.

Officers Steel, Barber, Reed and McMahon, who were wounded in the riot of May the 4th, were so far recovered as to be able to be present.

Felix Puschek was sworn and submitted plans of the Haymarket and several halls in the city known to be headquarters for the meetings of the anarchists

Police Inspector Bonfield next took the stand and related how the police attempted to disperse the unlawful assemblage of armed Anarchists, and detailed the circumstance of the bomb-throwing, already related. He also identified the following circular, by which the meeting was called:

"Attention, working men? Great mass-meeting to-night, at 7 o'clock, Haymarket square, between Desplaines and Halsted. Good speakers will be present to denounce the late atrocious act of the police, the shooting of our fellow working men yesterday afternoon. Working men, arm and appear in full force.
"THE COMMITTEE."

Some of the anarchist's indicted for conspiracy turned State's evidence. Gottfried Waller, a Swiss by nationality, a cabinet-maker by trade, formerly a socialist, and a member of the Lehr and Wehr Verein, testified that the latter organization comprised various armed groups of anarchists; that the letter "Y" in the *Arbeiter Zeitung* meant for the armed section to meet at Grief's hall; that he acted as chairman of the meeting of seventy or eighty persons, Engel, Fischer and Breitenfeld, the commander of the Lehr and Wehr, being present. The witness testified that Engel unfolded a plan whereby if a collision between the strikers and the police should occur, the word "Ruhe" would appear in the *Arbeiter* as a signal for the Lehr and Wehr and the Northwest group of anarchists to assemble in Wicker Park with arms. They should then storm the North avenue police station, and proceed thence to other stations, using dynamite and shooting down all who opposed them, and should cut the telegraph wires to prevent communication with the outside world. Engel said the best way to begin would be to throw a dynamite bomb into the police station, and that when the populace saw that the police were overpowered, tumult would spread through the city, and the anarchists would be joined by the working men. This plan, Engel said, had been adopted by the Northwest group. It was decided to appoint a committee to keep watch of affairs in the city and to call a meeting for the next night in the Haymarket. Fischer was directed to get the handbills calling the meeting printed. Those present at the preliminary meeting represented various groups throughout the city Fischer announced that the word "Ruhe" would mean that a revolution had been started. Engel put the motion, and the plan was adopted. The committee on action was composed of members from each group; the witness knew only one—Kraemer. The members of the armed groups were known by numbers, and witness number was 19.

Spies was questioned in January, 1885, at Grand Rapids, Mich., relative to these secret organizations, when he said that force must bring about the necessary reform which the ballot-box had failed to inaugurate and was incompetent to perform. Shook, of Grand Rapids, also testified that Spies had said that the secret drilled organizations of Chicago for the revolution of society numbered over 3,000, and that none except members of those organizations knew of the *modus operandi* by which they intended to wage their warfare.

Lieutenant Bowler testified to seeing men in the crowd fire upon the police with revolvers; officers S. C. Bohner and E. J. Hawley saw Fielden fire. In the line of proving up the conspiracy to incite the workingmen to violence, it was shown by the evidence of James L. Frazer, E. T. Baker, A. S. Leckie Frank

Haraster, Sergeant John Enright and officer L. H. McShane, that Spies and Fielden incited the mob to attack McCormick's Reaper Works and the non-union employes on May 3. Detective Reuben Slayton testified to having arrested Fischer at the *Arbeiter Zeitung* office. He had a loaded revolver hid under his coat; a file-grooved dagger and a fulminating cap, used to explode dynamite bombs. Theodore Fricke, former business manager of the *Arbeiter*, identified the copy of the "Revenge" circular as being in Spies' handwriting. Lieutenant William Ward testified to having commanded the Haymarket meeting to disperse in the name of the people of Illinois, and that Fielden cried, "We are peaceable," laying a slight emphasis on the last word.

William Seliger, of 442 Sedgwick street, testified that Louis Lingg boarded with him, and that himself, Lingg, Huebner, Manzenberg and Hewmann worked at making dynamite bombs of a spherical shape. He attended the various meetings. He identified the calls for the armed sections to meet in the *Arbeiter Zeitung*. Balthasar Rau brought the "Revenge" circular to Zephf's hall. Lingg worked at first on "gas pipe" bombs; they made forty or fifty bombs the Tuesday before the riot. Lingg said they were to be used that evening; he and Lingg carried a small trunk full of the bombs to Neff's hall, 58 Clybourne avenue, that evening, where they were divided up among the anarchists; besides the Northwest group the Sachsen Bund met at Neff's hall; witness, Lingg, Thieben and Gustave Lehmen and two others from the Lehr and Wehr Verein, left Neff's hall for the Larrabee street police station; Lingg said a disturbance must be made on the North side to prevent the police from going to the West side; Lingg wanted to throw a bomb into the station;

the police were outside, and they could not get near; the patrol wagon came along completely manned, and Lingg wanted to throw a bomb under the wagon ; he asked witness for fire from his cigar; witness went into a hallway and lit a match, and before he returned the wagon had passed : they returned to Neff's hall where he heard a bomb had fallen on the West side, and killed a great many; Hewmann blamed Lingg and said in an angry voice, "You are the cause of it all ;" they then went and hid their bombs under sidewalks and in various places, and went home ; Lingg first brought dynamite to the house about six weeks beforeMay 1, in a long wooden box ; he made a wooden spoon to handle it with in filling the bombs; witness belonged to the Northwest group, and his number was 72, Engel was also a member. [The bombs were here produced and Judge Gary ordered them removed immediately from the court room and from the building.] Seliger's testimony was unshaken on cross-examination. Mrs. Bertha Seliger corroborated her husband's testimony, testifying that at one time six or seven men were at work making bombs, and that after the Haymarket Lingg tore up the floor of a closet to secrete those he had on hand.

Lieutenant John D. Shea, Chief of the Detective force, testified to having assisted in the raid on the *Arbeiter Zeitung* office, May 5. The galley of type from which the "Revenge" circular was printed, copies of Herr Most's book, and other anarchistic literature. red flags and banners with treasonable devices, and a quantity of dynamite were found. The witness asked Spies if he wrote the "Revenge" circular, and he refused to answer. When he arrested Fischer he asked him where he was on the night of the Haymarket meeting. Fisher said in the *Arbeiter-Zietung* office with Schwab, and that Rau brought word that

Spies was at the Haymarket, that a big crowd was there, and they all went over. He had a belt, a dagger, and a fulminating cap on him when arrested, but he said he carried them for protection. I said: 'You didn't need them in the office.' He said: 'I intended to go away, but was arrested.' I also said: 'There has been found other weapons like this sharpened dagger; how is it you come to carry this?' He said he put it in his pocket for his own protection."

Detective William Jones testified that he had a locksmith open a closet in Spies office, and in a desk were found two bars of dynamite, a long fuse, a box of fulminating caps, some letters, and copies of both the celebrated circulars. At Fischer's home he found a lot of cartridges and a blouse of the Lehr und Wehr Verein. Officer Duffy found two thousand copies of the circular calling upon the working men to arm, and the manuscript of the "Revenge" circular in the *Arbeiter Zeitung* office. Herr Most's book, "The Science of Revolutionary Warfare," found in the *Arbeiter* office, was offered in evidence; also the manual for the manufacture of explosives and poisons.

Bernhard Schrader, a native of Prussia, five years in this country, a carpenter by trade, testified that he was a member of the Lehr und Wehr Verein; was at the meeting at Greif's hall the night of May 3, and he corroborated Waller's testimony throughout. Besides those mentioned by Waller, Schrader named Hadermann, Thiel and Danafeldt, as attendants at the meeting. He saw Balthauser Rau distributing the "Revenge" circulars at a meeting of the Carpenter's Union on Desplaines street. Witness was present also at the Sunday meeting on Emma street. It was here agreed to cripple the fire department, in case they were called out, by cutting their hose. Witness went to the meeting at 54 West Lake street in response to the signal "Y" in the *Arbeiter Zeitung*. He was at the Haymarket, but did not know who threw the bomb. The Northwest group of the Lehr und Wehr were armed with Springfield rifles. Witness' number in the organization was 3,312.

Lieutenant Edward Steele testified that when the police entered the Haymarket somebody cried out: "Here come the blood-hounds. You do your duty, and we'll do ours."

Lieutenant Michael Quinn testified that he heard this exclamation and that the man who made it was Fielden, just as he ceased speaking on the wagon. About the instant the bomb exploded, Fielden exclaimed: "We are peaceable!"

Lieutenant Stanton testified that the bomb exploded four seconds after his company of eighteen men entered the Haymarket. Every member of his company except two were wounded, and two—Degan and Redden—killed. The witness was wounded in eleven places. Officers Krueger and Wessler testified to having seen Fielden shoot at the police with a revolver.

Gustave Lehman, one of the conspirators, gave a detailed account of various meetings; the afternoon of May 4 he was at Lingg's house where men with cloths over their faces were making dynamite bombs; Huebner was cutting fuse; Lingg gave witness a small hand-satchel with two bombs, fuse, caps, and a can of dynamite; at 3 o'clock in the morning, after the Haymarket explosion, he got out of bed and carried this material back to Ogden's grove and hid it, where it was found by Officer Hoffman; money to buy dynamite was raised at a dance of the Carpenters' Union, at Florus' Hall, 71 West Lake street. Lingg took this money and bought dynamite; Lingg taught them how to make bombs. M. H. Williamson and Clarence P. Dresser, reporters, had heard Fielden, Parsons and Spies counsel violence; the latter at the *Arbeiter Zeitung* office had advised that the new Board of Trade be blown up on the night of its opening. George Munn and Herman Pudewa, printers, worked on the "Revenge" circular in the *Arbeiter Zeitung* office; Richard Reichel, office-boy, got the "copy" for it from Spies.

The most sensational evidence of the trial, as showing the inside workings of the armed sections of the socialists, and at the same time the most damaging as indicative of their motives and designs, was that of Detective Andrew C. Johnson, of the Pinkerton agency, an entirely disinterested person who was detailed in December, 1884, by his agency, which had been employed by the First National Bank to furnish details of the secret meetings which it was known were being held by revolutionary plotters at various places throughout the city. Johnson is a Scandinavian, thin-faced and sandy-haired, born in Copenhagen, and thirty-five years of age. He told his story in a calm, collected, business-like manner. Mr. Grinnell asked:

"Do you know any of the defendants?" Witness—"I do."

"Name them."—"Parsons, Fielden, Spies, Schwab and Lingg."

"Were you at any time connected with any group of the International Workingmen's Association?"—"I was."

"What group?"—"The American group."

"Were you a member of any armed section of the socialists of this city?"—"Yes, sir."

"When did you begin attendance at their meetings?"—"The first meeting I attended was the 22d of February 1885, at

Baum's pavilion. The last meeting I attended was the 24th of January of this year."

"At whose instance did you go to their meetings?"—"At the instance of my agency."

"Did you from time to time make reports of what you heard and saw at their meetings?"—"I did."

"Mr. Grinnell passed over to witness a bundle of papers and asked: "Have you in your hand a report of the meeting of the 22d of February, 1885?"—"Yes, sir."

"Were any of the defendants present at that meeting?"— "Yes, sir; Parsons was present."

"Refer to your memoranda and tell me what was said by Parsons at that meeting."—Objected to; overruled.—"Parsons stated that the reason the meeting had been called in that locality was so as to give the many merchant princes who resided there an opportunity to attend and see what the Communists had to say about the distribution of wealth. He said: 'I want you all to unite together and throw off the yoke. We need no president, no congressmen, no police, no militia, and no judges. They are all leeches, sucking the blood of the poor, who have to support them all by their labor. I say to you, rise one and all, and let us exterminate them all. Woe to the police or to the military whom they send against us.'"

"That was where?"—"At Baum's pavilion, corner of Cottage Grove avenue and Twenty-second street."

"Have you a report of any other of the defendants speaking at that meeting?"—"No, sir."

"What is the next memorandum that you have?"—"The next meeting was March 1. That night I became a member. I went to Thielen, who was at the time acting as treasurer and secretary for the association, and gave him my name and signified my willingness to join the association. He entered my name in a book and handed me a red card with my name on and a number."

" When and where was that?—"That was March 1, 1885, at Grief's hall, No. 54 West Lake street, in this city."

"Have you what was said and done at that meeting?"—" I have a report of it here."

" Who spoke?"—" Parsons, Fielden, Spies, and others."

" Any other of the defendants?"—" No sir."

" State what Fielden said, and then what Parsons said."—"A lecture was given by a man named Bailey on the subject of socialism and christianity, and the question arose as to whether christianity ought to be introduced in their meetings."

" What did Fielden, Spies and Parsons say there?"—"Fielden said that he thought this matter ought not to be introduced into their meetings. Parsons said, 'I am of the same opinion,' and Spies also said that it ought not to be introduced."

" Now state the next meeting."—" The next meeting was March 4, at the same place."

Who were present?—" Parsons, Fielden and Spies were present, and spoke."

" When was the memorandum made that you have of that meeting?"—" The same day, immediately after the termination of the meeting. Parsons said: ' We are sorely in need of funds to publish the *Alarm*. As many of you as are able ought to give as much as you can, because our paper is our most powerful weapon, and it is only through the paper that we can hope to reach the masses.' During his lecture he introduced christianity. Spies stood up and said: ' We don't want any christianity here in our meetings at all. We have told you so before.' Fielden made no speech."

"When was the next meeting?"—"March 22."

"Were any speeches made by any of the defendants there?" —"Yes, sir, Spies spoke, Previously a man named Bishop introduced a resolution of sympathy for a girl named Sorell. Bishop stated that the girl had been assaulted by her master. She had applied for a warrant, which had been refused her on account of the high social standing of her master. Spies said: 'What is the use of passing resolutions? We must act, and revenge the girl. Here is a fine opportunity for some of our young men to go and shoot Wight.' That was the man who had assaulted the girl."

"Do your reports contain references to speeches made by others?"—"They do,"

"You are only picking out speeches made by the defendants?" "That is all."

"When was the next meeting?"—"March 29, 1885, at Grief's hall, The defendant, Fielden, spoke at that meeting. He said: 'A few explosions in the city of Chicago would help the cause considerably. There is the new Board of Trade, a roost of thieves and robbers. We ought to commence by blowing that up.'"

"Were other speeches made at that meeting?"—"There were, but no others made by the defendants."

"When was the next meeting?"—"April 1, at Grief's hall. Spies, Fielden and Parsons were present at the meeting. Spies made a lengthy speech on this occasion. His speech was in regard to acts of cruelty committed by the police in Chicago; he spoke of the number of arrests made, and the number of convictions in proportion. He also referred to the case of the girl who preferred a charge of assault against police-sergeant Patton, of the West Chicago avenue station."

"Who else spoke there?"—"Fielden. Spies had said before that he had advised the girl to get a pistol and go and shoot the policeman. Fielden stood up and said; ·That is what she ought to do.'"

"What was the next meeting?"—"April 8, 1885, at Greif's hall. Parsons made a lengthy speech. He referred frequently in his address to the strike at the McCormick harvester works. He said: 'There is but one of two things for the men to do. They must either go to work for the wages offered them or else starve.' In concluding his remarks he referred to the strike at La Salle, Illinois. He said: 'To-morrow morning or the next day the authorities here in the city will probably send a trainload of policemen or militia to La Salle to shoot down the working people there. Now, there is a way to prevent this. All you have to do is to get some soap and place it on the rails and the train will be unable to move.' Parsons spoke at great length of the crimes, as he termed them, of the capitalists, and he said to those present that it was an absolute necessity for them to unite against them, as that was the only way they could fight the capitalists."

"Who else spoke there?"—"Fielden. He said it was a blessing something had been discovered wherewith the working men could fight the police and militia with their Gatling guns."

"What was the next meeting you had?"—"April 19. That meeting was held at No. 106 Randolph street, because the hall at No. 54 Lake street was engaged. At this meeting Parsons offered a resolution of sympathy for Louis Riel and the half-breeds in the Northwest who were in rebellion against the Canadian government. Neither Parsons nor Fielden spoke at the meeting."

"What was the next meeting?"—"April 22, at Greif's hall. Referring to the opening of the new Board of Trade building, Parsons said: 'What a splendid opportunity there will be next Tuesday night for some bold fellow to make the capitalists tremble by blowing up the building and all the thieves and robbers that are there.' At the conclusion of his speech he said that the working men of Chicago should form in processions on Market square Tuesday evening next, and he invited all those present to get as many of their friends as they could to join in the procession."

"Did any other of the defendants speak there?"—"Fielden said: 'I also wish to invite as many of you as can come and as many as you can get. Go around to the lodging-houses and get all you can to join in the procession—the more the merrier.'"

"When was the next meeting?"—"April 26, at Greif's hall."

"Did any of the defendants speak there?"—"There were present Parsons, Fielden, Spies. Parsons said: 'I wish you all to consider the misery of the working classes, and the cause of all the misery is these institutions termed government. I lived on snow-balls all last winter, but, by G—d! I won't do it this winter.'"

"What was the next meeting at which any of the defendants attended?"—"April 30, at Market square; Parsons and Fielden. Parsons said: 'We have assembled here to determine in which way best to celebrate the dedication of the new Board of Trade building, and to give the working men of Chicago a chance to state their views in the matter.' Fielden then said:

'I want all the working men of Chicago, the country, and the world in general to arm themselves and sweep the capitalists off the face of the earth.' Parsons then said: 'Every working man in Chicago must save a little of his wages every week until he has enough to buy a Colt's revolver and a Winchester rifle, for the only way that the working people will get their rights is by the point of the bayonet. We want you to form in procession now, and we will march to the Board of Trade. We will halt there, and while the band is playing we will sing the Marseillaise.'"

"Did you march in the procession, too?—"I did."

"Where were you in that line of march?"—"I was in the center of the procession."

"Did any of the defendants march with you?"—"Not with me, but in the procession Fielden, Spies, Parsons and Neebe marched."

"What was the next meeting?"—"There was something occured the night of May 30. I was standing at the corner of Washington street and Fifth avenue close behind Spies. That was Decoration day, and as the procession passed by, Spies said: 'A half-dozen dynamite bombs would scatter them all.' A little later a gentleman who was standing near remarked upon the fine appearance of the Illinois National Guard, who were then passing. Spies said: 'They are only boys, and would be no use in case of a riot. Fifty determined men would soon disarm them all.'"

"When was the next meeting?"—"The next meeting was on the Lake front, May 31, and Fielden and Parsons was there. Fielden said: 'It is only by strength and force that you can overthrow the government.' Parsons also spoke, but I don't recollect what he said."

"Go on to the next meeting."—"The next meeting was June 7, at Ogden's grove. There were present Fielden, Parsons and Spies. Fielden said: 'Every working man in Chicago ought to belong to organizations. It is of no use to go to our masters to give us more wages or better times. I mean for you to use force. It is of no use for the working people to hope to gain anything by means of an ordinary weapon. Every one of you must learn the use of dynamite, for that is the power with which we hope to gain our rights.' Schwab also spoke at that meeting in German, which I do not understand."

"When was the next meeting?"—"The next meeting was August 19, at Greif's hall. Parsons and Fielden spoke. Parsons referred to the late strike of the street-car employes, and said that if but one shot had been fired, and Bonfield had happened to be shot, the whole city would have been deluged in blood, and social revolution would have been inaugurated. The next meeting was August 24, at Greif's hall."

"Do you know of a fellow named Bodendecke speaking at those meetings?"—"Occasionally, but not frequently; I don't know where he is now. There were some twenty or twenty-three men present at that meeting, and twenty women."

"Name who were present."—"Besides the two defendants, Parsons, and Fielden, there was Baltus, Bodendecke, Boyd, Lawson, Parker, Franklin and Schneider."

"State what occured there."—"After being there a short time a man armed with a long cavalry sword and dressed in a blue blouse and wearing a slouch hat came into the room. He ordered all those present to fall in. He then called off certain names, and all those present answered to their names. He inquired whether there were any new members who wished to join the military company, and some one replied that there was. He then said: 'Whoever wants to join step to the front.' Myself and two others stepped to the front. We were asked separately to give our names. I gave my name, which was put down in a book, and I was then told that my number was 16. Previous to my name being put down in the book, a man to whom I was speaking asked whether there was any one present who knew me, or whether any one could vouch for my being a true man. The defendant, Parsons and Bodendecke spoke up and said they would vouch for me. The other two were asked their names in turn, and as they were properly vouched for, their names were entered in a similar manner in a book, and they were given numbers. The man who came into the room armed then inquired of two other men in the room whether they were members of the American group. Both said they were and he asked to see their cards. As they were unable to show cards they were expelled, as were two others. The doors were closed and the remainder were asked to fall in line, and we were drilled about three-quarters of an hour—put through a regular manual of drill, marching, countermarching, wheeling, forming fours, etc."

"Who drilled you?"—"The man that came in with the sword; I didn't ascertain his name. At the expiration of that time the drill-instructor stated that he would now introduce some of the members of the first company of the German organization. He went outside and in a few minutes returned accompanied by ten other men, dressed as he himself was, each one armed with a Springfield rifle. When they all got into the room he placed them in line facing us and introduced them as members of the first company of the Lehr und Wehr Verein. He said that he was going to drill them a little while to let us see how far they had got with their drill. He drilled them about ten minutes in a regular musket drill. At the end of that time a man in the employ of the proprietor of the saloon at No. 54 West Lake street came into the room with two tin boxes, which he placed on the table at the south end of the room. The drill-instructor then asked all those present to step up and examine the two tin boxes, as they were the latest improved dynamite bomb. I stepped to the front with the others, and examined the two tins."

"Describe them as near as you can.'—" They were about the size and had the appearance of ordinary preserved fruit cans. The top part unscrewed, and on the inside the cans were filled with a light-brown mixture. There was also a small glass tube inserted in the center of the can. The tube was in connection with a screw, and it was explained that when the can was thrown against any hard substance it would explode."

"Was that mixture a liquid?"—"Inside of the glass tube was a liquid."

"Was there anything around that glass tube?"—"Yes, sir; it was a brownish mixture."

"Was that a liquid?"—"No, sir; it looked more like fine sawdust."

"Did you feel of it?"—"I did not. The drill-instructor told us we should be very careful about selecting new members of company, because if we were not, there was no telling whom we might get into our midst. The next proceeding of the evening was to select officers. A man named Walters was chosen Captain, and Parsons was chosen Lieutenant. Some discussion arose as to what the company should be called. It was decided eventually that we should be called the International Rifles. The drill-instructor then suggested that we ought to choose some other hall, as we were not quite safe there. He added: 'We have a fine place at No. 636 Milwaukee avenue. We have a shooting range in the basement, where we practice shooting regularly.' Parsons inquired whether it was not possible for us to rent the same place. The drill-instructor informed him he did not know. The question of renting another hall was postponed, and our next meeting was fixed for the next Monday."

Mr. Salomon—"A meeting of what?"

Witness—"A meeting of the armed section of the American group."

Mr. Grinnell—"Who drilled that company that night?"—Witness—"That German, and Parsons and Fielden."

"When was the next meeting?"—"The following Monday, the 31st of August, at the same place. Parsons and Fielden were present, and others. That was a meeting of the armed section, and it was held at Greif's hall. Capt. Walters drilled us about an hour and a half. Afterward a consultation was held by the members of the company as to the best way of procuring arms. Some one suggested that each member should pay so much a week until a sufficient amount had been raised wherewith to purchase a rifle for each member of the company. Parsons said: 'Look here, boys, why can't we make a raid some night on the militia armory? There are only two or three men on guard there, and it is easily done.' This suggestion seemed to be favored by the members, and it was finally decided to put the matter off until the nights got a little longer."

Capt. Black—" Which matter was put off?"

Witness—" The raid on the armory."

Mr. Grinnell—" When was the next meeting?"—Witness—" September 3, 1885, at No. 54 West Lake street. Fielden made a speech there and said: 'It is useless for you to suppose that you can ever obtain anything in any other way than by force. You must arm yourselves and prepare for the coming revolution.' That was one of the ordinary meetings of the association. The next meeting was October 11, at Twelfth street Turner hall. Spies and Fielden were present. Fielden said: 'The Eight-Hour law will be of no benefit to the working men. You must organize and use force. You must crush out the present Government by force. It is the only way in which you can better your present condition.' I left with Fielden before the meeting terminated."

"When was the next meeting you attended?"—"The next meeting was December 20, at Twelfth street Turner hall. Fielden was present. He said: 'All the crowned heads of Europe are trembling at the very name of Socialism, and I hope soon to see a few Liskes in the United States to put away a few of the tools of the capitalists. The execution of Riel in the Northwest was downright murder.'"—"Was that an open meeting?"—"It was as far as I know. I saw no one refused admission."

"How about those other meetings you have mentioned, aside from the armed sections?"—"Aside from the meetings of the armed section I should say that they were public. I never saw any one refused admission."—"Was there any precaution taken?"—"A precaution was taken in this way: A member of the group was generally stationed at the door, and as each member entered the hall he was closely scrutinized. The next meeting was December 30."

"What place?"—"At No. 106 Randolph."

"Who spoke there?"—"Fielden. At this meeting a stranger asked a question, and Fielden replied to the question."

"Do you know what the question was?"—"The question was: 'Would the destruction of private property assist universal co-operation?' Fielden replied: 'Neither I or any body else can tell what is going to be in a hundred years from now, but this everybody knows: If private property is done away with, it would insure a better state of things generally. And we are trying all we can to teach the people the best way in which to bring about this change.'"

"Who was present at that meeting?"—"Fielden, only. The next meeting was January of this year, at Twelfth street Turner hall. Fielden and Schwab were present. Fielden, referring to the troubles in Ireland, said: 'If every Irishman would become a Socialist, he would have a better opportunity to secure home-rule for Ireland. I want all Irishmen to destroy all the private property they can lay their hands on.' He also referred to other matters. What he said had reference to Pinkerton's detective agency."

"What was it he said?"—"He said Pinkerton's detectives were a lot of cold-blooded murderers, and the worst enemies the working men had, and they were all in the pay of the capitalists."

"Is that all that was said there? Was that one of these ordinary opening meetings?"—"It was."

"What else happened?"—"Schwab also addressed this meeting in German. During his speech he was frequently applauded. The next meeting I attended was January 14, at No. 106 Randolph Street."

"January of this year?"—"Yes, sir."

"What was said at this meeting?"—"Before the meeting commenced the defendants, Fielden and Spies, had a conversation which I overheard."

"Where was that?"—"That was held in the hall near the door."

"State what you heard."—"Spies said to Fielden: 'Don't say very much about that article on Anarchists in an afternoon paper. You simply need to state that a reporter of the paper had an interview with me a few days ago, but that most of the statements of the paper are lies.'"

"How was that conversation carried on?"—"It was carried on quietly and was not meant for anybody else to hear."

"Capt. Black objected to the last part of the answer, and succeeded in having it stricken out.

"What was the tone of voice?"—"In whispers."

"When did they leave?"—"Spies further said: 'You must be careful in your remarks. You don't know who might be amongst us to-night.' Spies then went away and the meeting was called to order"

"By whom?"—"Fielden."

"What did he say?"—"He made a long talk, commenting on the articles that appeared. He said almost all of the statements were lies. He said in regard to dynamite bombs: 'It is quite true we have lots of explosives and dynamite in our possession, and we will not hesitate to use them when the proper time comes. We care nothing at all either for the military or the police. All of these are in the pay of the capitalists.' He further said that 'even in the regular army most of the soldiers are in sympathy with us, and most of them have been driven to enlist. I have had a letter from a friend out West. He told me that he had seen a soldier on the frontier reading a copy of the *Alarm*.' Others then made speeches. Afterward Fielden again spoke at the same meeting in regard to the question asked him, what was the Socialist idea of the eight-hour movement. Fielden said : ' We don't object to but we don't believe in it. Whether a man works eight hours a day or ten hours a day he is still a slave. We propose to abolish slavery altogether.' That is all of that meeting. Fielden said, the 24th of January, at a meeting held at No. 106 Randolph street—"

" What is the name of that, Jung's hall?"—" Yes, I believe it is Jung's hall. Fielden said good results were sure to follow the abolishment of private property."

" When did you quit this branch of your business?"—" The latter part of January last."

" Did you know then of Pinkerton's agency having any other men employed in the same line that you were employed in?"— " I knew there had been another man, but whether he was employed then I do not know."

"Have you lately, within the last few days, ascertained, and do you know the fact, that you have seen any Pinkerton men in these meetings?"—" That is so."

" But you did not know it at that time?"—" I did not know it at that time."

" How often did you drill with the armed section?"—" Only twice."

" How often did they drill?"—" Once a week."

"Have you got any information from any other members of the organization? If they drilled after that?"

Objected to and withdrawn.

"Did you ascertain from any of the defendants if they drilled after that?"—"I did not."

"Have you had any other talk with Parsons outside of these utterances?"—"I have."

"Have you had any talk with Spies, Fielden, Parsons, and other defendants as to the purposes of their organization?"—"I have talked frequently with Parsons and Fielden at various times and at various places. I cannot recollect as to what was said at each place and when it was said."

"Can you give me the substance or purport of what was said at any time?"

Captain Black objected, unless time and place were given.

"What was the object of the armed section as was expressed by the members?"—"At the first meeting of the armed section the discussion arose as to what the company should be called. Some one suggested that the company should be amalgamated with the German organization, and the company was to be called the Fourth Company of the Lehr und Wehr Verein. This idea was opposed, and finally it was decided that it should be called the International Rifles. It was further said and understood by all the members that in case of a conflict with the authorities the International Rifles were to act in concert with the Lehr und Wehr Verein, and obey the orders of the officers of that organization."

"What was said at any time as to when this revolution was to take place—when was to be the culmination of the conflict?"—"The 1st of May was frequently mentioned as a good opportunity."

"What 1st of May?"—"This present. As far as I remember it was at a meeting at Twelfth street Turner hall on one occasion in December, and it was the defendant Fielden that said the 1st of May would be the time to strike the blow. There would be so many strikes and there would be 50,000 men out of work—that is to say if the eight-hour movement was a failure."

"Have you ever met any of them at the *Arbeiter Zeitung* office?"—"I have."

"What conversation did you have?"—"I had a conversation with Parsons some time in March. The conversation took place in the *Alarm* office in the *Arbeiter Zeitung* building. This office is situated in the back of the building."

"Well, state what you remember of the conversation."—"I asked Parsons if he did not think it advisable to get some papers printed in the Scandinavian language, as I thought I could make use of them. I intended to distribute them among the Scandinavian people along Milwaukee avenue and that neighborhood. Parsons replied: 'Yes, it is a good idea, and the best thing you can do is to bring the matter up in our next meeting. Bring it up before the meeting, and I will see that it is attended to. It is no use, we must have the Scandinavians with us.'"

"Did you have any talk with any of these defendants about the purposes and objects of the social revolution, so called?"—"I have had numerous conversations with Fielden and Parsons but I cannot remember distinctly what was said."

"What was Parsons' relation to the *Alarm*?"—"He was the editor."

"Did you ever see a book by Most called 'The Modern Science of Revolutionary Warfare?' Look at that book and state whether you have seen it before."—"I have."

"Where?"—"I have seen it at meetings at Twelfth street Turner hall; at No. 54 West Lake street, and also at No. 106 Randolph."

"Who had charge of the distribution of it?"—"The Chairman."

"Of the respective meetings?"—"Yes, sir."

"Were they sold or given away?"—"They were sold."

"Do you know whether or not any steps were taken to distribute the *Alarm?*"

"There were a number of those present at that particular meeting who bought a number of copies of the *Alarm*, and said that they would try their best to sell them and obtain new subscribers."

"Do you know a man named Schneider and one Thomas Brown?"—"Yes, sir."

"Did they belong to the American group?"—"Both of them."

"Did they belong to the armed section?"—"Both of them."

"Where usually did the American group meet before the time you ceased your connection with it?"

"During the last few meetings it met at No. 106 Randolph street."

"Prior to that where did it meet?"—"It had met at No. 54 West Lake street, also at No. 45 North Clark street, and on the Lake front."

"Did you ever meet with the American group at No. 107 Fifth avenue?"—"No, sir."

"No. 636 Milwaukee avenue was the place mentioned as tne proper place for drilling. Were you ever there?"—"I was there.',

"Did they meet more than once there?"—"I don't know."

"Do you know what the hall is called?"—"I do."

"What is it?"—"Thalia hall."

"When you joined this organization did it cost you anything?"—"Ten cents."

"How often did you pay the contributions?"—"Once a month."

"How much?"—"Ten cents."

"When you joined the armed section did that require any special contribution?"—"No, sir."

"What was Fielden's office in the group of the armed section?"

"He was Treasurer and Secretary of the organization—of the group."

"Did he hold any office, or was he simply a private in the armed section?"

"He held no office while I attended there."

CROSS-EXAMINED.

Cross-examined by Mr. Foster:—"Where were you before you came here?"

"I was a police officer in England eight years."

"In uniform?"—"Part of the time."

"How long did you do detective service there?"—"Three years."

"At what place?"—"In Lancashire."

"How long have you been with Pinkerton?"—"Three years."

"What did you do before you became a detective here? Were you ever in any legitimate business?"

Mr. Grinnell—" In any *other* legitimate business? "

Witness—" I was storekeeper at the Windsor hotel."

"Was that meeting at Baum's hall a public one?"—"It was."

" March 1 you became a member?"—" Yes, sir."

" Were your antecedents inquired into?"—" No, sir."

" You just paid your ten cents and were received?"—" Yes, sir."

"Is not that your experience, that anybody who could pay 10 cents could be received?"—" Yes, sir."

"Did you ever see anybody excluded?"—" No, sir, except reporters. I have seen reporters excluded sometimes."

" Were not reporters generally freely admitted?"—" Not very often."

"They had seats for them and a table?"—" I don't know. I never saw more than one at a time there."

" Did you ever see anybody excluded by the doorkeeper?"
" No, sir."

"Did you ever have any ushers—anybody who got seats for strangers.

" No, sir; but I saw some of the old members get up and give their seats when strangers came in."

"You stated that Mr. Spies introduced resolutions in sympathy with a girl?"

"Somebody else introduced them but Spies opposed it. He said there was no use making resolutions."

"That is, the girl had had her day in court and it was no use passing resolutions?"

"He said it would be a good opportunity for some one to take a pistol and go and shoot Wight."

"You are sure Spies said that?"—"Yes, sir."

"You wrote out your report immediately with all the facts fresh in your mind."—"Yes, I wrote it that night."

"Didn't you write in your report [reading from it] that Keegan said that after Spies got through with his remarks?"

"Yes, but Mr. Spies said it also."

"You are sure of that?"—"Yes, sir."

"Will you show me the place in your report where this is said?"—"I don't find it."

"Then your memory is better now than it was immediately after the meeting?"

"It is considerably better now that I have refreshed it."

"A detective's memory gets better as the time goes on, does it?"

Mr. Grinnell objected to this kind of cross-examination.

Referring to the charges against Sergt. Patton, Mr Foster asked: "Were the circumstances stated that the girl had been grossly abused, but his brother officers stood round and swore him out?"

"It may have been."

"And was it not stated as a general expression that such a man ought to be shot?"

"It may have been."

In regard to the strike at La Salle, Mr. Foster made it appear as if Parsons had simply stated in general terms that if soap was put on the rails the train would not be able to move, but that he did not advise anybody to go and put the soap on. Fielden's remark that something had been discovered by which the working men could resist the police and militia, and Parsons remark that he would not live on snowballs another winter, were

OSCAR NEEBE.

represented by Mr. Foster in an equally innocent and harmless light. The cross-examination for the day concluded with the following questions and answers:

"You heard Fielden say: 'While we march toward the Board of Trade we will sing the Marseillaise hymn?'"—"Yes, sir."

"That you understood to be the French national hymn?"—"Yes, sir."

W. H. Freeman, a reporter, testified as follows:

"I was at the corner of Randolph and Desplaines streets. Saw Parsons speaking, and listened to what he had to say. Some one said Mayor Harrison was there and I tried to find him. There was a big crowd. Parsons said that Jay Gould was a robber, and asked what was to be done. Somebody shouted, 'Throw him in the lake.' Parsons said: 'No, that won't do. We must overthrow the system by which he was enabled to secure so much money.' He shouted frequently: 'To arms! to arms!' and the crowd applauded. There were six or eight persons on the wagon. Fielden, the next speaker, discussed legislation, saying that Martin Foran had admitted that it was impossible for the working men to get their rights through legislation, and that the people were fools to send such a man to Congress when he owned that the legislation could not better them. He justified the forthcoming revolution, saying it was just as proper as the colonial revolution. The police came up quietly and my first knowledge of it was the command to disperse. Then the bomb exploded. It made a terrible noise, and a moment after the firing commenced. Parsons, Spies and Fielden were on the wagon, and I think I saw Schwab there. I crouched down behind the wagon until after the firing was over; then I went to the Desplaines street station. On getting out on the street I saw two officers lying wounded. I spoke to them but they didn't answer, so I told the sergeant of a patrol-wagon about it."

Officer McKeogh testified. :

"I was at the Haymarket on the night of May 4. Parsons followed Spies, saying: 'I am a Socialist from the top of my head to the soles of my feet, and I'll express my sentiments if I die before morning.' Again he said. 'I pay rent for the house I live in.' Some one asked: 'What does the landlord do with the money?' Parsons replied: 'I am glad you asked that question. The landlord pays taxes, they go to pay the sheriff, the militia, and the Pinkertonites.' The crowd cheered, then Parsons cried: 'To arms! to arms!' and Fielden took the stand He said: 'The law does not protect you, working men. Did the law protect you when the police shot down your brothers at McCormick's? Did the law protect you when McCormick closed the doors of his factory and left you and your wives and children to starve? I say throttle the law; strangle it, kill it!'"

H. E. O. Heineman, formerly a reporter on the *Arbeiter Zeitung*, was asked :

"Mr. Heineman, you were formerly an Internationalist?"— "Yes, sir."

"When did you cease your connection with them?"— "About two years ago.

"Whom of the defendants do you know that were in that association or society before you left it?"—"Of my own knowledge I know none but one, that is Neebe. He used to belong to the same group that I did."

"Did you ever meet with any of the others at any of the

meetings?"—"Yes; Spies, Schwab, and I think, Parsons."

"That was about the time Herr Most came here and delivered some speeches?"—"Yes, sir."

"And it was on account of those speeches you severed your connection with the Anarchists?"—"Yes."

"Whom did you see on the speaker's wagon at the Haymarket?"—"I saw the speakers, Spies, Schwab and Fielden, and Rudolph Schnaubelt, whom I had formerly known from my connection with the Internationalists."

"You say Schnaubelt was on the wagon. How long after the cloud came up and the crowd thinned out did you see him?"—"I cannot say."

"Well, how long before the police came did you miss Schnaubelt?"—"I cannot say; perhaps ten minutes."

"You say Mr. Neebe was a member of the Internationalist organization. Now, you didn't have any passwords, did you? It wasn't an organization where you drilled, was it?"—"It was an avowed Socialistic order."

Another sensational witness was Harry L. Gilmer, a workman, who testified that he saw Spies and Rudolph Schnaubelt standing inside the mouth of the alley at the Haymarket; that Spies lit a match for Schnaubelt, who in turn lit the fuse of the bomb and threw it among the police. An effort was made to shake the testimony of this witness, which was not successful, and witnesses were then brought forward to impeach his veracity, but the state produced many prominent men who knew him, and who stated that they would believe him under oath.

Captain Frank Schaack, in charge of the East Chicago avenue police station, who unearthed the Anarchists' conspiracy after the Haymarket, was called to the stand on Thursday, July

29. Lingg's trunk was placed before him. He was asked:
"Do you know any of the defendants in this case?"

"I have seen Spies, Schwab and Parsons, and Engel and Lingg were arrested and confined in my station."

"When did you first converse with Lingg about this case?"

"About 3 o'clock on the afternoon of May 14. First I asked him his name. He told me. I asked him if he was at the meeting at 54 Lake street on Tuesday night. He said: 'Yes.' Then he said he made dynamite. I asked him what for. He said: 'To use then.' He looked excited. I asked why he disliked the police. He said he had a reason; the police clubbed the men at McCormick's. He said he was down on the police because they took the part of the capitalists. I said: 'Why don't you use guns instead of dynamite?' He said guns wouldn't do; that the militia would outnumber the Socialists. I asked him how he learned to make dynamite. He said out of books, and that he made bombs out of gas-pipe and out of lead and metal mixed. He said he got the lead on the streets and the gas-pipe along the river or anywhere he could."

"What other conversation did you have?"

"Lingg said he made those bombs and meant to use them. Then Mrs. Seliger accused him of making bombs a few weeks after he came to her house. I knew then that he had made a good many. John Thielen was arrested at the same time, and from him we got two bombs. I said to Lingg: 'This man says you gave him the bombs. What have you to say?' He looked at Thielen and shook his head, and Thielen said: 'Oh, it's no use, everything is known; you might just as well talk.' But Lingg refused to say anything."

"Anything else?"

"Well, this trunk here was brought to my office. Under the lining I found a lot of dynamite and some fuse and asked him if that was the kind of dynamite he used. He said it was; that he got it at a store on Lake street. There were three kinds of dynamite. He said he experimented once with a long bomb: that he put it in a tree, touched it off, and that it riddled the tree to atoms. I asked him if he knew Spies. He said 'Yes, for some time;' that he was often at the *Arbeiter Zeitung* office. I asked him how long he had been a Socialist. He said he'd been a Socialist as long as he could think."

"Did you have any conversation with Engel?"

"Yes, on the 18th, in the evening, I asked him where he was May 3. He said he worked for a man named Koch. I asked him if he made a speech at the meeting at 54 Lake street. He said no, but that he was at the meeting. The second time I talked with him his wife came. She brought him a bunch of flowers. He got excited, and cried: 'What good are those flowers to me? Here I am locked up in a dark cell.' Then his wife said: 'Papa, see what trouble you've got yourself into; why haven't you stopped this nonsense?' He said: 'Mamma, I can't. I am cursed with eloquence. What is in a man must come out. Louis Michel suffered for the cause. She is a woman; why should I not suffer? I am a man, and I will stand it like a man.'"

"How many bombs in all did you find?"—"Objected to.

"Tell the jury what experiments you made with those bombs."

"One bomb found in Lingg's room, which Schuettler said was loaded with a funnel, I put in a box two feet square and buried in the ground three feet deep at Lake View. Officers

Stift, Rehm and Loewenstein were there. We touched the
bomb off. It blew the box to pieces, fragments carried off the
branches of trees, and the ground was torn up for a great distance. This black dynamite, also found in Lingg's room, was
put in a beer keg. Part of this dynamite Lingg gave to Thielen,
and this is a fragment of a round bomb I experimented with.
On top of this bomb I had a round piece of iron thirty-four
inches wide, some heavy planks, a piece of steel forty-two inches
wide and weighing 180 pounds; then an iron boiler twenty-two
inches wide and fourteen inches high; then on top of that a
stone weighing 132 pounds. The stone was burst to pieces, nine
holes were shot through the iron boiler, the steel cover was
cracked, and the planks were split into kindling wood. Portions of the other bombs I cut off, and gave them to Profs.
Haines and Paton."

"There were bushels of bombs before the jury. Coils of
fuse was unwound. Dynamite in paper packages and in tin
boxes was displayed. The court-room looked like the interior of
an arsenal so far as the tremendous character of the explosives
were concerned. Pieces of metal, gas-pipe, tin cans, and iron
boxes rattled together. Capt. Schaack, pointing to the bombs,
said he got two from Hoffman, one from fireman Miller, and one
from Officer Loewenstein. He was not allowed to tell how
many bombs in all he received until the officers first told where
the bombs were found.

"Now about those conversations. Did Lingg say anything
about the use of those bombs?"

"He said he intended to use them against the Gatling-guns
of the militia; that a revolution was impending. I asked him
about that satchel he brought to Neff's place. He said he saw

one there. Then I asked him where he got the moulds to mould the round bombs. He said he made them out of clay; that they could be used about two times, then they were no good. He said he saw the 'Revenge' circular on the West side."

"Who did he say was at his place May 4?"—"He said about six in all, but he only knew the two Lehmans."

Capt. Schaack was asked by Mr. Ingham whether he experimented with fuse.

"I did. I also experimented with dynamite cartridges. I had one inserted into a stone weighing perhaps thirty pounds. The explosion broke this stone into atoms."

Cross-examined by Mr. Foster.—"What Lingg said to you, Captain, was substantially this: That there was to be a conflict between the police and the Gatling-guns on one side and the laboring men on the other, and that he was making these bombs to use when that time came?"

"That's about it, only he said the time had actually come."

"Those experiments you made were made for your own satisfaction?"

"They were made to enable me to testify to the character of the stuff that was found."

"As a matter of fact you woke up Engel in his cell after midnight to interrogate him, didn't you?"

"Well, I don't remember. If I did, I did, and I suppose I did. I had a right to do it."

"Do you know of two detectives at your station who went to Lingg's cell late at night and exhibited a rope saying they were going to hang him?"

"I do not, and I do not believe anything of the kind was done."

Officer Hoffman, of the Larrabee street station., testified that he found nine round bombs and four long ones under a sidewalk near Clyde street and Clybourn avenue.

"Who was with you at the time?"—"Gustav Lehman."

Under John Thielen's house the witness found two long bombs, two boxes of cartridges, two cigar boxes full of dynamite, one rifle, and one revolver.

"What else?"—"Lehman pointed out to me a can holding about a gallon, and this was filled with dynamite."

"Look at this box of caps. Where did you find them?"— "They were with the dynamite. They were all under the sidewalk on Clybourn avenue, back of Ogden's grove."

Assistant State's-Attorney Frank Walker opened the proceedings Friday, July 30, by reading extracts from Parsons' *Alarm*, dated May 2d of this year. It was a speech delivered by Parsons April 29, the night the new Board of Trade was dedicated, and that occasion afforded the speaker his subject. The speech was full of rabid utterances, of which the following are samples:

"To-night the property owners are dedicating a temple for the plunder of the people. We assemble as Anarchists and Communists to protest against the system of society founded on spoilation of the people." In conclusion Parsons advised his hearers to save their money and buy revolvers and rifles, and recommended the use of dynamite.

Under date of December 26, 1885, the *Alarm* contained a long description of what qualities should center in a revolutionist. "The revolutionist," it was said, "must dedicate his life exclusively to his idea, living in this world only for the purpose of more surely destroying it. He hates every law and science, and knows of but one science—that of destruction. He despises public sentiment and social morality. All his sentiments of friendship, love and sympathy must be suppressed. Equally must he hate everything that stands in the way to the attainment of his ends. He must have but one thought—merciless revolution; he must be bound by no ties, and must not hesitate to destroy all institutions and systems."

On February 6, 1886, the *Alarm* paid its respects to Captain Bonfield, and the attention of the revolutionists was called to the clubbing done by the police at the time of the car-men's strike, by saying: "American sovereigns, if you don't like this, get guns or dynamite."

The names of those appointed to act as a bureau of information for the Anarchists were printed in the *Alarm* under date January 9, 1886. Joseph Bock, B. Rau, August Spies, A. R. Parsons and Anton Hirschberger were the names given. On March 20, 1886, the *Alarm* said: "All argument is no good unless based on force."

On another occasion, speaking of the eight hour movement, it was said: "All roads lead to Rome; so must all labor movements lead to Socialism." Later the *Alarm* said: "One pound of dynamite is better than a bushel of ballots. Working men, to arms! Death to luxurious idleness!" All articles from which these extracts were taken had Parsons' name appended as the writer. April 24, the date of the last issue of the *Alarm*, the Knights of Labor were assailed "for attempting to prevent the people from exterminating the predatory beasts—the capitalists." Mr. Ingham reads from Herr Most's book a description of an infernal machine to burn down buildings. This apparatus is described as of wonderful efficiency and dirt cheap. It is read to secure the admission as evidence of the four tin boxes spoken of by Detective Jansen, who saw them exhibited at 54 West Lake street.

The Court is not sure the contents in both cases are the same, and Officer Coughlin, of the Chicago avenue station, is put on the stand to prove the character of the compound. He experimented with one can by means of a fulminating cap. He tried to explode the can but failed, then he attached a fuse and an explosion followed. A quantity of burning liquid, much resembling vitriol, was distributed in all directions, a stream was thrown five or six feet high, and for a space of ten feet in all directions the grass was set on fire, and it burned for fully five minutes.

Charles B. Prouty is called. He was formerly manager of a gun store on State street.

"Have you ever seen any of the defendants before?"—"I have seen Engel and Parsons."

"When did you converse with Engel last, before May 4?"—"Some time last fall. Mr. Engel and his wife called at the store and inquired for some big revolvers. They found one that suited them, to present to some society. They said they wanted 100 or 200 for this society. A week later they said this revolver would do and they wanted some 200 revolvers. I told them I thought I could get them, but when they came back the second time I found I couldn't. They were much disappointed and said they would go some place else."

"What was the price?"—"I think $5.50. They were either 44 or 45 calibre revolvers."

"What did you say about the price?"—"I told them that was very cheap and said they could make a handsome profit on them. They said they didn't want to make any profit; that the weapons were for a society."

Captain Black, on the cross-examination, brings it out that the witness sold the gun to Engel, thinking he wanted to go into some speculation.

W. J. Reynolds, also in the gun business at 73 State street, has seen Parsons, and he thinks Engel.

"When did you see Parsons relative to your buisness, and tell what it was?"

"I think it was in February or March. He came into the store and wanted to purchase about forty remodeled Remington guns. Parsons spoke to me several times about this purchase, but it was never made. Parsons seemed undecided."

"State whether your concern ever sold any rifle or revolver cartridges, which were to be delivered, and were delivered, at 636 Milwaukee avenue—Thalia hall?"

This question is overruled by the court unless the cartridges were delivered by the witness in person. Capt. Black takes the witness in hand and he said he never knew Parsons by name until yesterday, then that person was pointed out to him in court.

"That's all," says Capt. Black.—"Mr. Reynolds," says Mr. Grinnell, "was Parsons pointed out to you, or did you not point out the man you had seen before?"

"I pointed out the man I had seen before."

A manuscript in Spies' handwriting is offered in evidence. It is a manuscript of an editorial which was printed in the *Arbeiter Zeitung* of May 4 and captioned: "Blood and Powder as a Cure for Dissatisfied Working Men." In another part of the paper was the following: "This evening there is a great meeting at the Haymarket. No working men ought to stay away."

Manuscript in Schwab's handwriting is submitted. This matter appeared in the *Arbeiter Zeitung* May 4, and one passage is as follows: "The heroes of the club dispensed with their cudgels yesterday." This has reference to the riot at McCormick's.

Another extract; "Reports of the capitalist papers have all been dictated by the police." Still another: "The armory on the Lake front is guarded by military tramps." And another: "Milwaukee, usually so quiet, yesterday became the scene of quite a number of labor riots." Under date of May 3, Spies' paper said: "A hot conflict. The termination of the radical elements bring the extortioners in numerous instances to terms." January 5, 1885, Spies wrote concerning a report of a meeting at 54 West Lake street: "Comrade Spies, in the course of his speech said: 'And if we commence to murder we obey the law of necessity for self-preservation.'" January 19, 1885, the *Arbeiter Zeitung* contained a two column report of a meeting held at Mueller's hall. Dynamite, blood and bombs were the nice points dealt with, and the comments thereon was what the state wanted read. But first a translation should have been made, and to do this an adjournment is taken until 2 o'clock.

As the trial progressed public interest in the development of the Anarchist plot to overthrow law and order increased. The courtroom would not hold half of the people that applied for admission, and hundreds were turned away. Scattered throughout the courtroom were numerous red flags and banners of the Lehr und Wehr Verein and the various Anarchist groups. Detective James Bonfield was recalled to identify the flags and banners found at the *Arbeiter Zeitung* office. They were as follows: "In the Absence of Law all Men are Free;" "Every Government is a Conspiracy against the People;" "Down with all Laws;" "Fifteenth Section Boys Stick together;" "Proletarians of all Countries, unite;" "International Working People's Association of Chicago. Presented by the Socialistic Women's Society July 16, 1875."

Saturday, July 31, the state introduced more translations from the *Arbeiter Zeitung*. The paper of January 6, under the caption of "A New Military Law," contained the following editorials: "After the adoption of the law and its working we have learned a lesson. The vote of 1881 has shown that we are stronger than ever. There exists to-day an invisible network of Socialistic forces. We are stronger than ever."

On January 22, 1886, an editorial asked: "How can the eight-hour day be brought about? Why, every clear-headed man can see that the result can be obtained by no other means than armed force."

The next day it was said: "The rottenness of our social institutions cannot be covered up with whitewash. Capital sucks its force out of the labor of the working men. The misery has become unbearable. Let us not treat with our enemies on May 1. Therefore, comrades, arm to the teeth. We want to demand our rights on May 1."

Regarding the riot in London, a meeting was held at the Twelfth street Turner hall, Neebe presiding; Fielden the orator, and his speech and the proceedings were reported under date of February 15. Fielden said: "The time is not so far distant when the down-trodden in Chicago will rise like their brothers in London, and march up Michigan avenue, the red flag at their head." Schwab spoke, calling on the people to rally around the red flag of revolution. An editorial on February 17 said:

"Hundreds and thousands of reasons indicate that force will bring about a successful termination in the struggle for liberty." April 10 it was said: "What happened yesterday in East St. Louis may happen in Chicago. It is high time to be prepared to complete the ammunition and be ready."

On April 22 Spies wrote: "Working men, arm yourselves. May 1 is close at hand." Six days later he said: "What Anarchists predicted six months ago has been realized now. The power of the manufacturers must be met with armed working men. The logic of facts requires this. Arms are more necessary now than ever. It is time to arm yourselves. Whoever has not money sell your watch and buy firearms. Patience has been preached—the working men have had too much of patience."

On April 29 Spies wrote: "The wage slave who is not utterly demoralized should have a breech-loader in his house." And the next day he said: "As we have been informed the police have received secret orders to keep themselves in readiness for fear of a riot on Saturday next, to the working men we again say: Arm yourselves! Keep your arms hidden so that they will not be stolen by the minions of the law, as has happened before." In the Letter Box was the following: "A dynamite cartridge explodes not through concussion. A percussion primer is necessary."

January 5, in the *Arbeiter Zeitung*, a report said: "The meeting which the American group held at 54 West Lake street was one of the best meetings ever held in Chicago. Comrade Spies said: 'When we murder we put an end to general murder. We only follow the law of self-preservation.'"

On January 18 all working men were called to attend a

meeting at Steinmetz hall. 'To Arms," was the caption. "Those who desire instruction in drilling will not have to pay." At Mueller's hall, a few days later, Schwab made an address, saying: " We have made all preparations for a revolution by force." Spies said: " I have been accused by a paper that I tried to stir up a revolution. I concede this. What is crime, anyhow? When the working men try to secure the fruits of their labor it is called crime."

Guns, dynamite and prussic acid, Spies preached, should be given the working men, and " for every clubbed head in the ranks of the workingmen there should be exacted twelve dead policemen." In a long discourse on the means of action, Spies said : " In the action itself one must be personally at the place, to select personally that point of the place of action which is the most important, and is coupled with the greatest danger, upon which depends chiefly the success or failure of the whole affair. Otherwise the thing would reach the long ears of the police, which, as is known to every one, hear the grass grow and the fleas cough ; but if this theory is acted on, the danger of discovery is extremely small." " The Love of Self-Sacrifice," as manifested by those who were killed during the uprising of the Paris Commune, while fighting under the red flag, was the subject of a long address on March 22, and March 23 it was said the question of arming was the one uppermost in labor circles. Working men, it was held, ought to be armed long ago. Daggers and revolvers were easily purchased; hand-grenades were plentiful, and so was dynamite. The approaching contest should not be gone into with empty hands.

The State here rested its case.

CHAPTER IV.

UNDER A CLOUD. A STRUGGLE FOR LIFE. CONTESTING EVERY POINT BY SHREWD COUNSEL. BRAVING IT OUT.

THE DEFENSE.

Attorney Zeisler moved to have the jury sent from the room pending a motion, and this the Court refused to do, saying it was a vicious practice, and that the jury should hear all there was in a case.

Capt. Black—"The motion we desire to make is that your Honor now instruct the jury, the State having rested, that they find a verdict of not guilty as to Oscar Neebe; and we desire to argue that motion."

Counsel for the defense proceeded to argue the motion, and held that Neebe was not amenable; not having been present at the Haymarket, and having nothing to do with the *Arbeiter Zeitung* until after the arrest of Spies.

The Court—"If he had had prior knowledge of the participation in the Haymarket meeting the question would be quite different, but if there is a general advice to commit murder, and the time and occasion not being forseen, the adviser is guilty if the murder is committed. Whether he did participate, concurred, assented, or encouraged the publication of the *Arbeiter Zeitung* is a question for this jury upon the testimony that he was frequently there, and that so soon as Schwab and Spies were away he took charge. Everything in which his name has been mentioned must be taken together, and then what the proper inference is, is for the jury to say."

Capt. Black—" Does your Honor overrule the motion?"—The Court—"I overrule the motion."

Capt. Black—" We except, if your Honor pleases. We de-

COUNSEL FOR DEFENDANTS.

sire also to make a like motion, without arguing it, in behalf of all the defendants except Spies and Fischer."—Motion overruled.

Mr. Salomon then began the opening argument for the defense. There were two leading points in his argument:

1. There connot be accessories without a principal. The state must prove that somebody was a principal in committing murder before it can convict others as accessories.

2. The defendants did not throw the bomb; therefore they are not guilty.

"True, the defendants made bombs; true, they intended to use dynamite. What if they did?" asks Mr. Salomon. "They were preparing for a revolution by force of arms and by means of dynamite—but what has that to do with the case? Did they kill Matthias J. Degan, for which act they were specifically indicted? That is the question."

Mr. Salomon then argued that the State would have to prove that the object of the Haymarket meeting was to "aggressively kill the police." He pointed out that the defendants had consecrated their lives to the benefit of their fellow men. They did not seek McCormick's property for themselves—they did not want the goods in Marshall Field's store for themselves. Their methods were dangerous, but why were they not stopped at inception? They advocated force, because they believed in force. No twelve men—no 12,000 men—could root out Anarchy. Anarchy is of the head—it is implanted in the soul! As well attempt to root out Republicanism or Democracy! They intended revolution—a revolution similar to that of the Northern states against slavery, or of America against British oppression. They wanted to free the white slaves—the working classes.

They intended to use dynamite in furtherance of that revolution. But they did not expect, nor did they conspire to take, the life of officer Degan Lingg had the right to manufacture bombs and fill his house with dynamite, if he so pleased. There was no law against it. Mr. Salomon intimated that an attempt would be made to show who threw the bomb, or that it was thrown by somebody other than Schnaubelt; also that the police began the riot by shooting into the crowd; that Schwab was not at the meeting at all, and that when the bomb exploded Parsons and Fischer were in Zephf's hall drinking beer.

"We expect further to show you," said Mr. Salomon, "that this meeting had assembled peaceably, that its objects were peaceable, that they delivered the same harangues, that the crowd listened quietly, that not a single act transpired there previous to the coming of the police, for which any man in it could be held amenable to law. They assembled there under the provisions of our Constitution in the exercise of their right of free speech, to discuss the situation of the working men, to discuss the eight-hour question. They assembled there and incidentally discussed what they called the outrages perpetrated at McCormick's. No man expected that bomb would be thrown, no man expected that any one would be injured at that meeting."

The witness who gave, perhaps, the strongest evidence for the defense was Dr. James D. Taylor, an aged physician of the Eclectic school. On the direct examination, Captain Black asked:

"How old are you?" Answer—"I am seventy-six years of age."

"Where were you on May 4, in the evening?"—"At the Haymarket."

"Tell us when you reached the Haymarket."—"About twenty minutes before the speaking commenced."

"During that twenty minutes where were you?"—"I was standing in the alley—Crane's alley—near Desplaines street."

"How near to the west edge of the sidewalk?"—"Very close to it."

"How long did you occupy that position?"—"As long as the bullets would let me."

"How long was that?" asks Mr. Grinnell.—"I was the last man that left the alley after the bomb exploded."

"Did you hear the speeches at the Haymarket?"—"Oh, yes; distinctly."

"What did Spies say?"—"He spoke about Jay Gould, and some one said: 'Hang him,' and Spies said: 'No, it is not time for that.'"

'What did Parsons say?"—"He spoke of the necessity for union. The substance of his remarks was that if the working men expected to win they must unite."

"Did you notice the approach of the police?"—"I did; the first column came up close to where I was standing. They were so close I could touch them."

"Did you hear Fielden?"—"Yes."

"What did he say?"—"Well, he spoke about the law, and said: 'It is your enemy. Kill it, stab it, throttle it; if you don't, it will throttle you.'"

"Did you hear the command given to disperse?'—"Yes, sir."

"What did Fielden say?"—"He said: 'We are peaceable,' or 'This is a peaceable meeting.'"

"Did you see Fielden again?"—"I did. He got down out

of the wagon and came around where I was standing."

"Did you see him with a revolver?"—"I did not."

"Did you see him shoot at all?"—"Never. I did not."

"Did you see the bomb?"—"I did."

"Where did it come from?"—"About twenty feet, or perhaps forty, south of the alley, behind some boxes on the sidewalk."

"Now, tell what you saw."—"Well, the bomb looked to me like a boy's firecracker. It was then about five feet in the air. It circled in a southeast direction, and fell, I think, between the first and second columns of the police."

"When did the shooting commence?"—"Almost simultaneously."

"Did the firing proceed frrom the crowd, or the police?"—"It came from the street, near where the police were."

"Did you see or hear of any pistol shots from the crowd?"—"Not one."

"You say you went to the Haymarket the next morning. Did you make any examination of the neighborhood?"—"I did."

"D.d you find any marks of bullets in the walls around there?"—"Yes, a great many. They were in the north end of the wall of Crane Bros.' building. Then I examined a telegraph pole north of the alley, on the west side of the street. There were a great many perforations on the south side of this pole."

"Were there any perforations on the north side of the pole?"—"Not one."

"Did you visit the place a second time?"—"I did."

"For the purpose of examining this telegraph pole?"—Yes, sir."

"Tell the jury whether you found the pole there or not."—"It was not there."

"How long ago was that?"—"A week."

"And the pole was gone?"—"It was gone."

"What course did you take, doctor, in going out of the alley?"—"I took a zig-zag course."

"Doctor, are you a Socialist?"—"Yes, sir."

"Are you an Anarchist?"—"Not in the sense in which the term is usually employed."

"How long have you been a Socialist?"—"About fifty years. I was taught Socialism by Robert Owen, father of Robert Dale Owen."

"Do you know any of the defendants?"—"Yes. I know Parsons and Fielden well; Spies and Neebe slightly."

"Have you ever taken part in Socialistic meetings?"—Yes. I have spoken at meetings controversially.'

"Are you, or were you, a member of the International Working Men's Society?"—"I was."

"For how long?"—"Well, I continued a member until the organization was abandoned."

"What group were you a member of?"—"Of the American group."

"Where did you attend meetings?"—"At Greif's hall."

"What were the conditions of membership? Tell the jury whether those meetings were secret or public."—"They were public. The conditions of membership were—" This answer was objected to by the State, and the Court sustains the objection.

"How long have you been a member of the American group?"—"I think a year, or a little more."

"How often have you met Parsons and Fielden?"—"They have not been regular in their attendance."

"Now, taking them in their order, will you state what you heard them say, either on the Lake front or at any hall, regarding the use of force?" Captain Black withdraws this question at once upon consultation with his associates.

Mr. Ingham then took up the cross-examination: "How did you come to go to the Haymarket, doctor?"—"I happened to be in the neighborhood, taking my usual evening walk."

"Did you see any circular?"—"I did not."

"How did you come to attend the meeting, then?"—"I saw a great many people, who told me there was to be a meeting."

"Did you go at once to the alley?"—"I did."

"Are you sure you did not stop on the Haymarket?"—"I am sure I did not."

"Why, then, did you go in the alley?"—"To hear what was to be said."

"What time did you get there?"—"A little after 7 o'clock."

"And you stopped there all the time?"—"Yes."

"How long did you wait?"—"About twenty minutes."

"Then the meeting was opened?"—"It was."

"And you listened to Spies?"—"Yes."

"What did he say?"—"The substance of what he said was that the men had better go home, and not do any violence."

(The witness confounds Spies and Parsons. The former, according to other witnesses, made no reference to Jay Gould, but Parsons did. The doctor said also that Parsons told the men that the history of strikes showed all strikes to have proved a failure; that what was wanted was a change in the system.)

"Did you see Fielden all the time he was speaking?"—"I did."

"And he had no revolver?"—"He had not."

"Did you keep your eye on him all the time?"—"Every minute."

"You did not take your eye off him for a single minute?"—"Not half a minute."

"And you saw him just as he closed his speech?"—"I did. He got down out of the wagon and was standing close to me."

"Where did he go after the bomb exploded?"—"The Lord only knows what became of him. The demoralization was so great that I don't know. I think he was one of the first men to go down after the shell exploded."

"Well, how long did you remain there?"—"I was the last man to go up the alley. There was a great crowd ahead of me."

"Were the bullets thick?"—"Well, I should say they were."

"Yet you didn't run?"—"Well, I am an old man, and I don't care much."

"What did you do next, after leaving the alley?"—"I went farther down in the alley. I was the last man to go down the alley. There was a projection in the alley and I took refuge behind that."

"You were young enough then to want to live?"—"It wasn't that; I heard the police shooting. They were going back toward the Haymarket. I could tell that by the report of the shooting. Then I ran out on Desplaines street and dodged about till I got home.'

"Where did you dodge?"—"A good many places. The police were shooting all over. They were all excited. I saw them shooting as far up as Madison street. One policeman on

Madison street I saw point his revolver at a crowd of people on the street and say: 'D— you! you've got to die any way.' Then he fired his revolver at them."

"You say you saw the bomb when it was about five feet in the air?"—"Yes."

"Did you see the fuse?"—"Yes."

"What kind of a bomb was it?"—"Round."

"What happened after it exploded?"—"The demoralization was great."

"Did you hear any groans?"—"No."

"How long have you been a physician?"—"Forty years."

"What school?"—"Eclectic."

"Are you a graduate of any college?"—"Yes; Eclectic."

"You say you are a Socialist, but not an Anarchist as it is commonly defined. Are you an Anarchist as you understand that term?"—"I am."

"Do you believe in an oath?"—"I do."

"Do you believe that an oath adds anything to the obligation to tell the truth?"—"No. All honest men should tell the truth."

"That's all."

L. M. Moses, a grocer, and Austin Mitchell, who lived with Moses, testified that they would not believe the witness Gilmer under oath. The defense then introduced August Krumm, of 1036 West Twentieth street, a woodworker, by whom they expected to entirely offset Gilmer's evidence. From his evidence it was made to appear that Gilmer mistook Krumm for Spies, and that instead of lighting a bomb Krumm was engaged in nothing more harmful than lighting a pipe of tobacco. Mr. Foster conducts the examination, and the witness says he was at the

Haymarket meeting May 4, and saw Spies and Parsons there for the first time.

"How did you come to go there?"—"I had business down town; heard of the meeting and went there with a friend, A. M. Albright."

"Now, how close to the alley near Crane Brothers did you stand?"—"Very close. We stood there all the time from about 9.30 o'clock until the police arrived."

"Did you stand there all the time?"—"No; we were gone for a minute or two."

"Where did you go?"—"We went into the alley. I wanted to light my pipe. Albright came with me. He gave me a pipeful of tobacco and I went into the alley to light my pipe."

"What did you go into the alley for?"—"There was a wind on the street, and we went into the alley so the match would not go out."

"And Albright followed you?"—"Yes. He came to light his pipe."

"Whose pipe was lighted first?"—"Mine."

"Then his pipe was lighted?"—"Yes. He came over to me and lit his pipe from the match that lit my pipe, holding his head up close to mine."

"After you came out of the alley what did you see?"—"The police were there; then the explosion followed."

"Did you see Spies go into the alley?"—"I did not."

"Did you see anybody in the alley?"—"Yes. There were two or three men there, but I could not tell who they were. It was dark."

"Did anybody come into the alley while you were there?"
—"No."

"Could anybody pass into the alley without your knowing it?"—"No, sir; I stood up close to the building while I was lighting my pipe."

"Now, tell whether you saw a light in the air about that time or a little after."—"Yes; I saw a light like a match about twenty feet south of the alley on Desplaines street."

Mr. Grinnell takes the witness in hand. "You say you came down town on business. Who did you want to see?"—"A friend of mine."

"Who is he?"—"Adolph Winness."

"Where does he live?"—"I do not know."

"Where does he work?"—"I don't know now."

"What does he work at?"—"He is a woodworker."

"How did you expect to meet him then, if you did not know where he lived or where he worked?"—"He told me I could find him there."

"Find him where?"—"On Randolph street."

"When did you see him last?"—"That afternoon. He came out to see me."

"And he did not tell you where he worked?"—"No."

"Nor where he stopped?"—"No."

"Yet he said you could find him on Randolph street?"—"Yes."

"So he gave you the idea that he could be found out of doors, did he?"—"Well, he's around Randolph street a good deal."

"Where did you meet Albright?"—"In the alley."

"Near Crane Brothers?"—"Yes."

"What did you say?"—"I said: 'Hello, Albright,' and he said: 'Hello, Krumm.'"

"What else?"—"Did you say you came down town to see a friend?"—"Yes."

"Did you tell him the name of your friend?"—"No."

"Who was speaking then?"—"Parsons, I think."

"Tell what he said."—"He said something about Jay Gould."

"What did Spies say?"—"He said: 'A few words more, boys, and we'll go home.'"

"Spies said that, did he?"—"Yes."

"Which man is Spies?"—The witness confounds the men. Asked to indicate Spies he points to Fielden.

"How did you stand in the alley when the speaking was going on?"—"I had my back to the north wall."

"Did you stand that way all the time?"—"Yes, except when we lit our pipes."

"Then did you stand the same way after you lighted your pipes?"—"Yes."

"Then how could you see these men if you had your backs to the wall?"—"I looked over my head."

"You looked over your head all the time?"—"Yes, when we looked at the speakers."

"And you never saw these men before?"—"No."

"Yet from that point in the alley, the speakers eight feet or more distant, a crowd between you, you looking over your shoulders in the dark, you recognize these men the first time you saw them?"—"Yes."

"Where were the police when Fielden said. 'Now, a word

more boys, and we will go home'?"--They were coming up Desplaines street."

"Where was Spies then?"—"I don't know. I don't remember."

"Well, didn't you see Spies on the wagon?"—"Yes."

"When?"—"I don't think now. Early in the evening, I think."

"Now, when you were talking to Albright, did you talk about what the speakers were saying?"--"No."

"Did you talk about the eight-hour question?"—"No."

"What were you talking about?"—"About the shop."

"Now, where did you see the bomb?"--"It was about ten feet in the air, about twenty feet south of the alley. I didn't see it explode."

"No, of course not. It was too far south."

"There then was some boxes on the sidewalk, and you couldn't see?"--"I did not say there were any boxes on the sidewalk."

"Yes, but if there were any boxes there you would have seen them?"—"Yes. I would have seen them if they had been on the sidewalk."

"And you did not see them there?"—"I did not."

(All the other witnesses for the defense testified that a big pile of boxes stood on the sidewalk between the alley and a point where the bomb exploded.)

"And you say you did not see those boxes?"—"I did not."

"When were you at the Haymarket?"—"May 4."

"Were you ever there in your life?"—"Yes."

"How about a lamp post. Did you see one?"—"I don't

remember now, but I know there is one at the southeast corner of the alley."

"How do you know this?"—"I worked at the corner of Randolph and Jefferson streets for ten years, and remember it."

"How long ago was that?"—"Seven years ago."

"And you can remember that a lamp post stood at the southeast corner of the alley after the lapse of seven years?"—"I can."

"Where is your wife now?"—"Living on Sedgwick street."

"Whereabouts?"—"I don't know. I have not seen her for a year."

"How did you come to go to Salomon & Zeisler's office?"—"I saw a notice in the *Arbeiter Zeitung* asking for all that knew anything about the bomb throwing to call on them. I went there on Sunday."

"When did you see this notice?"—"Some time ago. I don't remember when."

"Did you talk with any one about this bomb throwing?"—"Yes, with Albright."

"Any one else?"—"No."

"Yet you saw the bomb in the air and heard the explosion but you did not talk to any one about what you saw?—"That's it."

M. T. Malkoff, the correspondent of a paper at Moscow, Russia, and formerly a writer on the *Arbeiter Zeitung*, testified that Parsons was in Zephf's hall, talking to his wife, Mrs. Holmes and the witness, when the bomb exploded. State's Attorney Grinnell elicits from the witness that he has been five years in this country, that he lived in New York and maintained himself by teaching the Russian Language. From New York, he went to Little Rock, then to St. Louis, and finally to Chicago, arriving here in 1884. "You came here with a letter of introduction to Spies?"—"No, sir. I obtained my position in the South through a letter of introduction from Spies."

"How did you come to get that letter?"—"I and a man named Clossie translated a romance from the Russian and sold it to Spies."

"That was a revolutionary novel?"—"It was not. It was a description—"

"Oh, I don't want to go into that. You know Herr Most?"—"I have seen him, but I don't know him."

"You know Justus Schwab? You had letters sent to his address?"—"That may be."

"You lived with Schwab in New York?"—"I did not."

"You lived with Balthazar Rau here, though, on May 4?"—"I did."

"Where?"—"At 418 Larrabee street."

"When did you leave Russia?"—"In 1882."

"Your bedroom was searched, wasn't it?"—"Yes, sir."

"Were the arms found there guns and bayonets, or any of them, belonging to you?"—"No, sir."

"Where did you live before you went to Rau's house?"—"With Mr. Schwab."

"One of the defendants?"—"Yes, sir."

"You are a stockholder in the *Alarm* company?"—"No, sir."

"You contributed money to that organization?"—"That may be."

"But did you not contribute money?"—"I did."

"How much?"—"Two dollars."

"You were a Nihilist in Russia?"—"No, sir."

"Are you not the agent here for the Nihilists in Russia?"—"No, sir. I am not an agent for any society in Russia."

"Did you not tell Mr. Hardy you were the agent for a Nihilistic society"—"No, sir. The reporters used to call me a Nihilist because I was Russian."

"What paper are you now working for?"—"The *Moscow Gazette*."

"Look at that letter; is that your signature at the bottom?"—"It is."

The letter is written in German and it is given to the translator, who is instructed to render it into English. "This letter is directed to a 'Mr. Editor.' What editor?"—"I think it was directed to Mr. Spies."

"That was before you came to Chicago?"—"It was."

"Then we offer it in evidence." The letter is, in substance, an inquiry as to whether or not Spies could use certain articles written by Malkoff. It goes on to say: "I have just completed another article treating of the secret revolutionary societies of Russia. I am a proletariat in the fullest sense of the word. Address your letter to J. H. Schwab, 50 First street, New York."

"Is that J. H. Schwab, Justus Schwab?"—"It is."

"Did you live with him in New York?"—"No, sir. I just got my mail there."

"Now," said Foster, "you say you were a proletariat. What do you mean by that term?"—"I understand it to be a man without any means of support."

"And you, having no money, had your mail sent to Justus Schwab because you had no home, eh?"—"Yes, sir."

"Now," asked Mr. Ingham, "I'll ask you if you did not use

the term proletariat in the sense in which Socialists always employ that term?"—"No, sir, I did not."

SAMUEL FIELDEN.

Samuel Fielden, one of the defendants who was speaking at the time of the bomb explosion, testified that he did not know who threw the bomb, and denied that he fired at the police with a revolver. He was cross-examined by Mr. Ingham for the State, who asked: "At what age did you come to the United States?"—"Twenty-one."

"Did you have any business before you came to the United States?"—"I went to work in a cotton mill at eight years of age, and worked in that mill until I left the country to come to the United States."

"How long have you been a Socialist?"—"I joined the Socialistic organization in July, 1884."

"How long have you been a revolutionist?"—"In the sense of an evolutionary revolutionist, I have been so for a number of years."

"How long have you been of the belief that the existing order of things should be overthrown by force?"—"I don't know that I have ever been convinced. I am of the opinion that the existing order of things must be overturned, but whether by force I don't know."

"How long have you believed in Anarchy?"—"Well, I believed in it shortly after I joined the organization—as soon as I came to think on the subject."

"You have been progressing from Socialism to Anarchism; and if you cannot convince the majority of the United States to your opinions, you propose to compel them by force?"—Objected to.

"How long have you preached Anarchy?"—Objected to.

"Was there any English-speaking group in the city that you know of?"—Objected to.

"Did you ever attend any meeting of any English-speaking group other than the American group in this city of that kind?"—"We tried to found one a year ago last winter on West Indiana street. I think we only held two meetings, and then we abandoned it."

"Any other group of them that you attended?"—"I don't remember any now."

"You have for the last two or three years been making speeches of Socialistic and Anarchistic character?"—"I have been making labor speeches; they were not always Socialistic or Anarchistic speeches."

"But you have made Socialistic and Anarchistic speeches?"—"Well, I have touched on Anarchy and Socialism, and sometimes my speeches might have been considered from the ordinary trades union standpoint, for all the anarchy there was in them."

"Have you ever made speeches on the Lake front and other Socialistic meetings?"—"Yes, on the Lake front, some on Market square, Twelfth street Turner hall, and at No. 106 Randolph street."

"Look at the copy of the *Alarm* of June 27, 1885, 'Dynamite; Instructions Regarding Its Use and Operation,' and signed 'A. S.' Say whether you ever saw it."—"I don't know that I have."

"Was there any reason why you did not walk when you

started home that night?"—"Yes. I did not wish to be arrested that night."

"You expected that you would be arrested?"—"Well, after that trouble I expected to be arrested."

"You were speaking when the police came up, and were making no inflammatory speech?"—"I did not incite anybody to do anything, to do any overt act. I told the people in general to resist the present socialistic system that oppressed them, and gave them no chance to earn a living."

"And yet you expected to be arrested?"—"I had read something of criminal proceedings, and I knew that the police would arrest everybody connected with that meeting in order to find the one who was responsible. I made an explanation before the Coroner's jury because I had a different idea of the police at that time. I thought if I made that statement and they inquired into the truth and were convinced of my innocence they would let me go. But I now see that I was mistaken."

"Did the police indict you?"—"I don't know who indicted me."

Redirect—"You have heard what has been said about your expression of throttling the law, of killing it, of stabbing it. Just state the explanation which you said you desired to make in regard to that."—"Well, it was just the explanation that a public orator would make when he was denouncing a political party. When he said he wanted to get rid of the Democratic party, for instance, he would kill it, stab it, or make way with it. The words would rush away with a public speaker, and in the hurry he could not add a lengthy explanation."

"You also read the reporter's notes in regard to snails and worms. and said there was no connection there. What were your words in reference to snails and worms, and the idea that you now remember?"—"Well, the idea that I intended to convey at that time was that when men were thrown out of work through no fault of their own, and it being a fact that has been proven and asserted on the floor of the House of Representatives that over a million of men are out of employment through no fault of their own—these men being driven about, become degraded and loathsome, and people look upon them with contempt, and yet it is no fault of their own; they have no part in producing the condition of things that throws them out of employment, and leads them to their abject condition."

"You did not know of the presence of a dynamite bomb or anything of that kind in the crowd?"—"No, sir; I did not even know of the presence of an unusual number of police at the station. I did not know that till after the meeting."

Henry Schultz, an elderly German, testified that "from 9 o'clock until the fight was over I was on the Haymarket; I stood in the middle of the steet, a little north of the wagon."

"How long had you been in Chicago at that time?"—"Two weeks. I am a tourist." [Laughter.]

"Have you been in the habit of attending meetings in the street?"—"No; but since I have been here seeing the sights I would stop at anything."

"Before the police came, did you see anything disorderly?"—"It was, as I know, peaceable, like a Fourth of July."

"Do you remember the speech of the first speaker?"—"I know the run of his talk; I kept it in my mind. He said, 'I didn't want to come here. Then they called me a coward, and I didn't like to be called a coward, and that is the reason I came.' A few words after that he said: 'They are only 500 yards from here. Maybe by to-morrow morning I will have to die.' I kept that on my mind. I left the meeting when the black cloud came up, and when the bomb exploded I looked around the corner, and I saw everything dark, and I thought the bomb must have blown out the lights." [Laughter.]

"What else did you seee?"—"I saw the policemen and they were all around. They had the ground. I saw some of the workmen run—they were about two blocks ahead of the police."

"Did you see the police come upon the working men?"— "They came pretty strong in Lake street, and they had the men in the gutter, and when they raised up they got another club."

Mr. Grinnell—"What is your business?"—"Doing nothing," replied Mr. Schultz, with a grin at the crowd, and the crowd laughed in a guarded way, because they did not wish to be fired out of the entertainment.

"How long have you been conducting that business?"— "About ten years. Before that I was mining in Montana."

"Where is your house in Portage City?"—"The next house to the courthouse," responded the witness with a cunning look at the Court, and there was another wild outburst of mirth from the audience. Mr. Schultz narrated a part of his early history, from which it appeared that before he became a millionaire he played the fiddle at dances; and in answer to a question as to when he began to be a musician, he said: "From nine years old. My father was a musician—it runs in the family."

"Do you play the violin since you have been in Chicago?" —"No; my money reaches so that I don't have to do anything." [Laughter.]

"The first speaker was Spies, wasn't it?"—"Oh, I can't promise anything," said Mr. Schultz, with a contortion of countenance which brought down the house. Judge Gary looked indignantly around and said: "Oh! be quiet!" and the crowd immediately became as demure as a Quaker meeting.

"What did Spies say about the police being so many feet away?"—"He said they was only five hundred yards from here and he was likely to die before morning. That was about all he said in that run of speech."

"Did you hear the first speaker say anything about 'To arms! to arms!'?"—"That was the man—I heard him."

"Where did you go when you left the meeting?"—"I went to wash my feet!"

The expression on Mr. Schultz's face, and the simplicity of the answer, upset the decorum of the spectators and they laughed right out in meetin,' regardless of the threatened penalty for such a glaring contempt of court. Judge Gary himself, however, assisted in the hilarity, and was very lenient with the offenders, a fellow-feeling evidently making him wondrous kind. Mr. Schultz a moment afterward had an opportunity to correct the impression that he was in the habit of touring around the streets of Chicago in his bare feet.

"Did you have your boots off when you were washing your feet?"—"Oh, no; I didn't wash my feet; I only washed the mud off my boots in one of them horse-troughs." Then Mr. Schultz treated the company to a choice selection of facial contortions, and got down out of the chair with the air of a man who has done his duty, his whole duty, and nothing but his duty.

MICHAEL SCHWAB.

The defendant, Michael Schwab, was put on the stand Monday, August 9. He testified that he went to the *Arbeiter Zei-*

tung office on the evening of May 4. A telephone message was received requesting Spies to speak at a meeting near Deering's Harvester works, on Clybourn avenue. The witness said he went to the Haymarket to find Spies, but failed. He did see Rudolph Schnaubelt, his brother-in-law, there. Witness then took a street car and went up Clybourn avenue; spoke twenty minutes at the meeting; stepped into a saloon and got a few glasses of beer, and then went to his home, on Florimond street, arriving about 11 o'clock P. M.

Mr. Foster asked: "Were you ever in the alley at Crane Bros.' that night with Mr. Spies?"—"No, sir."

"Did you walk west on Randolph street with Mr. Spies two blocks, then return with him?"—"No, sir."

"Did you see Mr. Spies that night?"—"No, sir."

"Did you see Mr. Spies hand your brother-in-law a package that night in the alley at Crane Bros.', and did you say anything like this: 'If that won't be enough, shall we get another one?'" —"No, sir."

"Did you see Mr. Spies at all that night?"—"No, sir."

"When did you see him at all for the last time that day?" —"In the afternoon. I did not see him again until the next morning."

Schwab said he had been a member of the Internationalist society since its organization. On the night of May 4 he went to the Haymarket on foot and walked through the Washington street tunnel. Balthazar Rau accompanied him as far west as Desplaines street.

"Are you an Anarchist?" asked Mr. Grinnell.—"It depends on what you mean. There are several definitions of that."

MICHAEL SCHWAB.

"Answer my question. Are you an Anarchist?"—"I can't answer that."

AUGUST SPIES.

Schwab stepped down and Spies took the stand. 'Give your full name to the jury," said Captain Black.

"August Vincent Theodore Spies," replies the prisoner.

He is thirty-one years old, and came to this county from Germany in 1872. Spies speaks with a marked accent, but very distinctly. He is cool and collected apparently, and sits back in the witness chair very much at ease.

He has been a member of the Socialistic Publishing Society, and that concern exercised control over the policy of the *Arbeiter Zeitung*, of which paper the witness was editor for six years. Spies said he was at a meeting on the "black road" on May 3. Spies reached the meeting on the "black road" about 3 o'clock in the afternoon. There was a crowd of perhaps three thousand present. Some men were speaking, but they were very poor speakers, and the crowd was not interested. Balthazar Rau was with him, and introduced him to the chairman of the meeting. It was called for the purpose of discussing the eight-hour question. While Spies was there a committee was appointed to wait on the bosses; then he was introduced, and spoke for possibly twenty minutes. Spies went on:

"I was almost prostrated. I had been speaking two or three times daily for the past two or three weeks, and was very much worn. I did not jump around and wave my hands as one witness testified here on the stand, and I made a very commonplace, ordinary speech. I told the men to hold together, to stand by their union, or they would not succeed. That was the substance of what I said. While I was speaking some one cried out in an unknown tongue, and about two hundred men detached themselves from the crowd and went on to McCormick's. Pretty soon I heard firing, and on inquiring what was the matter was told the men had attacked McCormick's men, and that the police were firing on them. I stopped for about five minutes, was elected a member of the committee; then I went to McCormick's. A lot of cars were standing on the tracks. The men were hiding behind these cars, others were running, while the police were firing on the flying people. The sight of this made my blood boil. At that time I could have done almost anything, I was so excited. A young Irishman came out from behind one of the cars. I think he knew me and said: 'What kind of —— business is this? There are two men over there dead; the police have killed them.' I asked him how many were killed. He said five or six, and that twenty-five or thirty were injured. I came down town then and wrote the report which appeared in the *Arbeiter Zeitung* the next day.'

" Did you write the 'Revenge Circular'?—" Yes; only I did not write the word 'Revenge.'"

" Can you tell how that word happened to put in the circular?"—" I cannot."

" How many of those circulars were distributed?"—" About twenty-five hundred."

" How soon was it written after your return to the office?"—" Immediately."

" At that time were you still laboring under the excitement incident to the riot?"—" I was."

" What was your state of mind?"—" I was very indignant. I knew from experience of the past that this butchering of peo-

ple was done for the express purpose of defeating the eight-hour movement." Spies is growing excited. Mr. Grinnell objects. The Court says his last answer is not proper and orders it stricken from the record.

"On the evening of May 4 you attended the Haymarket meeting?"—"I did."

"You were asked to speak there?"—"I was."

"When did learn there was to be a meeting?"—"About 8 o'clock that morning. I was advised there was to be a meeting and was asked to address it."

"What time did you reach there?"—"About 8:20 o'clock."

"Did you see the notice of that meeting in the *Arbeiter Zeitung?*"—"Yes; I put it in myself."

"Did you see a circular that day, calling for a meeting at the Haymarket?"—"Yes. It was the circular containing the line: 'Working men, arm yourselves and appear in full force.' When I read that line I said: 'If this is the meeting I am to address I will not speak.' He asked why. I said on account of that line. He said the circulars had not been distributed, and I said: 'If the line is taken out I will go.' Fischer was sent for and he told the men to have that line taken out."

"Who was this man that brought the circulars?"—"He was on the stand; Gruenberg is his name, I think."

"Was there any torch on the wagon?"—"No; I think the sky was clear and that the lamp was burning near the corner of the alley."

"Was that selection made by yourself, or upon consultation?"—"Well, I consulted with my brother Henry. He was with me all evening."

"After you got them together, what did you do?"—"Some

one suggested we had better move the wagon around on Randolph street, but I said that might impede the street cars. Then I asked where was Parsons. I was not on the committee of arrangements and had nothing to do with the meeting except to speak. One Schroder said Parsons was speaking then at the corner of Halsted and Randolph streets, and I went up to find him with my brother Henry and Schnaubelt."

"Did you see Schwab?"—"No, I did not. Schnaubelt told me Schwab had gone to Deering's."

"Did you go to Crane's alley with Schwab?"—"I could not very well do that, as I had not seen him that night."

"Just answer the question," cried Mr. Ingham.—"Well, I did not go to the alley. I did not even know there was an alley there." The witness denies the conversation Mr. Thompson alleges he overheard Spies engage in with Schwab. He said Schnaubelt cannot speak any English—that he has only been about two years in the country.

"Did Schwab say to you that evening: 'Now, if they come, we are prepared for them'?"—"No, sir; I did not see him that evening."

"Did you talk with Schwab on the east side of Desplaines street, about twelve feet south of the alley that evening?"—"I did not. I was not anywhere near that alley with any man."

"You remember what the witness Thompson said, that he saw you walk with Schnaubelt east on Randolph street; that he saw you hand him something; that you then returned to the meeting together. Is that true?"—"It is not. That man told a different story before the coroner's jury."

This last answer is ordered stricken out, and Spies was told to say nothing but in answer to questions. Spies was asked to tell what he said at the meeting. It was a short synopsis of the existing state of the labor world. First, he said that the meeting was to be a peaceable one; that it was not called for the purpose of creating trouble. Attention was directed to the strike at East St. Louis, where those who were active in the riots there were not Socialists nor Anarchists, but church-going people, and honest, sincere Christians. It was admitted by students that society was retrograding; the masses were being degraded under the excessive work they had to carry on. For twenty years the working men asked in vain for two hours less work a day, and that finally they resolved to take the matter in their own hands and help themselves. "About this time I saw Parsons, then I broke off. I was not in a state to make a speech. I was tired. I introduced Parsons, and he proceeded to address the meeting."

" What was the size of the crowd then?"—" About two thousand persons."

"Where did you go after finishing your speech?"—" I remained on the wagon."

" You spoke in English?"—" Yes. I made no speech in German that night. I was asked to do so, but was too tired. I introduced Fielden and he made a brief speech, then we intended to go home."

" What did Parsons say in his speech?"—" Parsons made a pretty good speech. He said of the dollar earned by the working men they got only fifteen cents, while the pharisaical class got eighty-five cents, and that the eight-hour movement was a still-hunt for that eighty-five cents."

" What do you remember of Fielden's speech?"—" Well,

Fielden did not say much. I don't remember now what he did say."

"Were you on the wagon when the police came?"—"Yes. I saw the police on Randolph street."

"At that time what was the size of the meeting?"—"It was as good as adjourned. About two-thirds of those present went, some going to Zepfh's hall when the black cloud came up."

"What did you hear when the command to disperse was given?"—"I was standing in the middle of the wagon, back of Fielden. I heard Captain Ward say; 'I command you, in the name of the people of Illinois, to disperse.' Captain Ward had a cane or club in his hand. Fidlden said to him: 'Captain, this is a peaceable meeting.' I started to get down out of the wagon. My brother Henry and one Legner helped me down. I was indignant at the thought that the police had come to disperse the meeting, as it was a quiet one. Just as soon as I reached the ground I heard a loud detonation. I thought the police had a cannon to frighten the people. I did not dream for a moment of a bomb, and I did not even then think the police were firing at the crowd. I thought the police were firing over their heads."

"Where did you go to?"—"I was pushed along by the crowd. I went to Zepfh's hall."

"Did you at any time that night get down from the wagon and go into an alley and light a bomb in the hands of Rudolph Schnaubelt?"—"I never did."

"Did you see Schnaubelt in the alley that night while Fischer was there?"—"I did not."

"You remember the witness Gilmer?"—"Yes."

"Is his story true?"—"Not a word of it."

"You remember Wilkinson, the reporter for the *Daily News?*"—"Yes. I had a conversation with him in January."

"Well, go on and tell us about it."—"He was introduced to me by Joe Gruenhut. He said he wanted to get some data wherewith to prepare an article on Anarchism, Socialism and dynamite, and all that. I happened to have four shells in my office. I had them for about three years. A man on his way to New Zealand gave me two bombs; another man some time after called at my office with two bombs, and wanted to know if their construction was proper. That's how I came to possess them. He wanted one to show to Mr. Stone. I let him take it. We went to dinner at a restaurent, and we conversed about society, its present state, and the trouble that was likely to ensue. We spoke about street warfare, as all this was contained in the papers every day. There was constant talk that so many wild-eyed Socialists were arriving every day, and I told him it was an open secret that there were 3,000 armed Socialists in Chicago, and we spoke about revolutions, and I said that in past ages gun-powder had come to the assistance of the downtrodden masses, and that dynamite was a child of the same parent, and was a great leveler."

"Do you remember the toothpick illustration?"—"Yes. I remember that, and also re-call speaking of the Washington street tunnel, saying how easy comparatively few men could hold that tunnel against a body of soldiers, but nothing was said about Chicago, nor was any time fixed for the revolution."

"You wrote the word 'Ruhe' for insertion in the *Arbeiter Zeitung* May 4?"—"I did."

"How did you come to do that?"—"The night before at 11 o'clock I received a letter as follows: *Mr. Editor:* Please insert in to-day's letter box the word 'Ruhe' in prominent letters."

"At that time did you know there was any import attached to the word?"—"I did not."

"When did you next hear of it?"—"The next afternoon Balthazar Rau asked me if the word was in the paper. I said: 'Yes.' He asked me if I knew the meaning. I said: 'No.' Then he said: 'The armed section had a meeting last night and adopted the word 'Ruhe' as a signal to keep their powder dry and be in readiness in case the police precipitated a riot.' I asked if that had anything to do with the meeting I was to address at the Haymarket, and he said: 'Oh, no; that's something the boys got up themselves.' I said it was very foolish, that it was not rational, and asked if there was no way in which it could be undone. Rau then went to see the people of the armed section and told them the word was put in by mistake."

"Were you a member of the armed section?"—"No, not for six year."

"Did you ever have dynamite and a fuse in your desk?"—"Yes, I had two packages of giant powder and some fuse in my desk for two years. I had them chiefly to show to reporters, they bothered me a good deal. They always wanted some sensation. Then, too, I wanted the dynamite to study it; I had read a great deal about explosives."

"Do you know anything about a package of dynamite found on the shelf in the closet of the *Arbeiter Zeitung?*"—"Absolutely nothing."

"Do you know anything about a revolver that was found in the *Arbeiter Zeitung* office?'—"No. I do not. I carried a revolver myself, but it was a good one."

"Did you carry a revolver?"—"Yes. I always thought it

was a good thing to be prepared. I was out late at night a good deal."

"Did you have a revolver that night?"—"No, it was too heavy. I left it with ex-Ald. Frank Stauber."

"You were arrested May 5?"—"Yes."

"Tell us how."—"Well, an officer—James Bonfield, I think —came to my office and asked for Schwab. He said Chief Ebersold would like to see him. Schwab asked me if he should go. I said yes, he might. Then the officer turned to me and asked me if my name was Spies. I said yes. Then he said Superintendent Ebersold would like to see me about that affair of last night. I went over there, unsuspectingly. I was never so treated before in all my life."

"Tell what happened?"—"Well, as soon as I got into the station Superintendent Ebersold started at me. He said: 'You dirty Dutch dog; you hound; you whelp—you, we will strangle you! We will kill you!'" Then they jumped on us, tore us apart from each other. I never said anything. Then they searched us, took our money, even our handkerchiefs, and would not return them to us. I was put in a cell, and have not had my liberty since."

Mr. Ingham cross-examined the witness. Spies said he came to this country when seventeen years old, and that he has lived in Chicago some thirteen years. The *Arbeiter Zeitung* was controlled by what Spies termed an "autonomous editorial arrangement;" that is, the powers of the several editors were co-ordinate, but the general policy of the paper was under the supervision of the board of trustees.

"Did you ever receive any money for the *Alarm?*"—"Yes."

"Did you ever pay out any money for the *Alarm?*"—"Yes."

"Did you ever write any articles for the *Alarm?*"—"I may have."

"How many bombs did you have in the *Arbeiter Zeitung* office?"—"Four, I think. Two I got from a man named Schwab. I forget now. He was a shoemaker. He went to New Zealand."

"How did this man come to give you those bombs?"—"He came to me and asked me if my name was Spies. I said yes. Then he asked me if I had seen any of the bombs they were making. I said no. Then he left them with me."

"Who did he mean by 'they'?"—"I don't know."

"Didn't he say who they were?"—"No."

"And you never saw him before or since?"—"No, sir."

"And when did you get these czar bombs?"—"I never got them. That is an invention of that reporter. A man came there while I was at dinner and left them there. He left the bombs with the bookkeeper. I never saw him before or after."

Mr. Ingham introduced a letter and a postal card found in Spies' desk, the reading of which, as translated by Mr. Gauss, created a great sensation. Spies acknowledged the writing as addressed to him by Johann Most, the noted Anarchist:

"DEAR SPIES:—Are you sure that the letter from the Hocking Valley was not written by a detective? In the week I will go to Pittsburgh, I have an inclination also to go to the Hocking Valley. For the present I send you some printed matter. There Sch. and H. also existed but on paper. I told you this some months ago. On the other hand, I am able to furnish "*medicine,*" and the "*genuine*" article at that. Directions for use are perhaps not needed with these people. Moreover, they were recently published in the "Fr." The appliances I can also send. Now, if you consider the address of Buchtell thoroughly reliable, I will ship twenty or twenty-five pounds. But how? Is there an express line to the place? Or is there another way possible? Polus the great seems to delight in hopping about in the swamps of the N. Y. V. Z., like a blown-up (bloated) frog. His tirades excite general detestation. He has made himself immensely ridiculous. The main thing is only that the fellow cannot smuggle any more rotten elements into the newspaper company than are already in it. In this regard the caution is important. The organization here is no better nor worse than formerly. Our group has about the strength of the North side group in Chicago, and then, besides this, we have also the soc. rev. 6, the Austrian and Bohemian leagues—three more groups. Finally, it is easily seen that our influence with the trade organizations is steadily growing. We insert our meetings only in the Fr., and cannot notice that they are worse attended than at the time when we yet threw the weekly $1.50 and $2 into the mouth of the N. Y. V. Z. Don't forget putting yourself into communication with Drury in reference to the English organ. He will surely work with you much and well. Such a paper is more necessary than the *Tooth*. This, indeed, is getting more miserable and confused from issue to issue, and in general is whistling from the last hole. Inclosed is a fly-leaf which recently appeared at Emden, and is, perhaps, adopted for reprint. Greetings to Schwab, Rau, and to you. Your

"JOHANN MOST.

"P. S.—To Buchtell I will, of course, write for the present only in general terms.

"A. Spies, 107 Fifth avenue, Chicago, Ill."

Mr. Gauss then read the following as his translation of the postal card:

"DEAR SPIES:—I had scarcely mailed my letter yesterday when the telegraph brought news from H. M. One does not know whether to rejoice over that or not. The advance in itself is elevating. Sad is the circumstance that it will remain local and therefore may not have the result. At any rate, these people made a better impression than the foolish voters on this and the other side of the ocean. Greeting and a hail. Your
"J. M."

W. A. S. Graham, a reporter for *The Times*, testified that he talked with the witness for the prosecution, Harry Gilmer, on the afternoon of May 5, and that Gilmer said the man who threw the bomb lit the fuse himself. "He said he saw the man light the fuse and throw the bomb, and that he could identify him again if he saw him. He said the man was of medium size and had a soft hat and whiskers. He said the man's back was turned to him."

At this stage the defense rested, and evidence in rebuttal was introduced. Justice Daniel Scully testified that in the preliminary examination of one Frank Steuner, charged with shooting from the wagon at the Haymarket, Officers Foley and Wessler did not testify that it was Steuner who fired on the police.

"Did the officers not say the man who jumped up from behind the wagon was a heavy man, with long whiskers (Fielden)?"
—"They did."

"Did not Officer Foley say he would be able to identify this man if he ever saw him again?"—"He did.'

John B. Ryan, an attorney who defended Steuner before

Justice Scully, testified that Steuner said at the time that the man who did the shooting was a short, heavy-set man with full whiskers.

United States District Attorney R. S. Tuthill, Charles B. Dibble, an attorney, Judge Chester C. Cole, of Des Moines, Iowa, E. R. Mason, Clerk of the United States District Court at Des Moines, George Crist, Ex-City Marshal of Des Moines, and Ex-Governor Samuel Merrill of Iowa, all testified to the good character of the witness Gilmer. They would believe him under oath. Governor Merrill had known Gilmer since 1872, and had given him employment.

As the great trial drew toward its close popular interest in the proceedings increased. The Criminal Court building was crowded with people daily long before the hour for opening court arrived, and many times the number who gained admission were turned away. On the day of the closing argument by the prosecution, and while the jury were deliberating over their verdict, extra precautions were taken to protect the administrators of the law. A cordon of police and deputy sheriffs surrounded the building, and no one was allowed to enter who could not be properly identified.

CHAPTER V.

ARGUMENTS FOR THE PROSECUTION AND DEFENSE.

Assistant State's-Attorney Frank Walker began the opening argument for the prosecution Wednesday, August 11. The speaker said:

"We stand in the temple of justice to exercise the law, where all men stand equal. No matter what may have been the deep turpitude of the crime, no matter what may have been the design, though it aim even at the overthrow of the law itself, no man ought to be convicted of the crime charged until proven guilty beyond all reasonable doubt. These men were presumed innocent at the outset until the proof presented by the State established their guilt. The defendants were charged with murder. Murder was defined to be the unlawful killing of a person in the peace of the people. An accessory was he who stands by and aids or abets or advises the deed, or who, not standing by, aids or abets or advises the deed, and such persons are to be considered as principals and punished. Whether the principals are punished or not, they are equally as guilty as the principals. When a number of persons conspire together to do a certain act, and when, in furtherance of this design, some one is killed, all those in the conspiracy are guilty of murder before the fact. The defendant's counsel have told you these men conspired to precipitate the social revolution, and though that conspiracy cost Matthias J. Degan his life, yet you are told these defendants are guilty only of murder. Was Luther Payne or Mrs. Surratt held guilty when in the execution of a conspiracy President Lincoln was killed? Neither Payne nor Surratt committed the deed, yet they were held guilty. There was a

COUNSEL FOR THE STATE.

conspiracy; it was designed to bring about another revolution. Booth killed President Lincoln, but all who participated in the conspiracy had to forfeit their lives.

"If a body of men, inflamed with resentment, proceed to pull down a building, or to remove an objectionable obstruction and death to some one ensues, each one of these men is individually responsible for the killing. Nobody knew this better than August Spies, the author of the 'Revenge' circular. Suppose that a body of men undertake to pull down a building; there is a common design to demolish that building, and a stone is thrown, not at any individual but at the building, and some one is struck by this stone and killed, all of those engaged in the execution of that common design are responsable for the killing of this one person. When there is an intent grievously to hurt and death is occasioned, then the offense is murder. Was this man [pointing to Fischer] in this conspiracy for murder? This man with his revolver a foot long and his file dagger with a groove? What is this groove for? It is for prussic acid. Was this man in the conspiracy?

Mr. Walker then read a passage from Most's "Revolutionary Warfare" telling how prussic-acid can be applied to groov d daggers, making them the more deadly. "This is the test: Was the bomb thrown in furtherance of the common design? If it was it makes no difference whether it was thrown by one of these conspirators here or not. Nobody had been advocating the use of dynamite but Socialists. Was there anybody who would throw a bomb except a Socialist? We have proved that Lingg made the bomb in furtherance of the common design. 'You have done this, Louis Lingg,' said Huebner, and Lingg went away and complained that he was blamed for doing the good work."

Mr. Walker reiterated that every one of the 3,000 men said by Spies to have participated in the conspiracy were equally guilty of the murder of Officer Degan. All the members of the Lehr und Wehr Verein were included in this charge. He pointed out the fact that nearly all of the witnesses for the defense are members of Anarchist bodies; that their sympathies are with the prisoners, and that it has been abundantly shown by their cross-examination that they would not hesitate to pervert the truth in order to shield their confederates from the consequences of their acts.

MR. ZEISLER FOR THE DEFENSE.

Mr. Zeisler, of the counsel for the defense, set to work at once to tear Mr. Walker's address to pieces. He accused the assistant State's Attorney of distorting the facts in the case, and attempting to bring about a conviction by working on the prejudices and suspicions of the jury. Mr. Walker impugned the motives and the characters of the defenses' witnesses. Mr. Zeisler continued:

"Who are their principal witnesses? The policemen who were at the Haymarket. And before we get through we will show that these men were not heroes, but knaves, led on by the most cowardly knave who ever held a public position. It has been proved that most of these policemen who went on the stand had been at one time or another members of the detective force, and the Supreme Court tells us that a detective is a liar!"

The speaker went on to attack the other State witnesses.

Detectives are taken from the criminal classes. Harry L. Gilmer, he said, is constitutional liar, and the only witness who has been impeached. Some of the reporters, he acknowledges, tell the truth, and on their statements the defense will partially rely to show the innocence of the prisoners.

"Nobody understands why the police came down to break up the meeting. Detectives have sworn here that after Mr. Parsons suggested that the meeting adjourn to Zephf's hall, and the sky clouded up, the crowd dwindled down to two hundred or three hundred men, and then came this army of 180 policemen, armed with clubs and revolvers, headed by this hero, Bonfield, the savior of his country, to break up this meeting of peaceable and unarmed citizens. Was this courageous, or was it cowardly? It was an assault in the eyes of the law. The counsel for the State have attempted to make you believe that these disciples of Herr Most took a match and lighted a bomb which Most says should have a fuse not longer than two inches. Doesn't it seem very probable that they would have lighted with a match this fuse, which would burn out in a few seconds, when they could have carried a lighted cigar to do it with? We have the testimony of a number of witnesses that Spies was not out of the wagon till the trouble began; and if Mr. Grinnell had had more sense in the prosecution of this case; if he had not been blinded by malice and prejudice; if he had not been influenced by the police conspiracy to send these men to the gallows, he would have seen the uselessness of attempting to secure a conviction by such testimony as that of Gilmer."

MR. INGHAM FOR THE PROSECUTION.

Mr. George Ingham addressed the jury for the prosecution.

He told them that there are verdicts which make history, and that theirs will be a history-making verdict. On the night of May 4, at 10 o'clock, Matthias J. Degan marched out of the Desplaines street station, full of life, and was soon afterward struck down by the hands of these defendants, not one of whom he had ever injured. The speaker told the jury again what "reasonable doubt" means. He said that the grand jury might have indicted 300 men instead of eight, but they saw fit to pick out the eight whom they deemed the leaders of the conspiracy against law and human life. There had been a good deal of talk, he said, about the constitutional right of free speech. The Constitution gave the people the right to meet and petition, but not to advise other people to commit murder. This right was based upon the old English common law, and in England was also found a definition of what constitutes incitement to murder. The case he was going to quote had also had another connection with the present one. It was brought in London in 1881 against Johann Most, who was then publishing his sheet, the *Freiheit*, in that city. It was shortly after the assassination of the Czar of Russia. He there advocated the assassination of all the heads of States, from Constantinople to Washington, and was convicted of inciting to murder. Mr. Ingham read the proceedings in the English court, the article upon which he was tried, and Lord Coleridge's decision. Then he said: "It is shown that these defendants—Spies, Parsons, Schwab and Fischer—were engaged in the publication of articles in which they advised the destruction of the police by force, in which they advised working men to arm themselves with dynamite and be ready whenever the conflict should come to destroy the police force. For the publication of any one of these articles the defendants could have been convicted of a misdemeanor. And when Fielden that night told the people that war had been declared and that they must arm themselves to resist what had never taken place, he was guilty of a misdemeanor, and for that reason, if for no other, the police had a right to disperse the meeting. The treatment that Herr Most received in London shows you that the only salvation of a community is to enforce the letter of the law without sentiment, that bloodshed may be avoided. Herr Most was convicted for the publication of that article, and no English policemen have been blown up with dynamite. He came to this country, and the policemen who have been blown up are the American officers right here in this city. If we have not enforced the law it is high time that we enforce it now."

Mr. Ingham then showed that the Haymarket meeting was a trap for the police designed for the purpose of leading them into a dark, dangerous place, the speeches being the bait, artfully increased until the police came to the alley and the bomb could be thrown. "Now who made the bomb? It is in evidence that Louis Lingg had been making bombs of a certain construction which Spies had said were superior, being of composite metal. It is in evidence that Lingg all the morning of May 4 was away from his house; that he upbraided Seliger for having made but one bomb. During the afternoon he was busy making bombs, and men came and went and worked at the bombs in his house. There is a story of a man who that day received bombs and dynamite from Lingg, showing that he distributed them." Mr. Ingham read to the jury the chemical analysis of the bombs furnished by Drs. Haines and Delafontaine. What is the answer to all this? That the bomb was not thrown from the alley, but from thirty-eight feet south of the alley. And if they had satisfied you of that, was it not still thrown by one of the Anarchists—one of the conspirators? The bomb came from the conspiracy. And the moment it resulted in the death of Degan the crime of conspiracy was merged into the crime of murder.

"When Sumter was fired on, when the flag was insulted, when the attempt was made to destroy the Government, it was an attempt merely to change the form of government. When the bomb in this war was thrown it was the opening shot of a war which should destroy all government, destroy all law, leave men free to live as they see fit, and leave nothing to guide but the strong arm. I believe for myself that humanity —not merely our people, not merely we of America, but that humanity the wide world over—has no hope or no safety save the law. Law is the very shield that guards the progression of the race; it is the palladium of the liberty and lives of all people. Law which does not punish murder breeds death. Jurors who from the merciful instincts of their hearts hesitate to convict the guilty, are, in reality, mercilesss as the grave, for by their verdict they people graves with the innocent victims of midnight assassination and fill the mind with deeds of blood. Innocent blood from the days of Abel till now cries to Heaven for vengeance; innocent blood that contaminates the ground upon which it falls, and from it spring up dragon's teeth. And now if you believe these men guilty, if you are satisfied beyond a reasonable doubt, as you cannot help but be, that these men were a party to a conspiracy unlawful in its nature, and that from that conspiracy a human life was taken, that they are murderers under that law, see to it that the majesty of the law of the state of Illinois is vindicated, and its penalties enforced. That is the demand upon you this day and this hour, not only of the people of the state of Illinois, but of humanity itself; for humanity, with all its fears, with all its hopes for future years, is hanging breathless on your fate."

MR. FOSTER FOR THE DEFENSE.

Mr. Foster, who followed for the defense, had not lived long in Chicago. He came in March from Davenport, Iowa, near which city he was born about forty years ago. He is of medium height and square build. His features are refined and intellectual. An abundant growth of rich auburn hair adorns his shapely head. Mr. Foster obtained considerable fame as a lawyer in his native state, took an active part in politics, and was one of the Blaine Electors in 1884, and was very active in the campaign of that year. After having made an energetic and finely-eloquent plea to the jury to cast aside all prejudice arising from hatred of the principles of the Anarchists, love of and loyalty to the land, inherent patriotism, and the teachings of the popular press, Mr. Foster proceeded, in order to set himself right, to tear down without apology the theory of the defense set up by Messrs. Salomon & Zeisler. He had no defense to make for Socialism—it is dangerous; Communism is pernicious, and Anarchism is damnable. Lingg had manufactured bombs, and he ought to be punished therefor; but he was on trial for throwing, not manufacturing bombs. Spies, Schwab and Fischer had no business to preach social revolution in America. If they were not satisfied with the state of things here they ought to have gone back to Germany and tried to reform things there. Mr. Fielden might have found occupation in teaching his brother Englishmen to be just to Ireland. Parsons he rebuked in an eloquent passage for his lack of patriotism. Having thus skillfully set himself right with the jurors, Mr. Foster proceeded to define the issue of the trial as he understood it, and as he wished the jury to understand it. He admitted the moral responsibility of some of the prisoners for the crime. He denied their legal responsibility.

"Our law knows no citizenship when a defendant is brought to the bar of justice. Our law is grand enough, our law is broad enough, the principles upon which our Government is founded are such that it matters not whether he be French, German, Irish, Italian, or wherever his birthplace may be. All men are equal before the law. They are all citizens of the United States except Louis Lingg. I believe the testimony shows that he has been in the country two years. I think that Spies said he came here in infancy. I know as a matter of fact that Neebe, born in the state of Pennsylvania, never was a foreigner. Schwab has been in this country long enough to be a citizen. Whether he is or not is entirely immaterial for the purposes of this case. I know that Fielden has been here more than twenty years. I know that Fischer has been in Chicago for the last ten to twelve years, and Engel for fifteen or twenty years. What is the importance of the suggestion that they are foreigners, and Germans, except that it is important to wring from you a verdict grounded on prejudice. * * * It was an open secret that the defendants were indicted for murder, conspiracy and riot, but I will only argue the question of conspiracy so far as it relates to the crime of murder. The question of Socialism was of no importance unless it was connected with the murder of Degan, and the defendants were not being tried for any offense but that of conspiracy which resulted in the muraer of Degan. The prosecution had oeen trying to toie the defendants out into the underbrush and assassinate them on immaterial issues; but the defendants' counsel were too smart to be seduced by the song of the siren. Suppose Spies *et. al.* did conspire to overthrow society and their conspiracy stopped there, then there was nothing to argue. A verdict rendered upon anything else than a conspiracy directly connected with the outrage perpetrated at the Haymarket, would fall to the ground and amount to nothing."

Referring to the popular clamor against the Socialists, Mr. Foster said: "Outside of you twelve gentlemen, the judge upon the bench, and counsel on either side, there is not a man in Chicago who has a right to say he has an opinion founded upon the facts in this case. If these men are to be tried on general principles for advocating doctrines opposed to our ideas of propriety, there is no use for me to argue the case. Let the Sheriff go and erect the scaffold; let him bring eight ropes with dangling nooses at the ends; let him pass them around the necks of these eight men; and let us stop this farce now, if the verdict and conviction is to be upon prejudice and general principles. We boast of our courts of justice, of our equitable law, but if the time has come, when men are to be prejudged before the trial and convicted upon general principles, all that is grand, sacred, noble and praiseworthy in our temples of justice will be destroyed. Considering the experience of us all in relation to this Haymarket tragedy, considering the facts that we know to be true, do you blame me for saying I am afraid of your passions? I am afraid of your prejudices." Holding up the Czar bomb, Mr. Foster exclaimed in a loud voice: "Hang Spies, and Neebe, and Schwab, and Parsons, and Fielden, and Fischer, and Lingg, and

Engel!" Taking up a tin dynamite can he continued: "Among other things, three tin cans were found under a sidewalk in the city. Strangle them to death, in part because these three cans were found! When were they in possession of any of the defendants? Never, so far as the testimony is concerned. When were they prepared and filled at the house of any of the defendants, or any of their associates? Never, so far as the testimony is concerned. And yet they are not only introduced in evidence, their contents examined and sworn to, but you are expected to smell them; you are asked to examine them at the risk of a headache, and they want your noses near to their tops. Why? Because they were found in the city of Chicago. And that is part of the testimony upon which the lives of these eight men are to be destroyed. But it is all in a lifetime; it is all part of the grand combination; it is all in the great conspiracy, because counsel tell us it is. Such evidence was never introduced in any court of justice in the civilized world without objection. It was said Herr Most described such things in his book on 'Revolutionary Warfare.' There is not a word of testimony that any of the defendants ever read that book. But that does not make any difference. They are Socialists—hang them. That does not make any difference. They are Communists—hang them; they are Anarchists—hang them. I always supposed that the lowest creature that possessed life was entitled to some consideration. I supposed there was not a thing in existence so low, so poor or loathsome, but had some rights, and I do not believe it now, except it be a Socialist, Communist or Anarchist. That puts them beyond the pale of civilization; it puts them beyond the protection of the law; it convicts them of itself."

W. P. BLACK AND WIFE.

CAPTAIN W. P. BLACK FOR THE DEFENSE.

On Tuesday, August 17, the fiftieth day of the trial, Captain W. P. Black, the leading counsel for the defense, made his plea. He said:

"May it please the Court, and Gentlemen of the jury: On the morning of May 5, 1886, the good people of Chicago were startled at the event which happened at the Haymarket. Fear is the mother of cruelty, and perhaps that will account in some measure for the bitterness with which the State has prosecuted this case. The serious question which confronts us, however, is to what extent, you, gentlemen, in your deliberations, may be influenced by passion or by prejudice. On the night of May 4 a dynamite bomb was thrown at the Haymarket in this city and exploded. It caused widespread havoc and loss of human life. But the moral responsibility for dynamite does not rest upon the Socialists. This explosive was given to the world by science. We might well stand appalled at the dread results this terrible agent is capable of producing. When a man is charged, or sought to be charged, with a crime, as in this case, the people must show who threw the bomb—who did the deed—and must show that these defendants were connected directly with the guilty man."

The speaker said that counsel for the State were wrong when one of them advised the jury that upon them it depended to maintain the law and government, because these defendants plotted against the state. They were revolutionists, it was said, but that was not true. There can be no revolution, though, except when the heart of the people rise to redress some great wrong.

"As to the witnesses for the State, the testimony of two of them, Gilmer and Thompson, who swore to having seen Schnaubelt throw the bomb, was impeached. Gilmer's story was utterly improbable in itself; the rational mind rejected it. Is it credible? Mr. Ingham has said Spies was the brainiest man among the Anarchists, and the greatest coward. The witness Gilmer testified that he saw Spies get down from the wagon and go into the alley with Schnaubelt; saw him strike the light, fire the bomb, and give it to Schnaubelt, who hurled it among the police. Is that credible? Remember, Spies, a man of brains, of more than average brains; would he light the match that fired that bomb, and the police almost upon him? Is that credible? It was also said Spies was a great coward. Then, if that were true, would he run the risk of lighting the bomb? The counter-proof was abundant. A half a dozen reputable citizens standing in the mouth of the alley had testified that they did not see Spies leave the wagon, and that he did not enter the alley before the bomb exploded. This was negative testimony, it was true, but considering the narrow space and how unlikely it was that Spies, whom they all knew, could enter the alley without being seen by the witnesses, it was conclusive. Again, two or three witnesses testified that Schnaubelt went home early in the evening, disappointed because there was no German speaking, and was not at the Haymarket when the explosion took place."

The circumstantial evidence presented by the State, and by which it was sought to enmesh the defendants, was next considered. The case of the state was substantially this. The meeting at the Haymarket May 4 was an incident in the carrying out of an organized scheme. August Spies was there to precipitate a conflict with the police. He put Parsons on the stand, who made a long harangue, but the police did not appear. Then Fielden was put up to speak. The police came, and the act was accomplished. But who called this meeting? Not Spies, not Neebe, not Parsons, not Schwab, nor Engel, nor Lingg, nor Fischer, as an individual act. It was the result of another meeting, held the night before at 54 West Lake street, and about which Spies knew nothing.

"Again, the State wished it to be understood that Spies, in order to get the men ripe for revolt, went out to McCormick's May 3, and forced himself on a meeting there. Then, having worked up his auditors to a pitch of excitement and inflamed them to attack the non-union men, he came down town and wrote the 'Revenge' circular, calling for the Haymarket meeting. But did he encourage the men at McCormick's to violence? The testimony, and it was not controverted, proved that he counseled peace; that he told the men to stand firm and to trust to concerted action for the attainment of their ends. The further circumstance proving that no violence was contemplated that night consisted in this, that when the black cloud came up and rain was threatened, an adjournment was proposed. Fielden had the stand at that time, but he, simple soul, begged a few minutes' delay, saying he had but little more to say, and then in all simplicity went on to say it. All this was in the line going to prove that Spies had no connection with the alleged conspiracy. The circular calling for the Tuesday night meeting referred to a specific object. Do not the circumstances," continued Captain Black, "prove that August Spies was not aware of the meeting held May 3? Do they not prove that he could have no share in the design of that meeting, of which the one at Haymarket, with its result, was an incident in the general conspiracy? As to the Haymarket meeting, was it not a lawful assemblage? Who first broke the laws? That meeting was called by a circular. It was called to denounce a grievance. Perhaps there was no real grievance, but if the projectors of the meeting thought there was they had the right to assemble. The Constitution given us by our forefathers who made the name of revolutionists glorious, gave us that right. That right was incorporated in the fundamental laws of the nation. One clause in the Constitution allows the people to assemble together in a peaceable manner to discuss their grievances, another provides that the people have the right to assemble together in a peaceable manner to discuss measures for their common good, and to instruct their representatives. I am not here to defend Socialism, nor do I contend that Anarchy has in it the elements of true reform, but I am here to defend these men. They are Socialists. That system centuries ago had the sanction of St. Augustine. John Stuart Mill is one of a great host of philosophers who have subscribed in fealty to Socialism.

"These defendants have the right to discuss the great wrongs of the working people. They have the right to try their remedy. They say that private property is robbery. That may be false. There is not a Catholic organization that is not founded on the idea of common co-operation. It was Plato's dream that the means of existence should be the common property of all. The Anarchist or Socialist was said to believe that every law of man was a bone of contention, intended for the benefit of one class only. The fact that these defendants are Anarchists is not a fact which would justify the jury in

JULIUS S. GRINNELL.

taking their lives. These men are not the lazy fellows pictured by the state."

STATE'S ATTORNEY JULIUS S. GRINNELL FOR THE PROSECUTION.

State's Attorney Grinnell closed for the State, and he began his remarks by criticising counsel for the defense for making heroes of the prisoners. The Anarchists were compared to the fathers of our country; they were pictured as martyrs, as men who sacrificed themselves for the welfare of human kind. If that be so, songs of praise should be sung, and the Anarchists ought to be garlanded with flowers. Captain Black had said that society was discriminating against the poor; that the struggle for existence was daily becoming harder. That was not true, for civil liberty was never before as widespread as it is at present. Mr. Grinnell said the case had received his entire attention since May 5. Government was on trial. Murder had been committed. It was sought to know who was responsible. For a few days after the Haymarket riot it was not thought it was more far-reaching than the results of the inflammatory speech-making. It was not until after the magnificent efforts of Captain Schaack that a conspiracy was developed. Then Schnaubelt was discovered. It was not until after Spies was arrested that it became apparent that a man was capable of the hellish act in which he was concerned. A mistake had been made. It was said the State would show who the bomb thrower was. This had not been done, owing to the inability of certain witnesses to make good on the stand the statements they had before made to the officers. These men were not Socialists, but Anarchists, and their creed is no government, no law. Until placed on the stand these men never hedged on that definition. It was sought to be shown that the defendants were barking dogs that would not bite. These men were on trial, law was on trial, Anarchy was on trial for treason. The penalty of treason is death. A man can commit an overt act of treason, and not kill anybody. Is it any the less treason because seven men are killed and sixty wounded? There is no statute of limitation for threats, when repeated threats resulted in the commission of the deed. For years past, on the Lake front and at the different so-called Socialistic halls in the city, these men had preached the use of dynamite, poison and daggers as a means of effecting the social revolution. The thing should have been stopped long ago. But that was foreign to the case. The men were here now on trial for murder. Their threats had been carried out. It did not matter whether any police officers had overstepped their duty; the jury had nothing at all to do with that. The accused were on trial for murder.

On the Lake front the Anarchists were wont to assemble under the red flag, which they described as the emblem of universal liberty. But there was but one flag of liberty—that was the Stars and Stripes; and it would always remain such if the gentlemen of the jury had the courage to uphold the law. Threats had been mouthed, dire vaporings were spread from one group to another to fill the people with terror, so that the social revolution might the more easily be accomplished. Mr. Grinnell holds that Spies wrote the "Revenge" circular premeditatedly. He reads it to the jury commenting on various passages contained therein, and makes it plain to the jury that Spies had an ulterior and sinister purpose in view when he penned the famous dodger. There were only two officers at McCormicks when the mob Spies was addressing broke loose and attacked the non-union men. The police were called, but why? To protect the McCormick property and the two officers from the fury of the mob as well as to save the non-union men from being killed. It was this sight—the coming of additional police—that made the blood of the valorous Spies boil. Knowing that no fatalities had taken place, or not knowing that any had occured, Spies posted down town, and the "Revenge" circular was written by him and in the hands of the printer before 5 o'clock that same afternoon. Balthazar Rau's name was mentioned every day, time and time again by the defense, but he was not called as a witness. They were afraid to put him on the stand. It was Rau who invited Spies to address the Haymarket meeting, and he was present when Spies made his speech. That was a kind of Marc Antony address, and to be understood one must read it between the lines. It was artfully calculated to inflame. It was a significant opening. The working men were told to come armed. Waller did come armed. The police should have broken up the meeting in its incipiency. If Bonfield had not gone down there at the time he did the riot would have been general. The reason more bombs were not thrown was that the other fellows in the conspiracy had not time to reach the scene. The man who threw the bomb obtained it from Lingg or Spies, and hurled it according to directions received from one or other of these men. Did Fielden shoot that night? For years past he has called the police bloodhounds; he said he would march down Michigan avenue with the red flag or the black flag, and preached "death to the capitalists and the police, our despoilers." This must be understood above all things; that the bomb was thrown in furtherance of the common design, no matter who threw it. Gilmer said Spies handed the bomb to Schnaubelt. Is that improbable? For years he preached the throwing of bombs. An article over his own signature is in evidence, and in this he gives directions as to the manner in which bombs should be ignited and hurled at the enemy. Who was Schnaubelt? Schwab's brother-in-law. He is the man who was arrested before the conspiracy was known and let go, then shaved off his whiskers, and has not been seen since. A peculiar circumstance, and the most significant of the case, was that when Spies was arrested he left the traces of his crime in his office. Bonfield arrested him. Spies said he went over to the Central station unsuspectingly. Had he known what was going to have happened he would have destroyed the "Ruhe" manuscript. It was the little mistakes that brought the criminal to justice, and there never was a criminal, big or little, that did not leave traces of his crime behind him.

Mr. Grinnell concluded by saying his labor was over; the jury's was just begun. They had the power to exact the lives of some of the prisoners, to others they might give a term of years in the penitentiary, and some again they might acquit. He would not ask the jury to take the life of Oscar Neebe. He would not ask the jury to do what he would not do himself. The proof was not sufficient to convict Neebe, but some of them, Spies, Fischer, Lingg, Engel, Fielden, Parsons and Schwab, ought to have the extreme penalty administered to them.

"Personally," said Mr. Grinnell, "I have not a word to say against these men. But the law demands that they be punished. They have violated the law, and you, gentlemen of the jury, stand between the living and the dead. Do your duty. Do not disagree. If you think that some of them do not deserve

JOS. E. GARY.

the death penalty give them a life sentence, out do not disagree. Gentlemen, this is no pleasant task for me, but it is my duty; do yours."

CHAPTER VI.

THE INSTRUCTIONS OF THE COURT.

In his instructions to the jury Judge Gary said: "The Court instructs the jury that whoever is guilty of murder shall suffer the punishment of death, or imprisonment in the penitentiary for his natural life, or for a term of not less than fourteen years. If the accused are found guilty by a jury they shall fix the punishment by their verdict.

"The Court instructs the jury as a matter of law that, in considering the case, the jury are not to go beyond the evidence to hunt up doubts, nor must they entertain such doubts as are merely chimerical or conjectural. A doubt to justify an acquittal must be reasonable, and must arise from a candid and impartial investigation of all the evidence in the case, and unless it is such that, were the same kind of doubt interposed in the graver transactions of life, it would cause a reasonable and prudent man to hesitate and pause, it is sufficient to authorize a verdict of not guilty. If, after considering all the evidence, you can say you have an abiding conviction of the truth of the charge, you are satisfied beyond a reasonable doubt.

"If it does so prove, then your duty to the State requires you to convict whosoever is found guilty. The case of each of the defendants should be considered with the same care and scrutiny as if he alone were on trial. If a conspiracy having violence and murder as its object is fully proved, then the acts and declarations of each one of the conspirators, before or after

May 4, which are merely narrative as to what had been or would be done, and not made to aid in carrying into effect the object of the conspiracy, are only evidence against the person who made them. What are the facts and what is the truth the jury must determine from the evidence, and from that alone. If there are any unguarded expressions in any of the instructions which seem to assume the existence of any facts, or to be any intimation as to what is proved, all such expressions must be discouraged and the evidence only looked to, to determine the facts.

" The Court instructs the jury as a matter of law that an accessory is he who stands by and aids, abets, or assists, or who, not being present, aiding, abetting, or assisting, has advised, encouraged, aided or abetted the perpetration of that caime. He who thus aids, abets, assists, advises or encourages shall be considered as a principal and punished accordingly. Every such accessory when a crime is committed within or without this state by his aid or procurement in this state, may be indicted and convicted at the same time as the principal, or before or after his conviction, and whether the principal is convicted or amenable to justice or not, and punished as principal.

" If the defendants attempted to overthrow the law by force and threw the bomb, then the defendants who were in the conspiracy were guilty of murder. If there was an Anarchistic conspiracy, and the defendants were parties to it, they are guilty of murder, though the date of the culmination of the conspiracy was not fixed. If any of the defendants conspired to excite by advice people to riot and murder, such defendants are guilty if such murder was done in pursuance of said conspiracy ; the impracticalness of the aim of the defendants is immaterial.

"Circumstantial evidence is competent to prove guilt, and if defendants conspired to overthrow the law and Degan was killed in consequence, the parties are guilty, and it is not necessary that any of the defendants were present at the killing.

"All parties to the conspiracy are equally guilty. Circumstantial evidence must satisfy the jury beyond reasonable doubt. In such case the jury may find defendants guilty. When defendants testified in the case they stood on the same ground as other witnesses."

THE VERDICT.

The jury retired at 2:50 o'clock Thursday, August 19. The first intimation that an agreement had been reached was when word was sent to the Revere house to prepare supper for the jury, it having been understood that unless a decision as to the fate of the prisoners was reached before 10 o'clock, supper would not be served at that time. Friday morning the excitement of the crowd in front of the Criminal Court building was something intense while the verdict was being awaited. There was none of the joking and laughing that is heard on the only other occasion that brings a mob to stand without those dreary walls—the execution of a convicted criminal. Such conversations as were held were in a low tone, and related solely to the one topic—the probable conviction of the eight prisoners who were waiting for the hour which was to mean life or death to them. Both sides of the street were lined with people who awaited anxiously for some tidings from the court within. An army of bailiffs and policemen guarded the big doors, and the surging masses were only kept back by sheer force. The limited number who obtained admission to courtroom were the reporters and the immediate friends and relatives of the defendants. The gaily-dressed women who had attended the trial since the start were not there. The court officials decided that the relatives of the prisoners should be allowed in the courtroom, and at 9:15 o'clock the sister of Spies, with another young woman, made her appearance. Shortly afterward the mother of Spies, accompanied by a younger son, also entered the courtroom and took a seat on the back benches. At 9:20 Mrs. Parsons entered the court room, accompanied by a woman who attended her throughout the trial. She was given a seat between two policemen. The row of seats farthest removed from the judge were occupied by a force of police officers. Next below, seated in the order named, were Henry Spies; Mrs. Spies, the prisoner's mother; Miss Spies; Chris Spies, and a young lady friend. Next below was Mrs. Martin. The ladies looked anxious. Mrs. and Miss Spies and Mrs. Parsons looked worn out, though the latter tried to appear unconcerned, and occupied her time in reading newspapers. It was 9:50 o'clock when the Judge came in. He looked nervous and excited. He was barely seated when Captain Black entered. The Captain took a seat near his wife. He had just paid a visit to his clients.

"Are they prepared for the worst?" asked Mrs. Black, anxiously.

"Prepared!" repeated the Captain. "Yes; fully prepared to laugh at death. They talk about the matter much more coolly than I can."

A moment or two later the prisoners were brought in. They were not given their usual seats, but placed in a row on a bench against the wall at the Judge's left, in the narrow aisle leading to the passage way to the jail. They sat in the same old order. Spies was at the head, next to the judge. All looked haggared and excited. Even the usually stocial face of Lingg wore an expression of anxiety. Fischer was deathly pale and trembled visibly. These pale and trembling wretches were the braggarts who a few short weeks before were boldly proclaiming the doctrines of Socialism and Anarchy on the Lake front, in Zephf's hall and the beer saloons of the North and West sides. They were the men who were advocating force and the use of dynamite, and the total annihilation of law and order, the theft of property, and murder of citizens. Their vapid mouthings were thrust upon assemblages of decent workingmen, their policy was Communism, their banner was the banner of blood, and their teachings were death and destruction. Bold and fearless as lions they appeared when indulging in flights of incendiary oratory. Like dumb, obedient beasts they bowed in submission before the most powerful scourge the law can wield—the death verdict.

The jurymen filed in and took their seats in the jury box. They looked determined and resolute. There was a death-like silence in the court. In a low voice the Judge asked: "Gentlemen, have you agreed?" F. E. Osborne, the foreman, rose and replied: "We have, your honor." Taking out two sheets of foolscap from his side coat-pocket, he handed them to Clerk Doyle, who glanced at them and handed them to the Judge, who slipped them apart, trembling so that the leaves shook violently. A whispered consultation between the Judge and the Clerk followed, and the document was returned to Mr. Doyle, who read:

"We, the jury, find the defendants, August Spies, Michael Schwab, Samuel Fielden, Albert R. Parsons, Adolph Fischer,

George Engel and Louis Lingg, guilty of murder, as charged in the indictment, and fix the penalty at death.

"We find the defendant, Oscar Neebe, guilty of murder in manner and form as charged in the indictment, and fix the penalty at imprisonment in the penitentiary for a term of fifteen years."

Not a sound came from the spectators. For a moment the courtroom was silent as the tomb. The prisoners were struck with horror. Spies' face blanched white as the paper on which his death sentence was written. His lips quivered, and he mechanically tapped the floor with his foot and nervously stroked his moustache. Neebe was completely stunned. The blood rushed to his face, and the perspiration stood out on his forehead in great drops. Schwab's yellow face seemed to look into vacancy, and he had a wandering, stupid stare. Parsons was visibly affected, but he kept himself up better than the rest, and maintained a certain air of nonchalance. He made an effort to flaunt a red handkerchief out of the window at the crowd on the outside, but was promptly checked by a bailiff. Fielden fairly quaked. He shook like an aspen leaf, and in every way showed his great fear. Fischer was ghastly. When the verdict was first being read he held a half-consumed cigar in his mouth, but when the death penalty was reached the weed fell from his lips to the floor. Lingg appeared sullen and stoical, but when the sentence was read his face flushed, and he was seen to tremble. Engel betrayed no emotion. When the verdict became known to the thousands assembled outside a great cheer rent the air.

Captain Black asked that the jury be polled. The jurymen answered with firm voices. Captain Black said he would desire to make a motion for a new trial. State's Attorney Grinnell said it would be impossible to dispose of the motion during the present term, but by agreement, the motion could be argued at the September term. This was agreed to by the defense.

The Court.—"Let the motion be entered and continued until the next term, and let the defendants be taken back to jail." Judge Gary then arose and addressed the jury as follows:

"GENTLEMEN OF THE JURY:—You have finished this long and very arduous trial, which has required a very considerable sacrifice of time, and some hardship. I hope that everything has been done that could possibly be done to make those sacrifices and hardships as mild as might be permitted. It does not become me to say anything in regard to the case that you have tried, or the verdict you have rendered; but men compulsorily serving as jurors, as you have done, deserve some recognition of the service you have performed besides the meager compensation you have received."

The Foreman of the jury said: "The jury have deputed to me the only agreeable duty, that it is in our province to perform, and that is to thank the Court and the counsel for the defense and for the prosecution, for your kindly care to make us as comfortable as possible during our confinement. We thank you."

The jury then filed out, and scarcely had they left the room when a shrill voice was heard, and Mrs. Schwab fell heavily to the floor. She was taken out into the fresh air by policemen, and soon revived. Mrs. Spies followed up this scene by going into hysterics, and also had to be assisted from the room. The other women kept their nerves, and after the first shock maintained composure. In the meantime the crowd had closed in on the prisoners, and were examining them from head to foot. The bailiffs, however, promptly put a stop to this, and led the condemned men away to their cells.

THE JURORS.

The twelve good men and true, who sat in judgment for so many long and weary days, are all Americans by birth. Frank S. Osborne, foreman of the jury, is a widower of thirty-nine, and the father of three sons. He is head salesman of the carpet department of Marshall Field's retail store, and came here from Columbus, Ohio. He is an Episcopalian.

Major James H. Cole, of Lawndale, the first juror accepted by both sides, was born at Utica, N. Y., forty-three years ago, and served throughout the Rebellion in the Forty-first Ohio Infantry. He came to Chicago from Chattanooga, Tennessee, six years ago, and though a bookkeeper by profession, is at present out of employment.

J. H. Brayton, principal of Webster Schoool, lives at Engelwood with his family, although a native of Lyons, N. Y. He had arranged a hunting and fishing excursion for the summer, which was ruined.

A. H. Reed is of the firm of Reed & Sons, of Reed's Temple of Music, 136 State street. He was born in Boston forty-nine years ago, but has been in the music business here for twenty-three years, living with his wife at 3242 Groveland Park. Mr. Reed is a Freethinker, but not an Atheist.

Andrew Hamilton, dealer in hardware, has lived in Chicago twenty years of the forty-one he has been on earth, and now lives with his wife at 1521 Forty-first street.

THE JURY.

C. B. Todd, forty-seven years old, was born in Elmira, N. Y., lived in Minnesota for sixteen years after the war, but is now a salesman in the Putnam Clothing House. He served in the Sixth New York Heavy Artillery. Mr. Todd lives at 1013 West Polk street.

H. T. Sanford is but twenty-four years old, and is a son of the late Lawyer Sanford, compiler of the Superior Court reports of New York. For fifteen months past he has been voucher clerk for the Chicago & Northwestern, but before coming to Chicago he was a petroleum broker at New York. He and his wife live at Oak Park.

S. C. Randall, the youngest man on the jury, was born in Erie county, Pennsylvania, in 1864, and in the three years he has been in Chicago he has been a hotel waiter, a milk peddler, and is now a salesman for J. C. Vaughan & Co., seedsmen, 45 La Salle street.

Theodore Denker, shipping clerk for H. H. King & Co., is twenty-seven years old, and lives at Woodlawn Park. He has lived in Chicago twenty-five years, and is not married.

Charles A. Ludwig is also twenty-seven years old, single, and is a clerk in the wood mantel shop of Charles L. Page & Co.

John B. Greiner is a clerk in the freight department of the Chicago & Northwestern Road, and lives at Humboldt Park. He is twenty-five years old, and single.

G. W. Adams, twenty-seven years old, travels in Michigan, selling paint for a Clinton street firm. He is a painter by trade, and lives with his brother at Evanston.

The following is the official Police Department report of casualties at the Haymarket:

CHAPTER VII.

THE CONSPIRACY AND MASSACRE. NAMES AND NUMBER OF KILLED AND WOUNDED. UNEARTHING THE PLOT. OFFICERS AT WORK AND CROWNED WITH SUCCESS. REPORT OF GRAND JURY.

NAME OF OFFICER.	STATION.	NATURE OF WOUNDS AND CIRCUMSTANCES.
August C. Killer	Third Precinct.	Shell wound in right side, and ball wound in left side. Wife and five children.
Thomas McHenry	" "	Shell wound in left kneee and three shell wounds in left hip. Single; has sister and blind mother to support.
John E. Doyle	" "	Bullet wound in back and calves of both legs; serious. Wife and one child.
John A. King	" "	Jaw bone fractured by shell, and two bullet wounds in right leg below the knee; serious. Single.
Nicholas Shannon	" "	Thirteen shell wounds on right side and five shell wounds on left side, also right foot and back; serious. Wife and three children.
MICHAEL SHEAHAN	" "	DIED MAY 9. Single.
James Conway	" "	Bullet wound in right leg. Single.
Patrick Hartford	" "	Shell wound right ankle, two toes on left foot amputated, bullet wound in left side. Wife and four children.
Patrick Nash	" "	Bruise on left shoulder by club. Single.
Arthur Conolly	" "	Two shell wounds in left leg, bones slightly fractured. Wife.
Louis Johnson	" "	Shell wound in left leg. Wife and four children.
M. M. Cardin	" "	Bullet wound in calf of both legs. Wife and two children.
Adam Barber	" "	Shell wound left leg, bullet wound in right heel, bullet not extracted. Wife and one child.
Henry F. Smith	" "	Bullet wound on right shoulder; quite serious. Wife and two children in California.
Frank Tyrell	" "	Bullet in right hip near the spine; bullet not removed. Single.
James A. Brady	" "	Shell wound in left leg, slight; injury to toes left foot and shell wounds in left thigh. Wife and two children; wife very sick at County Hospital.
John Ried	" "	Shell wound in left leg; bullet wound in right knee, not removed. Single.
GEORGE MULLER	" "	DIED MAY 6, at County Hospital. Single.
Patrick McLaughlin	" "	Bruise on right side, leg and hip; slight. Wife and three children.
Frank Murphy	" "	Trampled on, three ribs broken. Wife and two children.
Lawrence Murphy	" "	Shell wounds left side of neck and left knee; part of left foot amputated. Wife and three children.

NAME OF OFFICER.	STATION.	NATURE OF WOUNDS AND CIRCUMSTANCES.
John J. Barrett	Third Precinct.	Died May 6, at County Hospital; shot in liver. Wife.
Michael Madden	" "	Shot in left lung, will recover; killed his assailant after he was shot. Single.
Lieutenant Stanton	" "	Shell wound in right side, bullet wound in right hip, wounds inside both hips, bullet wound in calf of leg. Wife, seven children.
Matthias J. Degan	" "	Instantly Killed. Widower; father, mother and three sons.
Thomas Brophy	" "	Slight injury in left leg; reported for duty. Wife.
Bernard Murphy	" "	Bullet wound in left thigh, shell wound in right side of head and on chin; not dangerous. Wife.
Charles H. Fink	" "	Three shell wounds in left leg and two wounds on right leg, and slightly in thigh; not dangerous. Wife.
Joseph Norman	" "	Bullet passed through right foot, slight injury to fingers on left hand. Wife and two children.
Peter Butterly	" "	Bullet wound in right arm, shell wound in both legs, near knees. Wife and one child.
Alexander Jameson	" "	Bullet wound in left leg; serious. Wife and seven children.
Michael Horan	" "	Bullet wound in left thigh, not removed, slight shell wound on left arm. Single.
Thomas Hennessey	" "	Shell wound on left thigh; slight. Has crippled brother and two sisters to support.
William Burns	" "	Slight shell wound on left ankle. Single.
Thomas Redden	" "	Died May 16, at County Hospital. Fracture of left leg below knee, bullet wound in left cheek, bullet wound in right arm. Wife and two children.
James Plunkett	" "	Struck with club and trampled upon: on duty. Wife.
Charles W. Whitney	" "	Shell wound in left breast, shell not removed. Single.
Jacob Hansen	" "	Right leg amputated above the knee. Three shell wounds on left leg. Wife and one child.
Timothy Sullivan	" "	Bullet wound just above left knee. Has four children (Widower).
Martin Cullen	" "	Right collar bone fractured, and slight injury to left knee; not serious. Wife and five children.
Simon Klidzio	" "	Shot in calf of left leg; serious. Wife and three children.
Julius L. Simonson	" "	Shot in arm, near shoulder; very serious. Wife and two children.
John K. McMahon	" "	Shell wound on calf of left leg; shell not found; ball wound left leg, near knee; very serious. Wife and two children.
Simon McMahon	" "	Shot in right arm and two wounds on right leg. Wife, five children.
Edward W. Ruel	" "	Shot in right ankle, bullet not removed; serious. Single.

8

NAME OF OFFICER.	STATION.	NATURE OF WOUNDS AND CIRCUMSTANCES.
Alexander Halverson.	Third Precinct.	Shot in both legs, ball not extracted. Single.
Carl E. Johnson	" "	Shot in left elbow. Wife and two children.
Peter McCormick	" "	Slight shot wound in left arm. Wife.
Christopher Gaynor	" "	Slight bruise on left knee. Wife.
Timothy Flavin	Fourth "	DIED FROM WOUNDS, MAY 8. Wife and three children.
Nils Hansen	" "	DIED JUNE 14, at County Hospital. Shot in body, arms and legs, fingers paralyzed. Wife and six children.
S. J. Weineke	" "	Shot in left side of head, ball not found; serious. Wife and two children.
Patrick McNulty	" "	Shot in right leg and both hips; dangerous. Wife and three children.
Samuel Hilgo	" "	Shot in right leg; not serious. Single.
Herman Krueger	" "	Shot in right knee. Wife and two children.
Joseph A. Gilso	" "	Slightly injured in leg and back. Wife and six children.
Edward Barrett	" "	Shot in right leg; quite serious. Wife and six children.
Fruman Steele	" "	Slightly wounded in back; not serious. Single.
James T. Johnson	" "	Right knee sprained; not serious. Wife and three children.
Benjamin F. Snell	" "	Shot in right leg; at hospital. Single.
James H. Willson	Central Detail.	Seriously injured in abdomen by shell, and in left hand; very serious. Wife and five children.
Daniel Hogan	" "	Shot in calf of right leg and in left hand. Wife and daughter.
M. O'Brien	" "	Shell wound in left thigh. Wife and two children.
Frederick A. Andrew	" "	Wounded in leg; not serious. Married.
Jacob Ebinger	" "	Shell wound on back of left hand. Wife and three children.
John J. Kelly	" "	Slight wound by shell, left hand. Wife and three children.
Patrick Flavin	" "	Finger hurt by shell. Married.

Total number of wounded officers, 67.   Deaths, 7.

"BEHOLD HOW GREAT A MATTER A LITTLE FIRE KINDLETH!" The explosion at the Haymarket made 3 widows, 14 orphans, and left 119 children dependent upon public charity, pending the recovery of their wounded, or perhaps permanently maimed and crippled fathers.

The business men of the city and railroad corporations promptly gave over $50,000 for the relief of the families of the officers who were killed and wounded.

THE CONSPIRACY.

The search for, and the capture of the primef-actors in the Haymarket tragedy was at once commenced in earnest. The well organized and efficient force of brave men, under command of cool headed and well skilled officers, was sure to succeed. Captain F. Schaack, with six detectives, kept the entire Northwest group under the survilance of their argus eyes. Thielen turned informer and communicated important information which fitted exactly to supply a perfect chain of evidence. The *Yipsilon* and *Ruhe* signals were significant evidence toward proving conspiracy along with the other daily developments in in the case. Several officers and detectives were detailed to make a search of several houses on Sedgwick street, among which, one Seliger's, at No. 442. As the officers were nearing the house, Louis Lingg and one, Oppenheimer, were watching them with much interest and discussing the practicability of making a rush for their arms and kill the officers rather than have the arsenal of the Anarchist, with its appliances for the manufacture of infernal machines for the consumation of conspiracy and treason, fall into the hands of the officers of the law. But the ever vigilant officers secured possession of the house and removed all suspicious articles to the station. Lingg went immediately into hiding, but was on the 14 of May arrested in a little cottage on Ambrose street. Seliger was arrested in Meyer's carpenter shop, and Thielen coming to see what Seliger was arrested for was also taken into custody. Lingg became reckless and defiant. Many of the conspirators were run to earth by those six men and arrested. Assistant State's Attorney Furthman interviewed the prisoners in their native tongue and made a record of their statements.

RUDOLPH SCHNAUBELT.

who it is now believed was the man who threw the dynamite bomb with such deadly effect, was once arrested, but on temporary release decamped at once, which suspicious action led to a further investigation. But two weeks having elapsed since his release, he made good his escape from the country no doubt. About forty Socialists were arrested and discharged again. Neebe was once discharged and re-arrested as the case developed. Gilmer's evidence some days after the riot tended very much to strengthen the belief that Schnaubelt was the party who threw the bomb, and that it was thrown under the immediate supervision and by the direction of August Spies, which is in keeping with his public speech and the secret teachings by which he was endeavoring to establish, that system of revolutionary warfare supplemented by the organization known as the *Lehr und Wehr Verin*, which is synonymous with armed protection, or teaching secretly the use of weapons for the purpose of defense.

THE GRAND JURY.

The following is an abstract of their report:

To THE HON. JUDGE JOHN G. ROGERS: In presenting the bills of indictments which we have the honor herewith to submit, in what are known as the "Anarchist cases," we deem it proper to accompany the same with a few words of explanation. We have endeavored in our deliberations and in our findings to be guided strictly by the instructions delivered to us by the Court in regard to the liability of a citizen under the law for the abuse of the privilege of free speech. We have in this connection, upon the evidence adduced, found true bills only against

such persons as had, in their abuse of this right, been more or
less instrumental in causing the riot and bloodshed at Haymarket
square, the particulars of which we were called upon to
investigate. We have in some cases refused to find bills for
the reason that persons against whom evidence was presented
seemed to be the weak and ignorant tools of designing men, and
that it was our belief should they continue their evil associations
and practices after this calamity shall have shown them to what
it leads, that some future grand jury would give their cases
proper attention. So far as we are informed this is the first
appearance of dynamite as a factor in the criminal annals of this
state, and this is also the first organized conspiracy for the destruction
of human life, and the overthrow of law in any part
of this country that has employed this new and dangerous
agency. It is not surprising that the fatal and appalling success
which has attended this, its first introduction, should have inspired
terror in this community.

We find that the attack on the police on May 4 was the result
of a deliberate conspiracy, the full details of which are now
in the possession of the officers of the law, and will be brought
out when the cases shall be reached in court. We find that
this force of disorganizers had a very perfect force of organizers
of its own, and that it was chiefly under the control of the coterie
of men who were connected with the publication of their English
and German newspaper organs, the *Alarm* and *Arbeiter
Zeitung*. The evidence has shown conclusively to us that these
men were manipulating this agitation from base and selfish
motives, for the power and influence which it gave them, and
for the money which they could make out of it; that the large
majority of their followers were simply their dupes, and they

have collected in this way large sums of money from those followers, and from the working men of this city. That their plan was to involve, so far as they could, not only the Socialist and Communist organizations, with whom they claim some kindred, but also the labor societies and trades unions, to the end that in the midst of the excitement they were creating they could not only rely upon them as a source of revenue, but also have them to fall back upon in the event of their finally being made amenable to the law. Witnesses have come before us under protest and with fear and trembling lest their appearance before this jury should draw down upon them or upon their families the secret vengeance of this unknown enemy. Branches of industry in the city have remained paralyzed after all causes of disagreement between the employer and the employed had been adjusted, by the same fear inspired among the workmen, coupled with the feeling that the law is administered was impotent to afford protection to a man ready and willing to work for the support of his family. So exaggerated has been the popular notion as to the magnitude of this force that politicians have cringed before it, and political parties have catered to its vote. Processions have been tolerated upon our public streets carrying banners and inscriptions which were a shame and a disgrace to our city, and an affront to every law-abiding citizen. Public harangues have been permitted that were an open menace to law and order, and which in logical sequence have reached their culmination in the bloody outrage known as the Haymarket massacre. We believe that a proper enforcement of the law, as expounded by your Honor in the charge made to this Grand Jury at the beginning of its session, would restore confidence, correct existing evils, preserve the peace, and protect this community from the recurrence of a like disorder.

In conclusion, we desire, as citizens and as members of this Grand Jury, in this public way to express our most grateful acknowledgments of the debt owing to the officers and men of the police force of Chicago. By their heroic bravery and their conscientiousness and devotion to duty we believe that they have saved this city from a scene of bloodshed and devastation equal to, or perhaps greater than that witnessed during the Commune in Paris. We wish further, from the evidence that has been placed before us, to express our fullest confidence that the same force that has protected us by its bravery in the face of the enemy, aided by the skill and legal ability of our Prosecuting Attorney and his assistants, is quite competent to hunt these public enemies down, and to bring them before our courts of law with sufficient evidence of guilt to insure what they so richly deserve.

Wednesday, May 19, there appeared before the grand jury as a witness one Krendl, who is in the service of the City Water Department. This witness, it was said, testified that he saw a machinest, whose name was withheld, talking with Spies and Schwab at the Haymarket the evening of the tragedy. The witness watched the trio closely and saw them go toward Halsted street and then return to the wagon so frequently referred to in connection with the massacre. Upon their return the witness noticed that the machinist had something in his right coat-pocket which filled it up as an apple or base-ball might. His attention was directed to this fact because of the persistent manner in which the machinist kept guard over the mouth of the pocket with his hand.

M. M. Thompson followed the above witness, and described a certain person who was with Schwab and Spies during the early part of the evening, and this, in connection with Krendl's testimony, was considered important by the jury. It was stated at the time that Krendl was able to give the machinist's name, from having once been a Socialist.

It was afterward discovered that Schnaubelt was the machinist referred to. Fred. P. Rosbeck, a manufacturer of light machinery at No. 224 East Washington street, stated that Schnaubelt had been in his employ about five weeks previous to the Haymarket riot. He was a good workman, but a pronounced Socialist and Anarchist, and his rabid utterances had many others in the shop to incline to his views. Schnaubelt had a companion, August Lambrecht by name, who came to work for Rosbeck about the same time he did. They were very intimate, going and coming together, and carrying on a close relationship. Tuesday, May 4, Schnaubelt asked his employer for the day, saying he had some important business to attend to. He was granted a leave of absence, but returned to work promptly Wednesday morning. Seeking to enlist him in conversation, Mr. Rosbeck said:

"Rudolph, they had a big time at the Haymarket last night."

"Yes," said Schnaubelt, "a devil of a time."

Intending to further draw him out, the employer continued:

"You Anarchists didn't half do your job, though. Why didn't you use more bombs?"

"Because," he answered, "they didn't get up with them in time."

That evening Rosbeck told this story to a friend, who informed the detective, and the arrest was made Thursday morning. Wednesday Schnaubelt had a heavy beard and moustache. At the time of his arrest Thursday he had no beard and his moustache had been trimmed close to his lip. After his release by the police Schnaubelt returned to the shop and resumed work, but that Thursday night he informed Rosbeck that he might not return the next day. He said that he feared the detectives might search his house and then arrest him. He said Mrs. Schwab was his sister, and he was often at her house. If they searched Schwab's house it might lead to his (Schnaubelt's) arrest. He has not been seen since that Thursday night. His tools and clothes remained in the shop, as also did his unpaid wages. Rosbeck thought Lambrecht had knowledge of his friend's whereabouts. About the middle of May Lambrecht informed Rosbeck that Schnaubelt had instructed him to draw his salary and take possession of his clothes.

In his evidence before the jury M M. Thompson declared that he saw either Spies or Schwab—and he felt almost certain it was the latter—hand Schnaubelt the bomb while the trio were about fifteen feet from the wagon. Schnaubelt, he said, was in waiting for them when they came from Halsted street. Krendl testified that in his opinion Schnaubelt could not have been handed the bomb at the place designated, because he saw him go to Halsted street with the speakers, and return. He admitted, however, that Schnaubelt had something in his outside pocket when near the wagon.

Schnaubelt, when arrested by Detective Palmer, admitted to Lieutenant Shea that he was with Schwab that Tuesday night, but insisted that he left the wagon on which they were standing when it commenced to rain.

Various rumors as to Schnaubelt's whereabouts were received. A letter, said to be in the fugitive's handwriting, was received by the police some weeks after the riot, from Portland, Oregon. The writer poked fun at the chief and said that the fact that he was so far away was due to the stupidity of the detective force and Lieut. Shea's gullibility.

Subsequently the body of a man was found in the canal at Erie, Pa., which in features and in the clothes upon it corresponded to the description of Schnaubelt, and it was thought he had left Chicago as a stowaway in a vessel and had been drowned in trying to get ashore at Erie at night. The authorities, however, became convinced that this was not Schnaubelt. Some of the police have always believed that Schnaubelt left the city with Parsons the night after the bomb throwing, and after remaining in hiding with the latter near Omaha until Parsons decided to appear and stand trial, continued his flight South or West, September 15, 1886, H. F. Schaffer, a conductor on the Mexican Central Railroad, on his way to his home in Ohio, called on Chief of Police Ebersold and informed him that from a picture of Schnaubelt in the *Police News*, he thought he had identified the fugitive in the person of a jeweler in the City of Mexico, who spoke English with a German accent. Mr. Schaffer and a companion visited the jeweler frequently and endeavored to draw him out upon the subject of the Haymarket massacre, but the suspected person would not talk about the Anarchists. It is understood the police took measures to investigate this supposed clue.

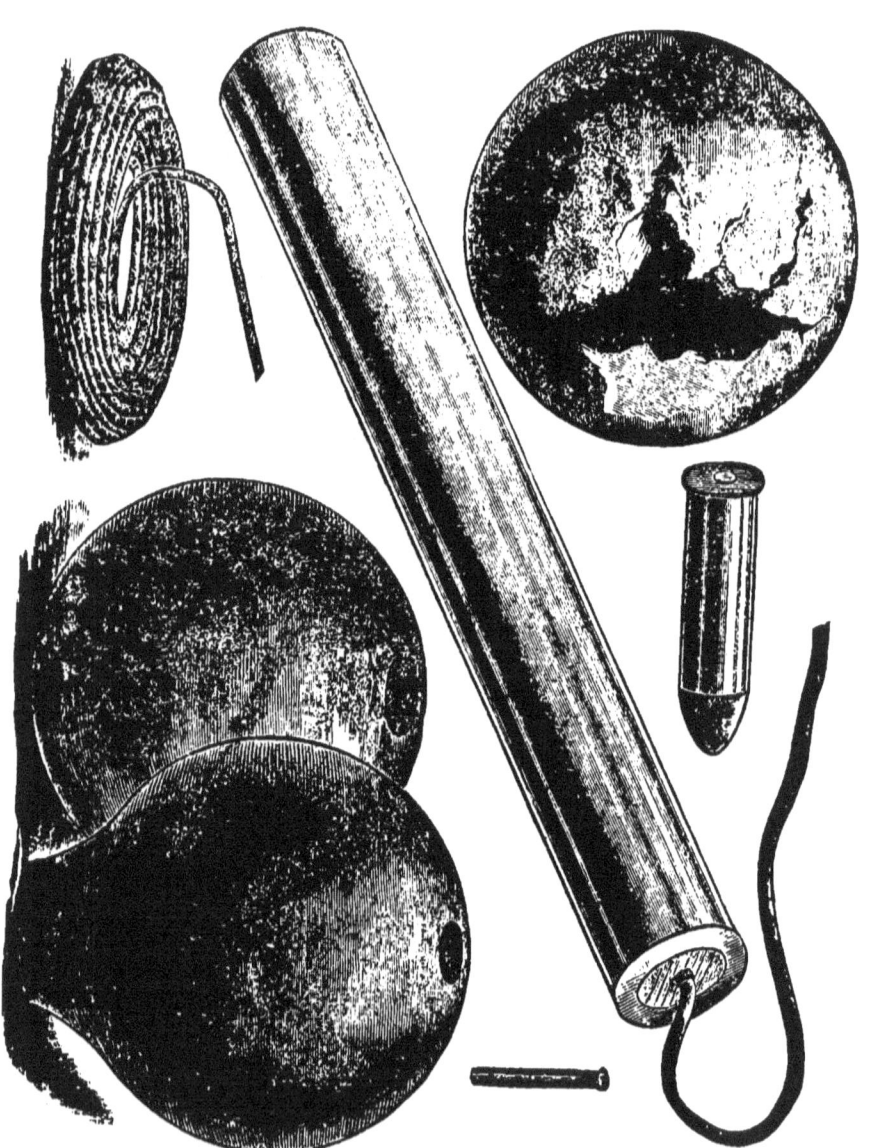

CHAPTER VIII.

COST OF ANARCHIST TRIAL. EXTRACTS FROM ZEITUNG. MOTION FOR NEW TRIAL. MOTION OVERRULED

COST OF THE ANARCHIST TRIALS.

It is estimated that the trials of the Anarchist conspirators for connection with the Haymarket massacre has cost Cook county and Chicago about $100,000. A calculation made by county officials at the close of the murder trial in August, placed the average cost since the night of the bomb throwing at $24,800 per month. Another estimate itemizes the daily expenses as follows:

State's-Attorney's office, stenographers, messengers, telegrams, interpreters, extra legal help (Mr. Ingham)	$200
Sheriff's office, bailiff's, jury fees, hotel bills for jury, etc.	150
Court Costs, Judge's salary, miscellaneous items	100
Detectives, policemen, witness fees	150
Criminal Court Clerk's office and other expenses	100

This makes a total of $700 a day, or $70,000 for the 100 days which the trial covered. The trials of the twenty-six persons indicted for conspiracy in connection with the murders bring the total cost up to $100,000.

In an interview Chief of Police Ebersold praised the brave and steady action of the police at the Haymarket, but for quick and active fighting gave the palm to the six officers who held a mob of two or three thousand men at bay at the McCormick works the day before the Haymarket affair. A mob tried to hang Officer Casey to a lamp-post, and he fought hand to hand against gread odds until rescued. Vaclav Dejnek, Frank Broda and a young man named Hess were indicted for this affair, and Dejnek was sentenced to serve one year in state's prison.

THE ARBEITER ZEITUNG.

The *Arbeiter Zeitung*, which was suppressed the morning after the riot, was re-issued almost immediately, and in one issue had the following comments on the trial:

"Has it come to this, in the land of Washington, Franklin and Jefferson? It is the Iron Must of historic development. Only those men who are economically independent can be truly free. Where there are poor and rich political freedom is a wretched lie. Mammon, the powerful idol, lowers freedom to a kitchen wench. As in Rome at the time of its decay Prætorian bands of foreigners upheld the rule of the Cæsars, so now the chief support of the money kings is the police force of the large American cities, which consists mainly of foreigners. The down-fall of the Republic is nigh. It will fall like all countries whose foundations crumble away in the course of time. All the weeping and wailing cannot delay catastrophe. The present is without hope, so we must strengthen ourselves by looking at the future. A new life will bloom from the ruins of the present social order. The society of the future will bridge over the abysses which open to-day before our eyes. All men will be equal. They will remember with a shudder the time when Prætorian bands could plot the massacre of thousands. Mammon will be cast down from his usurped throne, and Freedom will take the place with conquering power, to dwell with happy humanity forever and ever."

After the verdict was rendered Mr. Grinnell, in behalf of

the State, sent word to the new publishers of the *Arbeiter Zeitung*, that care must be taken by them that no attacks either on the jury or Judge Gary should appear in their paper, notifying them that if any such article should appear, the managers of the paper would be prosecuted for contempt of court.

The following was the result of the warning·

"OUTRAGEOUS!

"SEVEN OF THE DEFENDANTS SENTENCED TO DEATH, AND NEEBE GETS FIFTEEN YEARS.

"A Motion for a New Trial Made!

"The jury, through Osborne, its foreman, presented their verdict to Judge Gary this morning. When the result became known the detectives, who mingled freely with the crowd on the street, set up a loud cheering, and the judge became very pale—he did not expect such a demonstration. Grinnell, on the other hand, evidently expected such a verdict, and presumably with cause. Marshall Field and men of his stripe have entirely too much money. What do the people say to this verdict? They will look upon it as being impossible—incredible. We were not inclined to believe it at first, but we soon became convinced. Captain Black instantly made a motion for a new trial, which Grinnell did not oppose, and Judge Gary will hear this motion next term. If he overrules the motion, an appeal will be taken. We are not in a proper frame of mind to say more to-day."

THE VERDICT

fell like a bolt of lightning into the midst of Socialistic and

Anarchistic circles, believing as they did, that punishment could only be inflicted upon the perpetrator of the act of hurling the bomb. No wonder that consternation sat darkly upon each sullen brow like the pall of impending doom, as slowly from the jury came those words of fearful import which set them face to face with death, the verdict was applauded by the foreign and American press. Twenty-five representatives of reputable labor unions met condemning the action of the Socialists and thereby endorsing the verdict of the jury.

The Socialists of New York held indignation meetings denouncing the verdict and expressing sympathy with their unfortunate brethren of Chicago. Mrs. Black, in a letter dated Sept. 22, prophesied that in case the sentence was executed widespread revolution and destruction of property and life would immediately be inaugurated. On the 27th Capt. Black served a notice upon State's Attorney Grinnell for a new trial, on the ground that the verdict was not in keeping with the law; also that the court had allowed improper testimony, and had erred in his instructions. 1,191 men were called to serve as jurors in the case before the twelve elligable men were secured, and even then it was claimed by the defense that only ten of the twelve were competent.

On Friday, Oct. 1st, the Attorneys for the defense began their arguments for a new trial, drawing largely upon their imaginations to supply evidence in the case. They endeavored to introduce false affidavits from one Orrin Blossom, of No. 2,961 Wentworth Avenue, and A. Love, of La Grange, to impeach the testimony of Gilmer. But the wary State's Attorney Grinnell had one move to make which blocked their game. He had counter affidavits from Orrin Blossom and Love proving that

Love was not in the city on the night of the Haymarket riot after six o'clock, and that he never saw *Harry Gilmer*.

Three days were spent by the defense in argueing their claims for a new trial, and on October 7th Judge Gary rendered his decision in the case in the following language:

THE MOTION FOR A NEW TRIAL OVERRULED.

Judge Gary said:

In passing upon this motion for a new trial the case is so voluminous, there is such a mass of evidence, that it is impossible, within anything like reasonable limits, to give a synopsis or epitome. I do not understand that either upon the trial before the jury or upon the arguments of this motion before me there have been any arguments tending or intended to deny that all of the defendants, except Neebe, were parties to whatever purpose or object there was in view—that the other seven were combined for some purpose. I, of course, do not wish to attribute to the defendants' counsel any admissions which they have not made, but my impression is that there has been no argument tending or intending to deny that all the other seven, except Neebe, were engaged in the pursuit of some object. What it is, the counsel have debated before the jury and before me. Now, it is important to know what that object was, whether it was as counsel for defense have stated—merely to encourage working men to resist, if unlawful attacks were made upon them—or whether it was something else. There is no better way to ascertain what the object was, than to read what they have spoken and written as the object, while the events were transpiring. Now, from the files of their newspapers, which go back a good way, a good deal can be taken, which must of necessity be taken as the truth of what their object was. I have not had time and opportunity to arrange either the translations of the *Arbeiter Zeitung* or the files of the *Alarm*, and pick out those which in the fullest shape show what they were proposing to do. These translations from the *Arbeiter Zeitung* now come to my hands for the first time. I have here a translation of the *Arbeiter Zeitung*, January 11, 1885, headed "To Arms."

The Court proceeded to read numerous and lengthy extracts from translations offered in evidence of articles in the *Arbeiter Zeitung*, in which revolution by force was advised, and the approaching revolution, it was declared, would be greater than that of the last century. Among the extracts read were the following:

"Dynamite! Of all stuff, this is the stuff."

"The day draws near when the working people of America, in an outburst of passion and ungovernable rage, will revolt and demand the total abolition of the existing state of things which brings to the working classes so much misery and death. Have you all prepared yourselves with knives, pistols, guns and dynamite for the unavoidable conflict between labor and capital?"

"It was decided at the last mass-meeting at No. 54 West Lake street that the next meeting will be devoted to the consideration of the military laws and necessity of using force in the warfare between capital and labor."

"Each working man ought to have been armed long ago. Daggers, revolvers and explosives are cheap, and can be easily obtained."

"Those who want to talk to capitalists in earnest must be

prepared to attain their object by killing them. This can only be accomplished by systematic organization. The time for all this is short—look out—"

"In addition to all this," continued Judge Gary, "there is the testimony of witnesses that there was a combination which was formed as early as 1884, and that combination had for its purpose the changing of the existing order of things, the overthrow of government, and the abolition of all law. There can be no question in the mind of any one who has read these articles or heard these speeches, which were written and spoken long before the eight-hour movement was talked of, that this movement which they advocated was but a means in their estimation toward the ends which they sought, and that the movement itself was not primarily any consideration with them at all. The different papers and speeches furnish direct contradiction to the arguments of counsel that they proposed to resort to arms merely to resist any unlawful attacks which the police might make upon them, because these all show that their object was this: If, during the eight-hour movement, strikes occured, and if the employers chose to employ other men in the place of those who had struck, then these men so employed must be prevented by force from going to work, and if the police then undertook to resist the force so employed on behalf of the strikers; if the police undertook to prevent this force from being so employed, then that was the ground on which the police force was to be destroyed. There can be no doubt that that was an unlawful combination. It is impossible to argue that any set of men have the right to dictate to others whether they should work or not, and if they chose to work in defiance of their dictation, drive them away by force, and if the police undertook to prevent that force, then kill the police. It is impossible for an instant to support any such principle as that. The members of this combination publicly announce that they had no hope of winning the majority over to their side by argument, and no hope of attaining their object by getting rid of this majority by violence. There is no doubt that seven of the defendants were in the combination formed for that purpose. As to Neebe's part, there is the evidence of witnesses that he presided at meetings called by the class of people from whom this combination was drawn, and that he called meetings of the people who were engaged in the movement. There is evidence that he marched in the Board of Trade procession, the object of which was said to be the demolition of that building."

The Court proceeded to discuss all the evidence against Neebe, which tended to show that he was associated with the rest of the defendants in the encouragement of the movement which had for its object the destruction of the government. The Court resumed:

"On the question of the instructions whether these defendants, or any of them, did anticipate or expect the throwing of the bomb on the night of the 4th of May, is not a question which I need to consider, because the instructions did not go upon that ground. The jury were not instructed to find them guilty if they believed that they participated in the throwing of the bomb, or encouraged or advised the throwing of that bomb, or had knowledge that it was to be thrown, or anything of that sort. The conviction has not gone upon the ground that they did have any actual participation in the act which caused the death of Deegan, but upon the ground, under the instructions, that they had generally by speech and print advised a large class to commit murder, and had left the occasion, time and place to the individual will, whim and caprice of the individuals so advised, and that in consequence of that advice, and in pursuance of it, and influenced by it, somebody not known did throw the bomb that caused Deegan's death.

"There is no example in the law books of a case of this sort. No such occurance has ever happened before in the history of the world. I suppose that in the Lord George Gordon riots we might find something like this. Lord George Gordon was indicted for treason, and the government failed in its proof upon the trial as to what he had done. Very likely they did not want to prove it very strongly against him; I do not know; it is none of my business. If the bomb was thrown in pursuance of the prisoners' advice, the instruction as to the law of accessories before the fact applied to the case, and the instruction to the jury was proper. If the radical Prohibitionists should make up their minds that the only way to stop the liquor traffic was by destroying the saloons and killing the saloon-keepers, and if some crank should blow up a saloon with a bomb for whose manufacture the radicals had furnished specific directions, and in the explosion a saloon-keeper was killed, there could be no question but that the radical temperance men were guilty of murder. But there was no question that when some one said 'Hang McCormick,' or 'Hang Gould,' the reply was given to make no idle threats, but when they got ready to do anything, to do it."

The shorthand report of the speeches of Spies, Parsons and Fielden at the Haymarket meeting was then read, after which the Court said:

"Now, the general advice throughout was to each individual-man—I mean the general teachings on this subject of associated revolution—was to each individual-man to do it himself, without combination; that men working together in deeds of violence were to be avoided; that they were to go alone where one man only was required to accomplish the work, and where more than one man was required, as few as was necessary should be taken. Now, under these circumstances, in the inflamed state of the public mind at the time, each of these orators was still more inflaming the public mind when he advised the people to use force, and some man—I do not say identified, but unidentified—some man in that crowd, when the police approached, with a bomb of Lingg's manufacture, killed Deegan; all who have advised such action are guilty of his murder. If anything can be proved by circumstantial evidence, that is proved; that he threw that bomb in consequence of the influence of these teachings, this advise by speech and printing over a course of two years; that the man who threw that bomb had been educated up to it by the teachings of these defendants. The case, as I said before, is unprecedented. There is no example of any such crime having been committed; there is no precedent of any case like this having become the subject of judicial investigation; but the principle of law is well fixed. It is the boast of people who profess to admire the common law, that it adapts itself to human events, and that no situation or no new form of industry can arise but the common law has principles which may be applied."

The prisoners spoke in their own behalf before sentence was passed. The courtroom was crowded as usual. The police department was represented by Chief Ebersold, Capt. Schaack, and twenty officers. The prisoners wore a look of even greater anxiety than at the morning session. Parsons appeared particularly thoughtful and gloomy. The greater part of the session he sat with his cheek resting in his hand and taking less note of the proceedings than usual. Spies was laboring under great excitement. Before he began his speech Judge Gary repeated the caution he had before given the auditors to refrain from any demonstration of approbation or disapprobation during the session. He insisted that every one in the court should be seated, and seeing two men at the rear of the room seated on a table he compelled them to take chairs or sit on the floor. Everything was quiet as the grave when Spies began his address. During the impassioned passages he raised his voice and indulged in violent gesticulation. Neebe's utterance was quite rapid, and he spoke like one at home before an audience. His speech would have produced an impression on any jury. His voice is clear and resonant, and he has a better presence than any of the other defendants. Fischer spoke hesitatingly, and would probably not have spoken at all but for an uncontrollable desire to express his opinion of the State's Attorney and all representatives of the law. Lingg's rather handsome face was flushed, and his eyes flashed as he poured out his denunciation of Messrs. Grinnell and Bonfield. When he took his seat his face was covered with perspiration. He made the walls ring, and as each sentence had to be translated by Prof. Ficke, he had ample opportunity to deliver each sentence with renewed emphasis. Schwab read his speech in a clear, resonant voice, and it had been evidently prepared with much care.

CHAPTER IX.

REASONS WHY THE SENTENCE OF THE LAW SHOULD NOT BE EXECUTED UPON THEM. SPEECHES BY THE ANARCHISTS.

AUGUST SPIES.

"In addressing this Court I speak as the representative of one class to the representative of another. I will begin with the words uttered five hundred years ago on a similar occasion by the Venetian Doge Faliero, who, addressing the court, said: 'My defense is your accusation; the causes of my alleged crime, your history.' I have been indicted under the charge of murder as an accomplice of accessory. Upon this indictment I have been convicted. There was no evidence produced by the State to show or even indicate that I had any knowledge of the man who threw the bomb, or that I myself had anything to do with the throwing of the missile unless, of course, you weigh the testimony of the accomplices of the State's Attorney and Bonfield, the testimony of Thompson and Gilmer, by the price they were paid for it. If there was no evidence to show that I was legally responsible for the deed, then my conviction and the execution of the sentence are nothing less than a willful, malicious and deliberate murder—as foul a murder as may be found in the annals of religious, political, or any other sort of persecution. Judicial murders have in many cases been committed where the representatives of the state were acting in good faith, believing their victims to be guilty of the charge or accusation. In this case the representatives of the state cannot justify themselves

AUG. SPIES.

by a similar excuse, for they themselves have fabricated most of
the testimony which was used as a pretense to convict us—convict us by a jury picked to convict before this Court and before
the public, which is supposed to be the State. I charge the
State's Attorney and Bonfield with a heinous conspiracy to commit murder.

"I will now state a little incident which will throw light
upon this charge. On the evening on which the prætorian cohorts of the Citizens' Association, the Bankers' Association, the
Bar Association, and railroad princes attacked the meeting of
working-men at the Haymarket with murderous intent—on that
evening about 8 o'clock, I met a young man, Legner by name.
My brother was with me at the same time, and never left me
on that evening until I jumped from the wagon a few seconds
before the explosion came. Legner knew that I had not seen
Schwab that evening. He knew that I had no such conversation with anybody, as Marshall Field's protege, Thompson has
testified to. He knew that I did not jump from the wagon and
strike a match and hand it to the man who threw the bomb.
He is not a Socialist. Why didn't we bring him on the stand?
Because the honorable representatives of the State, Grinnell and
Bonfield, spirited him away. These honorable gentlemen knew
everything about Legner. They knew that his testimony would
prove the perjury of Thompson and Gilmer beyond any reasonable doubt. Legner's name was on the list of witnesses for the
State. He was not called, however, for obvious reasons. First,
as he stated to a number of friends, he had been offered $500
if he would leave the city, and threatened with direful things
if he should remain here and appear as a witness for the defense. He replied that he could neither be bought nor bull-

dozed to serve such a foul, damnable, dastardly plot. But when we wanted Legner he could not be found. Mr. Grinnell said—and Mr. Grinnell is an honorable man—that he himself had been searching for the young man, but had not been able to find him. About three weeks later I learned that the very same young man had been kidnapped and taken to Buffalo, N. Y., by two of the illustrious guardians of the law, two Chicago detectives. Let Mr. Grinnell, let the Citizens' Association, his employer, let them answer for themselves, and let the people—let the public—sit in judgment upon these would-be assassins. No, I reply, the Prosecution has not established our legal guilt, notwithstanding the purchased and perjured testimony of some, and notwithstanding the originality of the proceedings of the trial. And as long as this has not been done, and you pronounce the sentence of the appointed viligante committee acting as a jury, I say that you, the alleged servant and high priests of the law, are the real and only law-breakers, and in this case you go to the extent of murder. It is well that the people know this. And when I speak of the people I do not mean the few conspirators of Grinnell, the noble patricians who are murderers of those whom they please to oppress. Those citizens may constitute the state. They may control the state; they may have their Grinnells, Bonfields, and their hirelings. No, when I speak of the people, I speak of the great mass of working beasts, who unfortunately are not yet conscious of the rascalities that are perpetrated in the name of the people—in their name. They condemn the murder of eight men whose only crime is that they have dared to speak the truth. This murder may open the eyes of these suffering millions, may wake them up indeed. I have noticed that our conviction has worked miracles in this direction already. The class that clamors for our lives, the good and devout Christians, have attempted in every way, through their newspapers and otherwise, to conceal the true and only issue in this case, by designating the defendants Anarchists and picturing them as a newly-discovered tribe or species of cannibles, by inventing shocking and horrifying stories of their conspiracies.

"I believe with Buckle, with Paine, with Jefferson, with Emerson, with Spencer, and with many other great thinkers of this century, that the state of caste and classes, the state where one class dominates and lives upon the labor of another class and calls it order, should be abolished. Yes, I believe that this barbaric form of social organization, with its legalized thunder and murder, is doomed to die and make room for free society—volunteer associations if you like—universal brotherhood. You may pronounce your sentence upon me, honorable judge, but let the world know that in the year A. D. 1886, in the state of Illinois, eight men were sentenced to death because they had not lost their faith in the ultimate victory of liberty and justice. Read the history of Greece and Rome; read that of Venice. Look over the dark pages of the church and follow the thorny path of science. No change! No change!

"You would destroy society and civilization, as ever, upon the cry of the ruling classes. They are so comfortably situated under the prevailing system that they naturally abhor and fear even the slightest changes. Their privileges are as dear to them as life itself, and every change threatens these privileges. But civilization is a record whose steps are monuments of such changes. Without these social changes, always brought about against the will and against the force of the ruling classes, there would be no civilization. As to the destruction of society, which we have been accused of seeking, it sounds like one of Æsop's fables—like the cunning of the fox. We, who have jeopardized our lives to save society from the fiend that has grasped her by the throat, that seeks her life-blood and devours her substance; we, who would heal her bleeding wounds, who would free her from the fetters you have wrought around her, from the misery you have brought upon her—we are enemies. We have preached dynamite, it is said, and we have predicted from the lessons history has taught us, that the ruling class of to day would no more listen to the voice of reason than did their predecessors. They would attempt by brute force to stay the march of progress. Was it a lie, or was it the truth that we stated? * * * I have been a citizen of this city fully as long as Mr. Grinnell, and am probably as good a citizen as Grinnell. At least I should not wish to be compared to him. Grinnell has appealed time and again, as has been stated by our attorneys, to the patriotism of the jury. To that I reply, and I will simply use the words of an English literateur, 'Patriotism is the last resort of the scoundrel.' My friends' agitation in behalf of the disinherited and disfranchised millions, and my agitation in this direction, the popularization of the economic teachings in favor of the education of wage-workers, is declared to be a conspiracy against society. The word 'society' is here wisely substituted for state, as represented by the patricians of to-day. It has always been the opinion of the ruling classes that the people must be kept in ignorance. They lose their sevility, modesty, and obedience to the arbitrary powers that be, as their intelligence grows. The education of a blackman, a quarter of a century ago was a criminal offense. Why? Because the intelligent slave would throw off his shackles at whatever cost, my Christian gentlemen. Why is the education of the working classes to-day looked upon by a certain class as treason against the State? For the same reason! The State, however, wisely avoided this point in the prosecution of the case. From their testimony one would really conclude that we had in our speeches and publications preached nothing else but destruction and dynamite. * * * You, gentlemen, are the revolutionists. You rebel against the effects of social conditions which have tossed you by fortune's hand into a magnificent paradise. Without inquiring, you imagine that no one else has a right in that place. You insist that you are the chosen ones, the sole proprietors of forces that tossed you into the paradise. The industrial forces are still at work. They are growing more active and intense from day to day. There tendency is to elevate all mankind to the same level; to have all humanity share in the paradise you now monopolize. Can you roll back the incoming tide or angry waves of old ocean by forbidding it to dash upon the shore? So you can no more frighten back the rising waves of intelligence and progress into their unfathomable depths by erecting a few gallows in the perspective. You, who oppose the natural forces of things, you are the real revolutionists. You, and you alone, are the conspirators and destructionists."

ADOLPH FISCHER.

"Your Honor, you asked me why the sentence of death should not be passed upon me. I will not talk much. I will only say a few words, and that is that I protest against my being sentenced to death, because I committed no crime. I was tried here in this room for murder and I was convicted of Anarchy. I protest against being sentenced to death, because I have not been found guilty of murder. I have been tried for murder, but I have been convicted because I am an Anarchist. Although being one of the parties who were at the Haymarket meeting, I had no more to do with the throwing of that bomb, I had no more connection with it than State's Attorney Grinnell had perhaps.

"As I said, it is a fact, and I do not deny that I was one of the parties who called at the Haymarket meeting, but that meeting—(At this point Mr. Salomon stepped up and spoke to Fischer in a low tone, but Fischer waived him off and said: Mr. Salomon, be so kind. I know what I am talking about.) Now, that Haymarket meeting was not called for the purpose of committing violence and crime. No; but the meeting was called for the purpose of protesting against the outrages and against the crimes of the police committed on the day previous out at McCormick's. The next day I went to Wehrer & Klein and had twenty-five thousand copies of the hand bills printed, and I invited Spies to speak at Haymarket meeting. It is the fact, and I don't deny it, in the original of the 'copy' I had the line 'Working men, arm!' and I had my reasons, too, for putting those lines in, because I didn't want the working men to be shot down in that meeting as on other occasions. But as those circulars were printed and brought over to the *Arbeiter Zeitung* office, my comrade, Spies, saw one of those circulars. I had invited him to speak before that. He showed the circular and said: 'Well, Fischer, if those circulars are distributed I won't speak.' And I admitted it would be better to take those lines out; and Mr. Spies spoke. And that is all I had to do with that meeting. I feel that I am sentenced, or will be sentenced

ADOLPH FISCHER.

to death because I am an Anarchist, and not because I am a murderer. I have never been a murderer. I have never committed any crime in my life yet; but I know a certain man who is on the way to becoming a murderer, an assassin, and that man is Grinnell—the State's Attorney Grinnell—because he brought men on the witness stand whom he knew would swear falsely; and I publicly denounce Mr. Grinnell as being a murderer and an assassin if I should be executed. But, if the ruling classes think that by hanging us, hanging a few Anarchists, they can crush out Anarchy, they will be badly mistaken, because the Anarchist loves his principles more than his life. An Anarchist is always ready to die for his principles."

MICHAEL SCHWAB.

"It is not much I have to say, and I would say nothing at all if keeping silence did not look like a cowardly approval of what has been done here. To those, the proceedings of a trial of justice would be a sneer. Justice has not been done. More than that, could not be done. If one class is arraigned against the other class it is idle and hypocritical to talk about justice and fairness. Anarchy was on trial, as the State's Attorney put it in his closing speech. A doctrine, an opinion hostile to brute force, hostile to our present murderous system of production and distribution. I am condemned to die for writing newspaper articles and making speeches. The State's Attorney knows as well as I do that the alleged conversation between Mr. Spies and me never took place. He knows a good deal more than that. He knows all the beautiful works of his organizer, Furthmann. When I was before the Coroner's jury two or three witnesses swore very positively to having seen me at the Haymarket when Mr. Parsons finished his speech. I suppose they wanted at that time to fix the bomb-throwing on me, for the first dispatches to Europe said that M. Schwab had thrown several bombs at the police. Later on they found that would not do, and then Schnaubelt was the man. Anarchy was on trial. Little did it matter who the persons were to be honored by the prosecution. * * *

"As soon as the word is applied to us and to our doctrine it carries with it a meaning that we Anarchists see fit to give. 'Anarchy' is Greek, and means, verbatim, that we are not being ruled. According to our vocabulary Anarchy is a state of society in which the only government is reason; a state of society in which all human beings do right for the simple reason that it is right, and hate wrong because it is wrong. In such a society no compulsion will be necessary. The Attorney of the State was wrong when he exclaimed 'Anarchy is dead!' Anarchy up to the present time existed only as a doctrine, and Grinnell has not the power to kill any doctrine whatever. Anarchy, as defined by us, is called an idle dream, but that dream was called by God a divine blessing. One of the three great German poets and a celebrated German critic of the last century has also defined it. If Anarchy was the thing the State's Attorney makes it out to be, how could it be that such eminent scholars as Prince Krapotkine should say what he has said about it? Anarchy is a dream, but only in the present. It will be realized, for reason will grow in spite of all obstacles. Who is the man that has the cheek to tell us that human development has already reached its culminating point? I know our ideal will not be accomplished this year or next year, but I know it will be accomplished as soon as possible, some day in the future. It is entirely wrong to use the word Anarchy as synonymous with violence. Violence is something, and Anarchy is another. In the present state of society violence is used on all sides, and therefore we advocated the use of violence against violence, but against violence only as a necessary means of defense. I have never read Herr Most's book simply because I don't find time to read it; and if I had read it, what of it? I am an agnostic, but I like to read the Bible, nevertheless. I have not the slightest idea who threw the bomb at the Haymarket, and had no knowledge of any conspiracy to use violence that or any other night."

OSCAR NEEBE.

"Your Honor: I have found out during the last few days what law is. Before I didn't know it. I did not know that I was convicted because I knew Spies and Fielden and Parsons. I have met these gentlemen. I have presided at a meeting, as the evidence against me shows, in the Turner hall, to which meeting your Honor was invited. The judges, the preachers, the newspaper men, and everybody was invited to appear at that meeting for the purpose of discussing Anarchism and Socialism. I was at that hall. I am well known among the working men of the city, and I was the one elected chairman of that meeting. Nobody appeared to speak, to discuss the question of Labor and Anarchism or Socialism with laboring men. No, they couldn't stand it. I was chairman of that meeting; I don't deny it. I had the honor to be marshal of a labor demonstration in this city, and I never saw as respectable a lot of men as I saw that day.

"'They marched like soldiers, and I was proud that I was

marshal of those men. They were the toilers and the working men of this city. The men marched through the city of Chicago to protest against the wrongs of society, and I was marshal of them. If that is a crime, I have found out—as a born American—what I am guilty of. I always thought I had a right to express my opinion, to be chairman of a peaceable meeting, and to be marshal of a demonstration. My friends, the labor agitators, and the marshals of a demonstration—was it a crime to be marshal of a demonstration? I am convicted of that. I suppose Grinnell thought after Oscar Neebe was indicted for murder the *Arbeiter Zeitung* would go down. But it didn't happen that way. And Mr. Furthmann, too—he is a scoundrel, and I can tell it to you to your face. There is only one man that acted as a lawyer, and he is Mr. Ingham, but you three fellows have not.

I established the paper and issued it to the working men of the city of Chicago, and inside of two weeks I had enough money from the toilers—from hired girls, from men who would take the last cent out of their pocket to establish the paper—to buy a press. I could not publish the paper because the honorable detectives and Mr. Grinnell followed us up, and no printing house would print our paper, and we had to have our own press. We published our own paper after we had a press, bought by the money of the working men of the city. That is the crime I have committed—getting men to try and establish a working-man's paper that will stand to-day, and I am proud of it. They have not got one press—they have got two presses to-day, and they belong to the working men of this city. When the first issue came out, from that day up to the day now, your Honor, we have gained 4,000 subscribers. There are the gen-

LOUIS LINGG.

tlemen sitting over there from the *Freie Presse* and *Staats Zeitung*—they know it. The Germans of this city are condemning these actions. They would not read our paper. There is the crime of the Germans. I say it is a verdict against Germans, and I, as an American, must say that I never saw anything like that.

"Those are the crimes I have committed after the 4th of May. Before the 4th of May I committed some crimes. I organized trades unions. I was for the reduction of the hours of labor and the education of laboring men and the re-establishment of the *Arbeiter Zeitung*. There is no evidence to show that I was connected with the bomb throwing, that I was near it or anything of that kind. So I am only sorry, your Honor, if you can stop it or help it, I will ask you to do it—that is, to hang me, too; and I think it is more honor to die certainly than to be killed by inches. I have a family and children, and if they know their father is dead they will bury him. They can go to the grave and kneel down in front of it; but they can't go to Joliet and see their father convicted of a crime that he hasn't anything to do with. That is all I have got to say. Your Honor, I am sorry I do not get hung with the rest of the men."

LOUIS LINGG.

[Translated by Prof. H. H. Fick.]

"Court of Justice: With the same contempt with which I have tried to live humanely upon this American soil, I am now granted the privilege to speak. If I do take the word I do it because injustice and indignities have been heaped upon me right here. I have been accused of murder. What proofs have been brought in support of it? It has been proved that I assisted some man by the name of Seliger in manufacturing bombs. It has been furthermore stated that with the assistance of somebody else I have taken those bombs to 58 Clybourn avenue, but although one of these assistants has been produced as a State witness it has not been shown that one of these bombs was taken to the Haymarket. * * * * What is Anarchy? * * * The points that we are driving at have been carefully withheld by the State. * * * But it has not been said that by their superior force we are driven to our course. Contempt of court has been charged against us. We have been treated as opponents of public order. What is this order? Such order as represented by police and detectives? On the slightest occasion the representatives of this public order have forced themselves into our midst. The same police that aim to give protection to property embraces thieves in its ranks. * * * I have told Capt. Schaack that I was at a meeting of carpenters at Zephf's hall on May 3. He has stated that I admitted to him that I learned the fabrication of bombs from Most's book, 'Science of Warfare.' That is perjury. * * * It has been proved that Grinnell has used Gilmer for his purpose intentionally. There are points which prove that. * * * I say that these seven persons here, of which I am one, are murdered purposely by Grinnell. * * * Grinnell has the courage to call me a coward, right here in this court of justice, and Grinnell is a person who has connived with miserable subjects to go against me, to get testimony against me, to kill me. * * * Is life worth living? What are their purposes in thus murdering these men? Low egotism, which finds its reward in a higher position, and which yields a return of money. * * * But it has been said that the International association of working men was in itself a conspiracy, and that I was a member of this association. My colleague, Spies, has already stated to you how we were connected. * * * And that is the conspiracy that has been proved against me, and for that I am to end my life upon the gallows—an instrument which you consider a disgrace to me. I declare here openly that I do not acklowledge these laws, and less so the sentence of the Court. * * * I would not say a word if I was really guilty according to this foolish law, but even according to these laws that would not be respected by a schoolboy, not even these laws have been carried out to the full extent when I was found guilty. * * * You smile. You perhaps think I will not use bombs any more, but I tell you I die gladly upon the gallows in the sure hope that hundreds and thousands of people to whom I have spoken will now recognize and make use of dynamite. In this hope I despise you, and I despise your laws. Hang me for it."

GEORGE ENGEL.

[Translated by Mr. Gauss.]

"When I left Germany in the year 1872 it was by reason of my recognition of the fact that I could not support myself in the future as it was the duty of a man to do. I recognized that I could not make my living in Germany because the machinery and the guilds of old no longer furnished me a guarantee to live. I resolved to emigrate from Germany to the United States, praised by many so highly. When I landed at Philadelphia, on the 8th of January, 1873, my heart and my bosom expanded with the expectation of living hereafter in that free country which had been so often praised to me by so many emigrants, and I resolved to be a good citizen of this country; and I congratulated myself on having broken with Germany, where I could have no longer made my living, and I think that my past will show that, that, which I resolved I intended to keep faithfully. For the first time I stand before an American court, and at that to be at once condemned to death. And what are the causes that have preceded it, and have brought me into this court? They are the same things that preceded my leaving Germany, and the same causes that made me leave. I have seen with my own eyes that in this free country, in this richest country of the world, so to say, there are existing proletarians who are pushed out of the order of society."

After explaining how his dissatisfaction with the existing order of things led him to become a Socialist, Engel continued:

"I resolved to study Socialism with all my power. In the year 1878 I came from Philadelphia to Chicago, and took pains to eke out my existence here in Chicago, and believed that it would be an easier task to live here, than in Philadelphia, where I had previously in vain exerted my powers to live. I found that, that also was in vain. There was no difference for a proletariat, whether he lived in New York, or Philadelphia, or Chicago. * * * To make further investigations I tried to buy, from the money that I and my family earned, scientific books on those questions. I bought the works of Ferdinand LaSalle, Karl Marx and Henry George. After investigating these works I recognized these reasons why a proletariat could not exist, even in this country, as free as it is. I thought about the means by which that could be corrected. They praised to me this country where every man and every working man had a right to go to the ballot-box and choose his own officers. I scarcely believed that any citizen of the United States could have meant so honestly and well as I, when I turned my attention to politics, and took part in them. But even in this regard of freedom of the ballot-box I found myself mistaken. I learned to see that the working man was not free in his opinion, that he was not free in vote. It was in vain that the Socialistic party took pains in former times, honest pains, to elect honest officers. After a few vain attempts I found that it was impossible for a working man to free himself by means of the ballot-box, and to secure those things which were necessary for his existence. * * * In this city corruption even entered the ranks of the Social Democracy. I also obtained the conviction that through those men who put themselves over us as leaders, and occupied themselves with compromises, this was brought about, and then I left the ranks of the Social Democracy and gave myself over to the International which was then organizing; and what these men wanted, and what these men through their exertions sought to bring about was nothing more or less than the conviction that the freeing of the ruling classes could only be brought about by force, as have all revolutions been throughout history. This conviction, before I went over to those people, was obtained through study of the history of all lands. The history of all lands showed me that all advantages in a political, in a religious, and in a material direction, were always obtained only by the use of force; and if I confine myself to the history of this country where I am convicted, I take into consideration that the first emmigrants into this country and the first colonists, only freed themselves by force from the power of England. I afterward obtained the conviction that the slavery existing in this country, to the shame of the Republic, could only be put aside by force. And what does this history teach us? The man that spoke against existing slavery in this country was hanged, as it is intended that we should be hanged, to-day. In the course of time I became convinced that all those who spoke in favor of the ruling classes must hang. And what are the reasons for it? This Republic does not exist through, and its affairs are not conducted by, those persons who come into office by an honest ballot. * * * Under these conditions it is certainly not a wonder that there were men, noble men, noble scientific men, who have tried to find ways and means to bring back humanity to its original condition. And this is the social science to which I confess myself with joy. The State's Attorney said here 'Anarchism is on trial.' Anarchism and Socialism are, according to my opinion, as like as one egg is to another. Only the tactics are different. Anarchism has abandoned the ways pointed out by Socialism to free man-mankind, and has resolved no longer to bear the yoke of slavery, and, therefore, I say to the working classes, do not believe any longer in the ballot-box and in those ways and means that are left open to you; but rather think about ways and means when the time comes, when the burden of the people becomes intoler-. able. And that is our crime. Because we have named to the people the ways and means by which they could free themselves in the fight against Capitalism, by reason of that, Anarchism is hated and persecuted in every state. In spite of that and again in spite of it Anarchism will exist, and if not in public it will exist in secret, because the powers force it to act in secret. If the State's Attorney declares or thinks that after he has hanged these seven men and sent the other one to the penitentiary for fifteen years he has then killed Anarchism, I say, that will not be so. Only the tactics will be changed, and that will be all. No power in the world will tear from the working man his knowledge and his skill or opportunity in making bombs. I am convinced that Anarchism cannot be routed out,—if that was the case it would have been routed out in other countries long ago—in the least by our murdering the Anarchists. That evening when the first bomb in this country was thrown, I was sitting in my room; did not know anything about the conspiracy; did not know anything about that deed; did not know anything about the bomb; did not know anything about the conspiracy which the State's Attorney had brought about here. * * * Can you have respect for a government that only gives rights to the privileged classes, but to the working men not at all, although there are conspiracies in all classes and connections of the capitalistic class. Although we have only recently experienced that the coal barons came together, put up the price of coal arbitrarily while they paid less wages to their working men, and wherever those coal workers, those miners have come together to consider the bettering their conditions, their demands have always been very modest on the whole, then the militia appears at once upon the scene and helps those people, while they are feeding the miners with powder and lead. For such a government I have no respect, and can have no respect in spite of all their followers, in spite of all their police, in spite of all their spies.

"I am not a man who hates a single capitalist. I am not the man who at all hates the person of the capitalist. I hate the system and all privileges, and my greatest desire is that the working classes will at last recognize who are their friends and who are their enemies. Against the condemnation of myself by the capitalistic influence I have no word to say."

SAM FIELDEN.

Fielden prefaced his plea by reciteing a poem called "Revolution,' written by Freilegrath, a German poet:

"And tho' ye caught your noble prey within your hangman's sordid thrall,
And tho' your captive was led forth beneath your city's rampart wall;
And tho' the grass lies o'er her green, where at the morning's early red
The peasant girl brings funeral wreaths—I tell you still—she is not dead!

* * * *

"You see me only in your cells; ye see me only in the grave;
Ye see me only wandering lone, beside the exile's sullen wave—
Ye fools! Do I not live where you have tried to pierce in vain?
Rests not a nook for me to dwell, in every heart, and every brain?

* * * *

"'Tis therefore I will be—and lead the peoples yet your hosts to meet,
And on your necks, your heads, your crowns, will plant my strong, resistless
    feet!
It is no boast—it is no threat—thus history's iron law decrees—
The day grows hot, oh, Babylon! 'Tis cool beneath thy willow trees!"

Fielden continued: "It makes a great deal of difference, perhaps, what kind of a revolutionist a man is. The men who have been on trial here for Anarchy have been asked the question on the witness stand if they were revolutionists. It is not generally considered to be a crime among intellectual people to be a revolutionist, but it may be made a crime if a revolutionist happens to be poor. * * * If I had known that I was being tried for Anarchy I could have answered that charge. I could have justified it under the constitutional right of every citizen of this country, and more than the right which any constitution can give, the natural right of the human mind to draw its conclusion from whatever information it can gain, but I had no opportunities to show why I was an Anarchist. I was told

SAM'L FIELDEN.

that I was to be hung for being an Anarchist, after I had got through defending myself on the charge of murder."

Fielden related that he was born in Lancashire; that his first speech was made to starving operatives in the streets of his native town; that it was here he began to hate kings and queens; his first speech was in support of the operatives of Lancashire as against the sympathizers with the South in the American rebellion; he came to the United States in 1868 and was a Methodist exhorter in Ohio, and came to Chicago in 1869. Fielden detailed how he had come to be a Socialist and Anarchist; reviewing the various speeches he had made at meetings in Chicago; attacking the veracity of witnesses who had testified against him, and declaring himself the victim of illegal prosecution. He continued:

"From the time I became a Socialist I learned more and more what it was. I knew that I had found the right thing; that I had found the medicine that was calculated to cure the ills of society. Having found it, I believed it, and I had a right to advocate it, and I did. The Constitution of the United States, when it says: 'The right of free speech shall not be abridged,' gives every man the right to speak. I have advocated the principles of Socialism and social equality, and for that and no other reason am I here, and sentence of death is to be pronounced upon me. What is Socialism? Taking somebody else's property? That is what Socialism is in the common acceptation of the term. No; but if I were to answer it as shortly and as curtly as it is answered by its enemies. I would say it is preventing somebody else from taking your property. But Socialism is equality. Socialism recognizes the fact that no man in society is responsible for what he is; that all the ills that are in society are the production of poverty; and scientific Socialism says that you must go to the root of the evil. There is no criminal statistician in the world but will acknowledge that all the crime, when traced to its origin, is the product of poverty. * * * If I am to be convicted—hanged for telling the truth, the little child that kneels by its mother's side on the West side to-day and tells its mother that he wants his papa to come home, and to whom I had intended as soon as its prattling tongue should begin to talk, to teach that beautiful sentiment—that child had better never be taught to read; had better never be taught that sentiment to love truth. If they are to be convicted of murder because they dare tell what they think is the truth, then it would be better that every one of your schoolhouses were reduced to the ground and one stone not left upon another. If you teach your children to read they will acquire curiosity from what they read. They will think, and then will search for the meaning of this and that They will arrive at conclusions. And then if they love the truth, they must tell to each other what is truth or what they think is the truth. That is the sum of my offending. * * * The private property system then, in my opinion, being a system that only subserves the interests of a few, and can only subserve the interests of the few, has no mercy. It cannot stop for the consideration of such a sentiment. Naturally it cannot. So you ought not to have mercy upon the private property system, because it is well known that there are many people in the community with prejudices in their minds. They have grown up under certain social regulations, and they believe that those social regulations are right, just as Mr. Grinnell believes that everything in America is right, because he happened to be born here. And they have such a prejudice against any one who attacks those systems. Now, I say they ought not to have any mercy upon systems that do nor subserve their interests. They ought not to have any respect for them that would interfere with their abolishing them."

Fielden maintained that the throwing of the bomb at the Haymarket was a complete surprise to him; that he felt that he would be held in some respect, at least responsible, yet he resolved not to attempt flight; continuing: "I have said here that I thought when the representatives of the State had inquired by means of their policemen as to my connection with it, I should have been released. And I say now, in view of all the authorities that have been read on the law and accessory, that there is nothing in evidence that has been introduced to connect me with that affair. * * * The great Socialist who lived in this world nearly 1,900 years ago, Jesus Christ, has left these words, and there are no grander words in which the principles of justice and right are conveyed in any language. He said: 'Better that ninety-nine guilty men should go unpunished than that one innocent man should suffer.' Mr. Grinnell, I should judge from his statements here, is a Christian. I would ask him to apply that statement of the Great Teacher to the different testimony that has been given here, and the direct contrary in other places in the investigation of this case. Your Honor, we claim that this is a class verdict. We claim that the foulest criminal that could have been picked up in the slums of any city in Christendom, or outside of it, would never have been convicted on such testimony as has been brought in here if he had not been a dangerous man in the opinion of the privileged classes. * * * If my life is to be taken for advocating the principles of Socialism and Anarchy, as I have understood them and honestly believe them to be in the interests of humanity, I say to you that I gladly give it up; and the price is very small for the result that is gained. * * * We claim that so far as we have been able to find out in trying to find a cure for the ills of society, we have not found out anything that has seemed to fit the particular diseases which society in our opinion is afflicted with to-day, better than the principles of Socialism. And your Honor, Socialism, when it is thoroughly understood in this community and in the world, as it is by us, I believe that the world, which is generally honest, prejudiced though it may be, will not be slow to adopt its principles. And it will be a good time, a grand day for the world; it will be a grand day for humanity; it will never have taken a step so far onward toward perfection, if it can ever reach that goal, as it will when it adopts the principles of Socialism. * * * To-day, as the beautiful autumn sun kisses with balmy breeze the cheek of every free man, I stand here never to bathe my head in its rays again. I have loved my fellow men as I have loved myself. I have hated trickery, dishonesty and injustice. The nineteenth century commits the crime of killing its best friend. It will live to repent of it. But, as I have said before, if it will do any good, I freely give myself up. I trust the time will come when there will be a better understanding, more intelligence, and above the mountains of iniquity, wrong and corruption, I hope the sun of righteousness and truth and justice will come to bathe in its balmy light an emancipated world. I thank your Honor for your attention."

A. R. PARSONS.

Parsons made a speech addressed in the main to working

A. R. PARSONS.

men, starting out with the recital of a poem by George Heinig, entitled "Bread is Freedom." He continued:

"Your Honor, if there is one distinguishing characteristic which has made itself prominent in the conduct of this trial it has been the passion, the heat, and the anger, the violence both to sentiment and to feeling, of everything connected with this case. You ask me why sentence of death should not be pronounced upon me, or, what is tantamount to the same thing, you ask me why you should give me a new trial in order that I might establish my innocence and the ends of justice be subserved. I answer you, your Honor, and say that this verdict is the verdict of passion, born in passion, nurtured in passion, and is the sum totality of the organized passion of the city of Chicago. For this reason I ask your suspension of the sentence, and a new trial. This is one among the many reasons which I hope to present to your Honor before I conclude. Now, your Honor, what is passion? Passion is the suspension of reason; in a mob upon the streets, in the broils of the saloon, in the quarrels on the sidewalk, where men throw aside their reason and resort to feelings of exasperation, we have passion. There is a suspension of the elements of judgment, of calmness, of discrimination requisite to arrive at the truth and the establishment of justice. I hold, your Honor, that you can not dispute the proposition that I make that this trial has been submerged, immerced in passion from its inception to its close, and even at this hour, standing here upon the scaffold as I do with the hangman awaiting me with his halter, there are those who claim to represent public sentiment in the city, and I now speak of the capitalistic press—that vile and infamous organ and monopoly of hired liars, the people's oppressors." Parsons claimed to have been for thirty years identified with labor interests, and said: "And in what I say upon this subject relating to the labor movement or to myself as connected in this trial or before this bar, I will speak the truth, though my tongue should be torn from my mouth and my throat cut from ear to ear, so help me God." The speaker then went into statistics, claiming that 9,000,000 out of the 12,000,000 voters in the United States were actual wage workers. He attacked the citizens' Association as an organization of millionaires, and claimed that the Court should stand between the accused and their persecuters. 'Where," he asked, "are the ends of justice observed, and where is truth found in hurrying seven human beings at the rate of express speed upon a fast train to the scaffold, and an ignominious death? Why, if your Honor please, the very method of our extermination, the deep damnation of its taking off, appeals to your Honor's sense of justice, of rectitude, and of honor. A judge may also be an unjust man. Such things have been known. We have in our histories heard of Lord Jeffreys. It need not follow that because a man is a judge he is also just. * * * Now, I hold that our execution, as the matter stands just now, would be judicial murder, and judicial murder is far worse than lynch law—far worse. But, your Honor, bear in mind please, this trial was conducted by a mob, prosecuted by a mob, by the shrieks and the howls of a mob, an organized powerful mob. The trial is over. Now, your Honor, you sit there judicially, calmly, quietly, and it is now for you to look at this thing from the standpoint of reason and from common sense. * * * Now, the money-makers, the business men, those people who deal in stocks and bonds, the speculators and employers, all that class of men known as the money-making class, they have no conception of this labor question; they don't understand what it means. To use the street parlance, with many of them it is a difficult matter for them to 'catch onto' it, and they are perverse also; they will have no knowledge of it. They don't want to know anything about it, and they won't hear anything about it, and they propose to club, lock up, and if necessary strangle those who insist on their hearing this question. Now, your Honor, can you deny that there is such a thing in the world as the labor question? I am an Anarchist. Now strike! But hear me before you strike. What is Socialism, briefly stated? It is the right of the toiler to the free and equal use of the tools of production, and the right of the producer to their product. That is Socialism. The history of mankind is one of growth. It has been evolutionary and revolutionary."

Parsons went into an explanation of the wage question and the relations of capital and labor, asserting that employers in owning capital and leaving nothing to the wage slave but the price of his work, had produced a conflict which would intensify as the power of the priviledged classes over the non-possession of property classes increased. He continued: "We were told by the Prosecution that law is on trial; that government is on trial. That is what the gentlemen on the other side have stated to the jury. The law is on trial, and government is on trial. Well, up to the conclusion of this trial we, the defendants, supposed that we were indicted and being tried for murder. Now, if the law is on trial, and the government is on trial, who has placed it upon trial? And I leave it to the people of America whether the prosecution in this case have made out a case; and I charge it here now, frankly, that in order to bring about this conviction the Prosecution, the representatives of the State, the sworn officers of the law—those whose duty it is to the people to obey the law and preserve order—I charge upon them a willful, a malicious, a purposed violation of every law which guarantees every right to every American citizen. They have violated free speech. In the prosecution of this case they have violated a free press. They have violated the right of public assembly. Yea, they have even violated and denounced the right of self-defense. I charge the crime home to them. * * * My own deliberate opinion concerning this Haymarket affair is that the death-dealing missile was the work, the deliberate work of monopoly—the act of those who themselves charge us with the deed. I am not alone in this view of this matter. What are the real facts of that Haymarket tragedy? Mayor Harrison of Chicago has caused to be published his opinion, in which he says: "I did not believe that there was any intention on the part of Spies and those men to have bombs thrown at the Haymarket.' He knows more about this thing than the jury that sat in this room, for he knows—I suspect that the Mayor knows—of some of the methods by which some of this evidence and testimony might have been manufactured. I don't charge it, your Honor, but possibly he has had some intimation of it, and if he has he knows more about this case and the merits of this case than did the jury who sat here. * * * Before the trial began, during its prosecution, and since its close, a Satanic press has shrieked and howled itself wild, like ravenous hyenas, for the blood of these eight working men. Now, this subsidized press, in the pay of the monopoly and of laborers and slavers, commanded this Court and commanded this jury and this Prosecution to convict us. As a fitting climax to this damnable conspiracy against our lives and liberty, what follows? O hide your eye now! hide it! hide it! As a fitting climax to this damnable conspiracy against our lives and liberty some of Chicago's millionaires proposed to raise a purse of $100,000 and present it to the jury for their verdict of guilty against us. This was done, as everybody knows, in the last days of the trial, and since the verdict so far as anybody knows to the contrary, this blood money has been paid over to that jury. * * * Condemned to death! Perhaps you think I do not know what for? Or maybe you think the people do not understand your motives? You are mistaken. I am here, standing in this spot awaiting your sentence, because I hate and loathe authority in every form. I am doomed by you to suffer an ignominious death because I am the outspoken enemy of coercion, of privilege, of force, of authority. It is for this you make me suffer. Think you the people are blind, are asleep, are indifferent? You deceive yourselves. I tell you, as a man of the people, and I speak for them, that your every word and act and thoughts are recorded. You are being weighed in the balance. The people are conscious of your power—your stolen power. They know you; that while you masquerade as their servants you are in reality playing the role of master. The people—the common working people—know full well that all your wealth, your ease and splendor, have been stolen from them by the exercise of your authority in the guise of law and order. I, a working man, stand here and to your face, in your stronghold of oppression, and denounce to you your crimes against humanity. It is for this I die, but my death will not have been in vain. I guess I have finished. I don't know as I have anything more to say.

Your Honor knows all I know about this case. I have taken your Honor's time up that I might be able to lay this thing, the whole thing, before you, reserving nothing; opening my mind and heart, telling you the truth, the truth, and the whole truth. I am innocent of this offense. I had no connection with that Haymarket tragedy. I know nothing of it. I am not responsible for it. I leave the case in the hands of your Honor."

SENTENCE PRONOUNCED.

Parsons spoke altogether nearly nine hours, and the addresses of all the prisoners occupied three days. Thousands of people were turned away during the closing days, and the scene in the courtroom when sentence was pronounced was peculiarly impressive. At the close of Parsons' remarks Judge Gary delivered the following remarks, and pronounced the death sentence:

" I am quite well aware that what you have said, although addressed to me, has been said to the world; yet nothing has been said which weakens the force of the proof or the conclusions therefrom upon which the verdict is based. You are all men of intelligence, and know that if the verdict stands, it must be executed. The reasons why it shall stand I have already sufficiently stated in deciding the motion for a new trial. I am sorry beyond any power of expression for your unhappy condition and for the terrible events that have brought it about. I shall address to you neither reproaches nor exhortation. What I shall say, shall be said in the faint hope that a few words from a place where the people of the State of Illinois have delegated the authority to declare the penalty of a violation of their laws, and spoken upon an occasion solemn and awful as this, may come to the knowledge of and be heeded by the ignorant, deluded and misguided men who have listened to your counsels and followed your advice. I say in the faint hope; for if men are persuaded that because of business differences, whether about labor or anything else, they may destroy property and assault and beat other men, and kill the police, if they, in the discharge of their duty, interfere to preserve the peace, there is little ground to hope that they will listen to any warning. It is not the least among the hardships of the peaceable, frugal and laborious poor to endure the tyranny of mobs, who, with lawless force, dictate to them, under penalty of peril to limb and life, where, when and upon what terms they may earn a livelihood for themselves and their families. Any government that is worthy of the name will strenuously endeavor to secure to all within its jurisdiction freedom to follow the lawful avocations and safety for their property and their persons, while obeying the law, and the law is common sense. It holds each man responsible for the natural and probable consequences of his own acts. It holds that whoever advises murder is himself guilty of the murder that is committed pursuant to his advice, and if men band together for a forcible resistance to the execution of the law and advise murder as a means of making such resistance effectual, whether such advice be to one man to murder another, or to a numerous class to murder men of another class, all who are so banded together are guilty of any murder that is committed in pursuance of such advice. The people of this country love their institutions, they love their homes, they love their property. They will never consent, that by violence and murder, those institutions shall be broken down, their homes despoiled, and their property destroyed. And the people are strong enough to protect and sustain their institutions and to punish all offenders against their laws; and those who threaten danger to civil society, if the law is enforced, are leading to destruction whoever may attempt to execute such threats. The existing order of society can be changed only by the will of the majority. Each man has the full right to entertain and advocate by speech and print such opinions as suits himself, and the great body of the people will usually care little what he says. But if he proposes murder as a means of enforcing he puts his own life at stake. And no clamor about free speech or the evils to be cured or the wrongs to be redressed, will shield him from the consequences of his crime. His liberty is not a license to destroy. The toleration that he enjoys he must extend to others, and not arrogantly assume that the great majority are wrong and may rightfully be coerced by terror, or removed by dynamite. It only remains that for the crime you have committed, and of which you have been convicted after a trial unexampled in the patience with which an outraged people have extended to you every protection and privilege of the law which you derided and defied, that the sentence of that law be now given. In form and detail that sentence will appear upon the records of the Court. In substance and effect it is that the defendant Neebe be imprisoned in the State Penitentiary at Joliet at hard labor for the term of fifteen years. And that each of the other defendants, between the hours of ten o'clock in the forenoon and two o'clock in the afternoon of the third day of December next, in the manner provided by the statute of this state, be hung by the neck until he is dead. Remove the prisoners."

Stay of sentence in the case of Neebe was granted until December 3, the date set for the execution of the other principles;

MRS. PARSONS.

and the counsel for the condemned Anarchists announced that they should file a bill of exceptions before the Illinois Supreme Court, and petition for a supersedeas.

CHAPTER X.

MISCELLANEOUS MATTER. ARBEITER ZEITUNG. MRS. LUCY PARSONS. HER ARREST IN OHIO. HER ARREST IN CHICAGO. HERR MOST ENDORSING THE BOMB-THROWING. THE PANIC HE COULD CREATE IN A BIG CITY IN THIRTY MINUTES WITH 3000 BOMBS IN THE HANDS OF 500 REVOLUTIONISTS.

As the trial progressed many new and sensational developments were made. Dr. Ernst Schmidt was constituted chairman of the committee of an organization, taking charge of matters pertaining to raising money for the defense. F. Bielefeld became business manager of the *Arbeiter Zeitung*. In all the important cities meetings were held in the interests of the condemned men. Mrs. Lucy Parsons, wife of the condemned anarchist, went on a lecturing tour to replenish the exchequer of the defendants, but public opinion in many places was against her, and she found it difficult in many places to obtain halls in which to speak. At Akron, Ohio, she was arrested for holding a meeting in defiance of the order of the mayor of that city. She has for years been an active anarchistic agitator, and her proclivities for public speech-making has brought her often before the public. She was arrested September 23 for a violation of the ordinance prohibiting the distribution of circulars on the street of Chicago. In New York, Herr Most, through his paper, the *Freiheit*, indorsed the bomb-throwing, saying: "Its work was thorough. Such bombs can be made by anybody, without much trouble, of an evening. Think of 500 revolutionists provided, say, each with six of these things, working in concert, so that, for example, in the wide range of a great cosmopolitan city within half an hour the fragments were to go flying in various suitable places, who will gainsay that by this means such a panic could be created that a comparatively small number of determined men might get possession of all commanding points in the place in a giffy? Nobody. The bomb in Chicago was legally justified, and, in a military sense, excellent. All honor to him who produced and made use of it."

For this, and similar incendiary utterances, Most was arrested and sentenced to serve a year in Sing Sing prison. He was living with Lena Fischer, alias Mary Georges, at 198 Allen street, under the name of West, and when captured was found in hiding under the woman's bed. The woman was thought to be a sister of Adolf Fischer, one of the condemned Chicago anarchists, but this was denied.

MISS NINA VAN ZANDT,

who has constituted herself the heroine of Anarchistic notoriety by developing a tender passion for the notorious Spies, is a young lady of eighteen years of age, with a fine form and a fair share of personal attractions; neither a pronounced blonde, nor yet a brunette, but seemingly occupying the middle ground, between. Nina is the daughter of the superintendant of the great Kirk soap factory of Chicago, and the heiress apparent to quite a fortune. She is of a dashing romantic disposition; fond

of flowers, birds and dogs. She fell a victim to the ardent glances of the humorous editor as the sequence of having made his acquaintance while inserting an advertisement in the *Zeitung* to recover her lost pug, to whom she was much attached. Through the efforts of Spies she recovered her pet canine, and while performing the duty of expressing her gratitude to the editor she was smitten, and yielded passively to her fate. She became so infatuated in her attachment and attentions to Spies that in February, 1887, a marriage license was procured for the purpose of becoming his wife in the jail, but the sheriff forbade the ceremony as illegal and unprecedented. It was then determined that the ceremony should take place by proxy. Spies' brother became the proxy, and the ceremony took place before Justice Englehardt in the town of Jefferson. Justice Englehardt made returns of the marriage to the county clerk, who refused to recognize the return, pronouncing the ceremony illegal. This wife, in name only, was placed on exhibition in wax in one of the dime museums, when the cheeky manager was served with an injunction; but this young would-be wife compromised the matter, it is thought, on condition that part of the emmoluments went into a fund for the benefit of her condemned lord.

MRS. OSCAR NEEBE

died quite suddenly in March, 1887. Neebe, under guard of Jailor Folz, visited the bedside of his dying wife and by official clemency remained some time with his children, and everything was done for the condemned men that could be done in the name of humanity under the circumstances.

CHAPTER XI.

SUPERSEDEAS GRANTED. UNITED STATES SUPREME COURT'S DECISION SUSTAINING THE ORIGINAL VERDICT. PARSONS' LETTER TO GOVENOR OGLESBY. LINGG DEFIANT. THEY REFUSE TO SIGN A PETITION ASKING FOR EXECUTIVE CLEMENCY. THEIR IMPERTINENT LETTERS TO GOVERNOR OGLESBY.

THE SUPERSEDEAS GRANTED.

There was no doubt from the beginning that the supersedeas asked for in behalf of the condemned anarchists would be granted. Capt. W. P. Black and Hon. Leonard Swett, who had been retained to present the petition and make the argument for a new trial, met Chief Justice Scott at Bloomington by appointment, Nov. 25, 1886, and he directed the writ of error to issue. The only thing of substance which Justice Scott said at the entering of the order was to call attention to the following language in Mooney vs. The People, CXI. Illinois, page 388 — an opinion by the full court :

Recognizing to the fullest extent the rule of law that the jury in their deliberations are judges of the facts and the weight of the evidence in criminal cases, yet the law has imposed on the court the solemn and responsible duty to see to it that no injustice is done by hasty action, passion, or prejudice, or from any other cause on the part of the jury. This duty the court may not omit in any case.

It is almost needless to state that the anarchists were well

RICHARD OGLESBY.
Governor of Illinois.

pleased with their temporary reprieve, and opportunity to have their able counsel argue for a rehearing of their case. The arguments were finished March 18, 1887, before the Supreme Court at Ottawa, States Attorney Grinnell and Attorney-general Hunt appearing for the State. The decision was rendered Wednesday, September 14, before the full bench of Supreme justices, being read by Judge Magruder, of Chicago. It will thus be seen that the Supreme Court gave the questions at issue full and ample consideration during a period of nearly six months. The court-room was crowded by an expectant throng, and the announcement of the decision was foreshadowed by impressive solemnity. In a condensed review like this it would be manifestly impossible to give a decision comprising upwards of 60,000 words, and covering every point and detail of the case. It is sufficient to state that the decision was unanimous on the part of the justices. Even Justice Mulkey, who was thought to lean toward a new trial, declared that, after having fully examined the record and given the questions arising on it his very best thought, with an earnest and conscientious desire to faithfully discharge his whole duty, he was fully satisfied that the opinion reached vindicates the law and does complete justice between the people and the defendants, fully warranted by the law and evidence.

Chief Justice Sheldon made the following announcement: "In this case the court orders that the sentence of the Criminal Court of Cook county on the defendants in the indictment of August Spies, Michael Schwab, Samuel Fielden, Albert R. Parsons, Adolph Fischer, George Engel, and Louis Lingg, be carried into effect by the sheriff of Cook county on Friday, November

11 next, between the hours of 10 o'clock in the forenoon and 4 o'clock in the afternoon of that day."

The formal order for the execution of the anarchists was received by Sheriff Matson, of Cook county, Monday, September 26. The guards inside and patrol outside the jail had been doubled upon receipt of the news that the Supreme Court had sustained the verdict. Monday night Oscar Neebe was quietly removed from the jail in a carriage and taken to Joliet by train by Deputy Sheriffs Gleason and Spear, Neebe being handcuffed securely to the latter officer. Neebe's companions and outside sympathizers did not know of his removal. Neebe said to a reporter of the *News* that he had abandoned all hope. He said he would rather step upon the gallows with his companions than to go to prison; related what he had accomplished for employees of Chicago breweries and the grocery clerks, in getting their hours shortened; was unrepentant of his part in the conspiracy, and said: "What I have done I would do again, and the time will come when the blood of the martyrs about to be sacrificed will cry aloud for vengeance, and that cry will be heard, aye, and that, too, before many years elapse."

EFFORTS TO SAVE THE ANARCHISTS HAD FAILED.

Upon receipt of the news of the affirmation of the sentence by the Supreme Court, A. R. Parsons sent to the newspapers an appeal, "To the American People," in which he maintained his innocence; declared that his speeches were lawful; condemned the evidence of detectives; refused executive clemency, concluding in the words of Patrick Henry, "I know not what course others may take, but as for me, give me liberty or give me death."

A. R. Parsons's open letter to the American people in which he justifies his actions, maintains his innocence, and refuses executive clemency, ran as follows, under date of September 22, 1887:

"To the American People — *Fellow Citizens:* As all the world knows, I have been convicted and sentenced to die for the crime of murder, the most heinous offense that can be committed. Under the form of law two courts — viz: the Criminal and Supreme courts of the State of Illinois — have sentenced me to death as an accessory before the fact to the murder of Officer Degan on May 4, 1886. Nevertheless, I am innocent of the crime charged, and to a candid and unprejudiced world I submit the proof:

PARSONS MAINTAINS HIS INNOCENCE.

" In the decision affirming the sentence of death upon me the Supreme Court of the State of Illinois says: 'It is undisputed that the bomb was thrown that caused the death of Degan. It is conceded that no one of the defendants threw the bomb with his own hands. Plaintiffs in error are charged with being accessories before the fact.' If I did not throw the bomb myself it becomes necessary to prove that I aided, encouraged, and advised the person who did throw it. Is that fact proved? The Supreme Court says it is. The record says it is not. I appeal to the American people to judge between them.

"The Supreme Court quotes articles from the *Alarm*, the paper edited by me, and from my speeches running back three years before the Haymarket tragedy of May 4, 1886. Upon said articles and speeches the court affirms my sentence of death as an accessory. The court says, 'The articles in the *Alarm* were most of them written by the defendant Parsons, and some of them by the defendant Spies,' and then proceeds to quote these articles. I refer to the record to prove that of all the articles quoted only one was shown to have been written by me. I wrote, of course, a great many articles for my paper, the *Alarm*, but the record will show that only one of these many quoted by the Supreme Court to prove my guilt as an accessory was written by me. This article appeared in the *Alarm* December 6, 1884, one year and a half before the Haymarket meeting. As to Mr. Spies, the record will show that during the three years I was editor of the *Alarm* he did not write for the paper half a dozen articles. For proof as to this I appeal to the record.

"The *Alarm* was a labor paper, and, as is well known, a labor paper is conducted as a medium through which working people can make known their grievances. The *Alarm* was no exception to this rule. I not only did not write 'most of the articles,' but wrote comparatively few of them. This the record will also show.

"In referring to my Haymarket speech the court says: 'To the men then listening to him he had addressed the incendiary appeals that had been appearing in the *Alarm* for two years. The court then quotes the incendiary article which I did write, and which is as follows: 'One dynamite bomb properly placed will destroy a regiment of soldiers, a weapon easily made, and carried with perfect safety in the pockets of one's clothing.'"

SIMPLY A QUOTATION FROM GENERAL SHERIDAN.

"The record will show by referring to the *Alarm* that this

is a garbled extract taken from a statement made by Gen. Philip Sheridan in his annual report to Congress. It was simply a reiteration of General Sheridan's statement that dynamite was easily made, perfectly safe to handle, and a very destructive weapon of warfare. The article in full as it appeared in the *Alarm* is as follows: 'Dynamite—The protection of the poor against the armies of the rich—in submitting his annual report, November 10, 1884, Gen. Philip Sheridan, commander of the United States army, says: "This nation is growing so rapidly that there are signs of other troubles, which I hope will not occur and which will probably not come upon us if both capital and labor will only be conservative. Still, it should be remembered, destructive explosives are easily made, and that banks, United States sub-treasuries, and large mercantile houses can be readily demolished and the commerce of entire cities destroyed by an infuriated people with means carried with perfect safety to themselves in the pockets of their clothing."'

"The editorial comment upon the above as it appeared in the *Alarm* is as follows: 'A hint to the wise is sufficient. Of course General Sheridan is too modest to tell us that himself and army will be powerless in the coming revolution between the propertied and the propertyless classes. Only in foreign wars can the usual weapons of warfare be used to any advantage. One dynamite bomb properly placed will destroy a regiment of soldiers; a weapon easily made and carried with perfect safety in the pockets of one's clothing. The First regiment may as well disband, for if it should ever level its guns upon the workingmen of Chicago it can be totally annihilated.

"Again the court says: 'He (Parsons) had said to them (referring to the people assembled at the Haymarket) Saturday,

April 24, 1886, just ten days before May 4, in the *Alarm* that had appeared: "Workingmen, to arms! War to the palace, peace to the cottage, and death to luxurious idleness! The wage system is the only cause of the world's misery. It is supported by the rich classes, and to destroy it they must be either made work or die. One pound of dynamite is better than a bushel of ballots! Make your demand for eight hours with weapons in your hands to meet the capitalist bloodhounds —police and militia—in the proper manner."'

"The record will show that this article was not written by me, but was published as a news item. By referring to the columns of the *Alarm* the following comment appears, attached to the above article, viz: 'The above hand-bill was sent to us from Indianapolis, Ind., having been posted all over that city last week. Our correspondent says that the police tore them down wherever they found them.'

"The court continuing, says: 'At the close of another article in the same issue he said: "The social war has come, and whoever is not with us is against us."' Assistant State's Attorney Walker read this article to the jury, and at its conclusion stated that it bore my initials and was my article. It is a matter within the knowledge of every one present that I interrupted him and called his attention to the fact that the article did not bear my initials, and that I was not its author. Mr. Walker corrected his mistake to the jury.

"Now these are the three articles quoted by the Supreme Court as proof of my guilt as an accessory in a conspiracy to murder Officer Degan. The record will prove what I say.

HIS SPEECHES WERE ALL RIGHT.

"Now as to my speeches—all of them, with one exception

purporting to be my utterances at the Haymarket, are given from the excited imaginations and preverted memories of newspaper reporters. Mr. English, who alone took shorthand notes and swore to their correctness, reports me as saying. ' It is time to raise a note of warning. There is nothing in the eight-hour movement to excite the capitalist. Don't you know that the militia are under arms and a gatling gun is ready to mow you down? Was this Germany, or Russia, or Spain? [A voice: "It looks like it."] Whenever you make a demand for eight hours' pay or increase of pay the militia and the deputy sheriffs and the Pinkerton men are called out and you are shot and clubbed and murdered in the streets. I am not here for the purpose of exciting anybody, but to speak out, to tell the facts as they exist even though it shall cost me my life before morning!' Mr. English continuing, said: 'There is another part of it (the speech) right here It behooves you, as you love your wife and children, if you don't want to see them perish with hunger, killed, or cut down like dogs on the street—Americans, in the interest of your liberty and your independence, to arms; arm yourselves!'

"This, be it remembered, is a garbled extract, and it is a matter of record that Reporter English testified that he was instructed by the proprietor of his paper to report only the inflammatory portions of the speeches made at the meeting.

THE MAYOR HEARD THE SPEECH.

"Mayor Harrison, who was present and heard this speech, testified before the jury that it was simply 'a violent and political harangue' and did not call for his interference as a peace officer. The speech delivered by me at the Haymarket, and which I repeated before the jury is a matter of record and undisputed, and I challenge any one to show therein that I incited any one to acts of violence. The extract reported by Mr. English, when taken in connection with what preceded and what followed, cannot be construed by the wildest imagination as incitement to violence. Extracts from three other speeches alleged to have been delivered by me were made more than one year prior to May 4, 1886, are given. Two of these speeches were reported from the memory of the Pinkerton detective Johnson. These are the speeches quoted by the court as proof of my guilt as accessory to the murder of Degan. Where, then, is the connection between these speeches and the murder of Degan? I am bold to declare that such connection is imperceptible to the eye of a fair and unprejudiced mind. But the honorable body, the Supreme Court of Illinois, has condemned me to death for speeches I never made, and for articles I never wrote. In the affirmation of the death sentence the court has 'assumed,' 'supposed,' 'guessed' 'surmised,' and 'presumed' that I can and did 'so and so.' This the record fully proves.

"The court says: 'Spies, Schwab, Parsons and Engel were responsible for the articles written and published by them, as above shown; Spies, Schwab, Fielden, Parsons and Engel were responsible for the speeches made by them respectively, and there is evidence in the same record tending to show that the death of Degan occurred during the prosecution of a conspiracy planned by the members of the international groups who read these articles and heard these speeches.'

OBJECTS TO THE PINKERTON MEN.

"Now, I defy any one to show from the record the proof

that I wrote more than one of the many articles alleged to have been written by me. Yet the Supreme Court says that I wrote and am responsible for all of them. Again—concerning the alleged speeches—they were reported by the Pinkerton detective Johnson, who was, as the record shows, employed by Lyman Gage, president of the First National Bank, as the agent of the Citizens' Association, an organization composed of the millionaire employers of Chicago.

"I submit to a candid world if this hired spy would not make false reports to earn blood-money. Thus, it is for speeches I did not make, and articles I did not write I am sentenced to die, because the court 'assumes' that these articles influenced some unknown and still unidentified person to throw the bomb that killed Degan. Is this law? Is this justice?

"The Supreme Court, in affirming the sentence of death upon me, proceeds to give further reasons, as follows: 'Two circumstances are to be noted. First, it can hardly be said that Parsons was absent from the Haymarket meeting when he went to Zepf's Hall. It has already been stated that the latter place was only a few steps north of the speakers' wagon and in sight from it. We do not think that the defendant Parsons could escape his share of the responsibility for the explosions at the Haymarket because he stepped into a neighboring saloon and looked at the explosion through a window. While he was speaking men stood around him with arms in their hands. Many of these were members of the armed sections of the international groups. Among them were men who belonged to the International Rifles, an armed organization in which he himself was an officer, and with which he had been drilling in preparation for the events then transpiring.'

"The records of the trial will show that not one of the foregoing allegations is true. The facts are these: Zepf's Hall is on the northeast corner of Lake and Desplaines streets, just one block north of the speakers' wagon. The court says 'it was only a few steps north of the speakers' wagon.' The court says further that 'it can hardly be said that Parsons was absent from the Haymarket meeting when he was at Zepf's Hall.' If this is correct logic, then I was at two different places a block apart at the same instant. Truly the day of miracles has not yet passed. Again, the record will show that I did not 'step into a neighboring saloon and look at the explosion through a window.' It will show that I went to Zepf's Hall, one block distant, and across Lake street, accompanied by my wife and another lady, and my two children (a girl of five and a boy of seven years of age), they having sat upon a wagon about ten feet from the speakers' wagon throughout my speech; that it looked like rain; that we had started home and went into Zepf's Hall to wait for the meeting to adjourn, and walked home in company with a lot of friends who lived in that direction. Zepf's building is on the corner and opens on the street with a triangular door six feet wide. Myself and ladies and children were just inside the door. Here, while waiting for our friends and looking toward the meeting, I had a fair view of the explosion. All this the record will show.

ABOUT THE BOMB.

"It would seem that, according to circumstances, a block is at one time 'a few steps' or a 'few steps' is more than a block, as the case may suit. The logical as well as the imaginative faculties of the Supreme Court are further illustrated in a most striking manner by the credence of the court to the 'yarn' of a 'reporter,' who testified that Spies had described to him the Czar' bomb, and the men who were to use them as follows. 'He spoke of a body of tall, strong men in their organization who could throw bombs weighing five pounds 150 paces. He stated that the bombs in question were to be used in case of conflict with the police or the militia.'

"The court gives this sort of testimony as proof of the existence of a conspiracy to murder Degan. Wonderful credulity. To throw a five-pound bomb 150 paces or yards is to throw it 450 feet or a quarter of a mile.

"Gulliver, in his travels among the Brobdingnag race, tells us of the giants he met, and we have also heard of the giants of Patagonia. But we did not know until now that they were mere Lilliputians as compared with the 'anarchist Swedes' of Chicago.

"The court proceeds to say, "While he (Parsons) was speaking, men stood around him with arms in their hands.' The record as quoted by the court shows that only one man flourished a pistol, not a number of men Again, the court says, 'Most of the men were members of the armed sections of the "International groups,"' thus making it appear that many of these men (when there was only one who was even alleged to have exhibited a pistol) were armed.

"The court says: 'Among them were men who belonged to the "International Rifles," an armed organization in which he himself was an officer, and in which he had been drilling in preparation for the events then transpiring.'

"Now I Challenge the Supreme Court or any other honorable gentleman to prove from the record that there ever existed such an organization as the armed section of the American group, known as the 'International Rifles.' It cannot be done. The record shows that some members of the American group did organize the 'International Rifles,' which never met but four or five times; was never armed with rifles or any other weapons, and was disbanded nearly a year before the 4th of May, 1886.

"The Pinkerton man Johnson says that dynamite bombs were exhibited 'in the presence of the "International Rifles."' It will take corroborative testimony before the American people will credit the statements of such a man engaged for such a purpose; and it is well known that Supreme courts have decided that the testimony of detectives should be taken with great caution.

HE APPEALS TO THE PEOPLE.

"I appeal to the American people, to their love of justice and fair play. I submit that the record does not show my gilt of the crime of murder, but on the contrary it proves my innocence.

"Against me in this trial all the rules of law and evidence have been reversed in that I have been held as guilty until I proved my innocence. I have been tried ostensibly for murder, but in reality for anarchy. I have been proved guilty of being an anarchist and condemned to die for that reason. The State's attorney said in his statement before the court and jury in the beginning of the trial: 'These defendants were picked out and indicted by the grand jury. They are no more guilty than the thousands who follow them. They are picked out because they are leaders. Convict them and our society is safe,' and in their last appeal to the jury the prosecution said: 'Anarchy is on trial. Hang these eight men and save our institutions. These are the leaders. Make examples of them.' This is a matter of record.

A WORD FOR HIS COMRADES.

"So far as I have had time to examine the records I find the same fabrication and perversion of testimony against all my comrades as exists against myself. I therefore again appeal to to the American people to avert the crime of judicial murder. And this appeal I have faith will not be in vain.

"My ancestors partook of all the hardships incident to the establishment of this Republic. They fought, bled, and some of them died that the Declaration of Independence might live and the American flag might wave in triumph over those who claim the 'divine right of kings to rule.' Shall the flag now, after a century's triumph, trail in the mire of oppression and protect the perpetration of outrages and oppressions that would put the older despotisms of Europe to shame?

"Knowing myself innocent of crime I came forward and gave myself up for trial. I felt that it was my duty to take my chances with the rest of my comrades. I sought a fair and impartial trial before a jury of my peers, and knew that before any fair-minded jury I could with little difficulty be cleared. I preferred to be tried and take the chances of an acquittal with my friends to being hunted as a felon. Have I had a fair trial?

PARSONS REFUSES EXECUTIVE CLEMENCY.

"The lovers of justice and fair play are assiduously engaged in an effort to thwart the consummation of judicial murder by a commutation of sentence to prison. I speak for myself alone when I say that for this I thank them and appreciate their efforts. But I am an innocent man. I have violated no law; I have committed no offense against any one's rights. I am simply the victim of the malice of those whose anger has been aroused by the growth, strength and independence of the labor organizations of America. I am a sacrifice to those who say: 'These men may be innocent. No matter. They are anarchists. We must hang them anyway.'

"My counsel informs me that every effort will be made to take this case before the highest tribunal in the land, and that there is strong hope of a hearing there. But I am also reliably informed that from three to five years will elapse before the Supreme Court of the United States can hear and adjudge the case.

"Since surrendering myself to the authorities, I have been locked up in close confinement twenty-one hours out of every twenty-four for six days, and from Saturday afternoon till Monday morning (thirty-eight hours) each week in a noisome cell, without a ray of sunlight or a breath of pure air. To be compelled to bear this for five or even three years would be to suffer a lingering death, and it is only a matter of serious consideration with me whether I ought to accept the verdict as it stands rather than die by inches under such conditions. I am prepared to die. I am ready, if needs be, to lay down my life for my rights and the rights of my fellow-men. But I object to being killed on false and unproved accusations. Therefore I cannot countenance or accept the efforts of those who would endeavor to procure a commutation of my sentence to an imprisonment in the penitentiary. Neither do I approve of any further appeals to the courts of law. I believe them to be all alike—the agency of the privileged classes to perpetuate their power, to oppress and plunder the toiling masses. As between capital and its legal rights, and labor and its legal rights, the courts of law must side with the capitalistic class. To appeal to them is in vain. It is the appeal of the wage slave to his capitalistic master for liberty. The answer is curses, blows, imprisonment, and death.

"If I had never been an anarchist before, my experience with courts and the laws of the governing class would make an anarchist of me now. What is anarchy? It is a state of society without any central or governing power. Upon this subject the court, in its affirmation of the death sentence, defines the object of the International Working Peoples' Association as follows:

"'It is designed to bring about a social revolution. Social revolution means the destruction of the right of private ownership of property, or of the right of the individual to own property. It means of the bringing about of a state of society in which all property should be held in common.'

HE REFERS TO THE SCRIPTURES.

"If this definition is right, then it is very similar to that advocated by Jesus Christ, for proof of which I refer to the fourth and fifth chapters of the Acts of the Apostles; also Matthew xxi., 10 to 14, and Mark xi., 15 to 19.

"No, I am not guilty. I have not been proved guilty. I leave it to you to decide from the record itself as to my guilt or innocence. I cannot, therefore, accept a commutation to imprisonment. I appeal—not for mercy, but for justice. As for me, the utterance of Patrick Henry is so appropos that I cannot do better than let him speak:

"'Is life so dear and peace so sweet as to be purchased at the price of chains and slavery? Forbid it, Almighty God! I know not what course others may take, but, as for me, give me liberty or give me death.' A. R. PARSONS,

"Prison Cell 29, Chicago, Ill., Sept. 21, 1887."

THE CASE BEFORE THE FEDERAL SUPREME COURT.

The anarchists were not lacking in funds to secure every chance of reprieve or commutation, as contributions had poured into their coffers swelling the sum total over $50,000. Every opportunity was accorded to the condemned men to place their case in as favorable a light as possible before the Federal Court. But the flagrant and far-reaching character of their crime gave little hope to the unbiased that the judges composing that honorable body would interfere. Following our readers will find Attorney Grinnell's argument before the United States Supreme Court. Also General Butler's defense for the impenitent yet doomed men.

GRINNELL'S ARGUMENT BEFORE THE UNITED STATES SUPREME COURT.

Mr. Grinnell, addressing the court, said that it had not been his intention to take part in the oral argument, and that he came here primarily for the purpose of assisting Mr. Hunt by means of his familiarity with the record in this case. He thought that by the presentation of the law and the facts yesterday it was clearly shown that there was no federal question involved, and that the court was without jurisdidtion to grant the writ of error. The assignments of error in the lower court, and the parts of the record relating to the jurors Denker and Sanford had been printed and were in the court's hands. In all the twenty-eight assignments of error there was no reference directly or indirectly to the constitution of the United States or any of its amendments. There were some things, he said, which were here generally conceded, and one of them was that the constitution itself confers no rights which need be here considered. It is simply a limitation of the rights of the legislative power in dealing with the rights of citizens.

THE QUESTION OF JURISDICTION.

The constitution of the State of Illinois contains almost all the provisions which are embraced in the constitution of the United States. This court had settled, he believed, the question of jurisdiction as far as the first ten amendments are concerned, and also, he thought, under the fourteenth amendment. The only clause of the latter which could figure here was that " no State shall deprive any person of life, liberty, or property without due process of law." Whatever affects liberty and life is made by this clause to affect also property. If the court has jurisdiction of this case under this provision of the amendment then every State question relating to property, such as special assessments, the condemnation of property, etc., might be brought to this court for review.

The Chief Justice—" Because they take property without valuation by a jury."

Mr. Grinnell—" Yes, your honor, in some cases they do, especially in the matter of drainage, where the proceedings may be before a justice of the peace."

PEREMPTORY CHALLENGES.

Mr. Grinnell said he thought it to be conceded that a State

Legislature had a right to prescribe how many peremptory challenges should be allowed in the formation of a jury. The common law of Illinois had been radically changed in this respect, and both prosecution and defendant now stood on an equal footing. Each defendant was entitled to twenty peremptory challenges, and as the eight defendants in this case acted in concert and were all consulted, each of them had practically 160 peremptory challenges. The State had a like number. The defendants exhausted all of their 160 peremptory challenges before a jury was obtained and the State availed itself of its priviledge to the extent of fifty-two challenges He maintained, however, that no federal question would be involved even if the State allowed only one peremptory challenge to one side and 160 to the other. It was the State's right. In this case there were 931 men called into the jury box and examined in order to obtain twelve jurors.

JURORS SANFORD AND DENKER.

No objection was raised to any one of the twelve jurors with the single exception of Sanford. Denker was challenged for cause after a brief examination; the challenge was overruled and the defense accepted, but they then proceeded with a further and more elaborate examination of him, and it is shown by the record that after this second examination they desired to keep him, that they did keep him, and that they did make no further exception. When Denker was taken the defense had left 142 peremptory challenges and they could have used one of these challenges to get rid of him if they had been very deirsous of so doing. They had forty-three peremptory challenges left after eleven jurors had been sworn. These forty-three challenges they frittered away frivolously for the purpose of taking some possible advantage. Their peremptory challenges were then exhausted, and they had to either take a juror or show cause why he should be rejected.

The examination of Sanford, the last juror, clearly demonstrated, Mr. Grinnell said, that the defense were more ready to take him than the State was. Not a single juror was put upon the defense to exhaust their peremptory challenges. Whenever a man said that he had talked with a witness or any one who was present at the Haymarket meeting, or that he had attended the coroner's inquest he was rejected for cause.

EULOGIZING THE JURY.

Speaking of the jury as a whole, Mr. Grinnell said: "I wish and am constrained to pay one tribute to that jury. It exemplified American citizenship in this country more than any jury that was ever looked upon. It embraced all walks of life. Three of them earned their living by manual work. They came from all parts of the country and one of them was born on foreign soil. They were not a class jury. They were honest citizens with the solemn duty devolving upon them of determining what should be done with those men. No judge could look in the faces of that jury without saying: 'They are intelligent; they represent American citizenship; they are fit to be trusted with the rights of freemen under our constitution.' There was not a capitalist on that jury. They were all common-place small dealers and intelligent men."

Mr. Grinnell said he would challenge any one to show that a single member of that jury was not a competent juror, not only under the jury law of Illinois, but under the common law.

"Congress," he said, "had recognized the right of States to make their own jury laws."

Section 800 of the Revised Statutes provides that "jurors to serve in the courts of the United States in each State respectively shall have the the same qualifications and be entitled to the same exemptions as jurors of the highest court of law in such State may have and be entitled to at the time when such jurors for service in the courts of the United State are summoned."

Almost every State in the North, he said, now had its new jury law, and these laws have been sustained by the highest State courts.

THE SEIZURE OF SPIES' PAPERS.

Proceeding to the question of "unreasonable search and seizure" in Spies' office, he said it did not strike him as being any part of this case. He was not here to offer any apologies for his own conduct. He then recited at some length the circumstances of the bomb-throwing in the Haymarket, the search of the *Arbeiter Zeitung* office, the prying open of Spies' desk, the finding of dynamite and letters there, the breaking open of Lingg's domicile, and the finding in his trunk of dynamite bombs precisely like the one thrown. Mr. Grinnell was interrupted at this point by General Butler, who said he should want to cross-examine him if it was competent for him to do so.

Mr. Grinnell—"You shall have that privilege, General."

Mr. Grinnell, resuming, said that such seizure was not a thing which this court could regulate. It had said in the Ker kidnaping case that it was not for the court to determine how he (the prisoner) got here. The court simply said: "You are here." The things seized in the search of these prisoners' premises " were there," and it was for the court to determine whether they were legally there. The only question was, "Are these things testimony?" and that was not an inquiry for the court.

SIMPLY EVIDENCE.

Forgery, murder, and other crimes had to be proved, Mr. Grinnell said, by such evidence. "The pistol found in the hand of the assassin Guiteau was forcibly taken from him, and his papers, if I remember rightly, were overhauled. They were 'there' (that is, in the court), and it was nobody's business how they got there. That the search and seizure in this case was an unreasonable search and seizure from the point of view of the defendants I have no doubt."

In conclusion Mr. Grinnell said: "It strikes us from our standpoint that the foundation of the constitution is less likely to be impaired by refusing to grant this writ than by granting it."

THE GENERAL'S INDIVIDUALITY.

After a great deal of rambling talk about the composition of the jury, dissatisfaction with the record, lack of time for preparation, the sentencing of the prisoners in their absence and that of their counsel, the injustice done them by "unreasonable search and seizure," etc., General Butler said that if all these things could be done the question was to be debated whether this government would not be a little better if it were overturned into an anarchy than if it were to be carried on in this fashion.

"I have no fear," he said, "of being misunderstood upon

this question. I have the individuality of being the only man in the United States that condemned and executed men for undertaking to overturn the law. There were thousands of them. And for that act, please your honors, a price was set on my head as though I were a wolf, and $25,000 was offered to any man that could capture me, to murder me, by Jefferson Davis and his associates, and who, if they were here at your bar, trying to ascertain whether they should have an honest and a fair trial for their great crimes, and they called upon me— their lives in danger—I should hold it to be my duty to stand here and do all that I might to defend them. That is the chivalry of the law, if I understand it, and if I don't it is of not much consequence, for I am quite easily and quickly passing away."

INHERENT RIGHTS OF CITIZENS

After some further talk General Butler said he agreed fully that the first ten amendments to the constitution were limitations of federal power and not restrictions of the rights of the States. The "privileges and immunities" however, claimed by these prisoners were privileges inherent in each one of the citizens of the several States of the United States, because in vast majority we were British subjects and had certain privileges and immunities inherited under the common law and magna charta, and among them, and the most thoroughly known and defined were the trial by jury for all high crimes, exemption from search and seizure without warrant of law, protection from self-accusation when a witness, and not to be deprived of life, liberty, or property without due process of law. We claim that all the rights, privileges, and immunities that belonged to a

British subject under magna charta belong to each citizen of the United States; and that as new citizens of the United States were made, not citizens of States, by naturalization, these rights, priviliges, and immunities came to them as citizens of the United States. The effect of the fourteenth amendment was to guarantee these rights, privileges, and immunities to the citizens of all the States.

MEANING OF "DUE PROCESS OF LAW."

The words "due process of law" as contained in the fourteenth amendment, and as used to define one of these guaranteed rights, mean "by the law of the land," not the law of a county, a province, or a State, but the law of the country—the whole country. That is the law of the land, and was so understood by our forefathers as due process of law. Any other meaning given to "due process of law" as it is used in the fourteenth amendment would make it simply ridiculous and frivolous, because any State may enact a "due process of law" according to that State, by which a man's life may be taken and from which not a single right or immunity of citizenship can protect him. Any law a State may make after the passage of this amendment for dealing with the rights of a citizen of the United States becomes wholly inoperative, because the "law of the land" must forever remain fixed as at that moment, not to be changed in regard to its citizens without a change of organic law, and for some purposes not to be even so changed.

THE CASES OF FIELDEN AND SPIES.

General Butler then proceeded to a consideration of the special and peculiar questions raised by the cases of Fielden and Spies who are foreigners. He contended that treaties were the supreme law of the land, and that these prisoners were entitled, by virtue of treaties with Germany and Great Britain, to all the rights and privileges of American citizens at the time such treaties were made. A State had no power to try these men by one of its own laws which was not the law of the land at the time the treaties were ratified. He did not mean, he said, that a foreigner could come into a State and break its laws with impunity and that the State could not touch him. But he did mean that the State could only try him in accordance with the law of the land—the whole land—at the time the treaty with his government was made. This, he said, was an important question to every American citizen, because in return for the concession made by this government in the treaty with Great Britain the government of that country had made similar concessions to us. Suppose that a citizen of the United States should go to Ireland and should make some remarks about the advantages of a republican form of government, and should be arrested and tried by the crimes act in violation of the treaty. Would we not stand up and say that this man must be tried by a fair and impartial jury? He must be tried as an Englishman would have been tried at the time the treaty was made, and he cannot be dealt with in a more summary way under a later law.

GENERAL BUTLER'S ARGUMENT.

If this should happen, General Butler said, he hoped that the English authorities would not be able to hold up to him a decision of the United States Supreme Court sustaining the right to try an Englishman by the local law of a State which was nothing but a swamp and a howling wilderness at the time the treaty was ratified.

Returning to the rights of States, General Butler said that he was not prepared to deny that a State might change its organic laws with the consent of all its citizens, but such change would not bind a citizen of another State who had not assented to them.

IMPARTIAL JURIES AND NEWSPAPER LIES.

After some desultory remarks about the record and the necessity of laying it before the court, and another reference to breaking open safes and desks, General Butler said: "There is no doubt that the prisoners were entitled to a trial by an impartial jury—a stupid jury, if you please—because I don't think a man who reads newspapers is any more competent to try a case —rather worse if he pays any attention to their lies." As enunciated by chief justices of the Supreme Court an impartial juror, he said, is one who "stands in freedom of mind, without bias or prejudice, and is indifferent." The petitioners were not tried by such a jury and are entitled to protection under the federal constitution.

"If" he said, "the court is to give me jurors as prejudiced as some of those in this case I had better go to a land of Hottentots, for they would not allow me to be stolen and taken back into Illinois." General Butler's allusion is to the kidnaping of Ker, referred to by counsel on the other side in defending their search and seizure.

In reply to Mr. Grinnell's statement that the records would show that the defense were more ready to take the last juror (Sanford) than the State was, General Butler said that they were compelled to accept the last juror. Their peremptory challenges were exhausted and they could do nothing else. Under these circumstances they talked to him and coaxed him, and tried to get him into a state of mind as favorable to their side as they could. That was what the parts of the record referred to by Mr. Grinnell would show, and nothing more.

NO WAIVER OF RIGHTS IN CAPITAL CASES.

General Butler then referred to the assertion of counsel on the other side that the petitioners had waved some of their rights through not insisting upon them by exception or objection at the proper time, and that therefore, they were estopped from asserting these rights now in this court. He contended, however, that when a man was on trial for his life there was no such thing as a waiver or estoppal. In capital offences a prisoner cannot waive wittingly or unwittingly anything that will affect the issue. In support of this contention he cited the opinion of Chief Justice Shaw in the case of Dr. Webster. The prisoners, he maintained, could not now be barred out because they had not raised sufficiently formal objections.

General Butler then returned again to the "unreasonable searches and seizures" complained of by the petitioners, and said his associate, Mr. Tucker, had characterized the proceeding as a "subpœnæ duces tecum," executed by a locksmith. "Why your honors," he exclaimed, "they searched under a burglary, headed by the State's attorney on his own admission—no miserable policeman or half-witted constable, but the State's prosecuting attorney does the burglary, steals the papers, and says you can't help that. He puts it with a sort of triumph, and yet we are told that our immunities and privileges are not invaded, and our remedy is to sue for trespass. What a beautiful remedy! Sue the State's attorney and be tried by such a jury as the laws of Illinois would give. Better be in a place not to be named for comfort."

PRISONERS ABSENT WHEN SENTENCED.

As a final reason why the writ should be granted, General Butler urged that the prisoners had been sentenced to death in their absence, and without being asked whether they had any reason to give why sentence of death should not be pronounced upon them. The record, he said, did not show that they were absent when sentenced, but they could prove it. The record showed that they were present, but they could prove by half Chicago that this was a mistake.

In conclusion, General Butler said: "May I, in closing, make one observation? If men's lives can be taken in this way, as you have seen exhibited here to-day, better anarchy, better be without law, than with any such law." General Butler then thanked the court for its indulgence and took his seat.

UNITED STATES SUPREME COURT'S DECISION NOVEMBER 2, 1887

Is as follows:

The court holds in brief: First, that the first ten amendments to the constitution are limitations upon federal and not upon State action: second, that the jury law of Illinois is upon its face valid and constitutional, and that it is similar in its provisions to the statute of Utah, which was sustained in this court in the case of Hopt vs. The Territory of Utah; third, that it does not appear in the record that upon the evidence the trial court should have declared the juror Sanford incompetent; fourth, that the objection to the admission of the Johann Most letter and the cross-examination of Spies, which counsel for the prisoners maintained virtually compelled them to testify against themselves, were not objected to in the trial court, and that therefore no foundation was laid for the exercise of this court's jurisdiction, and fifth, that the questions raised by General Butler in the cases of Spies and Fielden upon the basis of their foreign nationality were neither raised nor decided in the State courts, and therefore cannot be considered.

The writ of error prayed for was consequently denied.

There was no dissenting opinion.

The above decision of the Supreme Court was received by the condemned anarchists with coolness amounting to indifference. A. R. Parsons then handed the copy of a letter sent to Governor Oglesby to the *Daily News* for publication, as follows: "*To His Excellency Richard J. Oglesby, Governor of the State of Illinois*—DEAR SIR: I am aware that petitions are being signed by hundreds of thousands of persons addressed to you, beseeching you to interpose your perogative and commute the sentences of myself and comrades from death to imprisonment in the penitentiary. You are, I am told a good constitutional lawyer and a sincere man. I therefore beg of you to examine the record of the trial, and then conscientiously decide for yourself as to my guilt or innocence. I know that as a just man you will decide in accordance with the facts, the truth, and the justice of this case. But I write to reiterate the declaration made in my published appeal to the people of America September 21, 1887. I am guilty or I am innocent of the charge for which I have been condemned to die. If guilty, then I prefer death rather than to go ' like the quarry slave at night scourged to his dungeon. If innocent then I am entitled to and will accept nothing less than liberty. The records of the trial made in Judge Gary's court prove my innocence of the crime of murder. But there exists a conspiracy to judicially murder myself and imprisoned companions in the name and by virtue of the authority of the State. History records every despotic, arbitrary deed of the people's rulers as having been done in the name of the people, even to the destruction of the liberties of the people.

"I am a helpless prisoner, completely in the power of the authorities, but I strongly protest against being taken from my cell and carried to the penitentiary as a felon. Therefore, in the name of the people, whose liberty is being destroyed; in the name of peace and justice, I protest against the consummation of this judicial murder, this proposed strangulation of freedom on American soil. I speak for myself, I know not what course others may pursue, but for myself I reject the petition for my imprisonment. I am innocent, and I say to you that under no circumstances will I accept a commutation to imprisonment. In the name of the American people I demand my right—my lawful, constitutional, natural, inalienable right to liberty. Respectfully yours,

"A. R. PARSONS, Prison Cell 29."

On receipt of the decision of the Federal Court not to interfere in the anarchists case, the doomed men were sullen. Louis Lingg, the bomb-maker, was blatant and defiant, and said to his attendants, "I will never die on the scaffold," he continued, "I hate and defy you all." A week before the execution Lingg said: "I approach my last moment cheerfully, but I will not go alone." This was significant language, and no doubt was an allusion to the fact that he intended to use the bombs, afterwards found in his cell for the purpose of producing an explosion in the jail that might have resulted in the death of scores of victims. Lingg, Engle, Fischer and Parsons refused absolutely and persistently to sign any petition to His Excellency, Governor Oglesby, for executive clemency in the commutation of their sentence to imprisonment. The following is a copy of letters from Lingg, Engle and Fischer to Governor Oglesby. They demand liberty or death:

COOK COUNTY JAIL, November 1.—An open letter to Mr. R. J. Oglesby, Governor of the State of Illinois.

Dear Sir: I am aware that petitions are being circulated and signed by the general public, asking you to commute the sentence of death which was inflicted upon me by a criminal court of this State. Anent the action of a sympathizing and well-meaning portion of the people, I solemnly declare that it has not my sanction. As a man of honor, as a man of conscience, and as a man of principle, I cannot accept mercy. I am *not guilty* of the charge in the indictment——of murder. *I am no murderer*, and cannot apologize for an action of *which I know I am innocent*. And should I ask "mercy" on account of my principles, which I honorably believe to be true and noble! *No!* I am no hypocrite, and have, therefore, no excuses to offer with regard to being an anarchist, because the experiences of the past eighteen months have only strengthened my convictions. The question is: *Am I responsible for the death of the policemen at the Haymarket?* and I say no, unless you assent that every abolitionist could have been responsible for the deeds of John Brown. Therefore I could not ask or accept "mercy" without lowering myself in my self-estimation. If I cannot obtain *justice* from the authorities and be restored to my family, then I prefer that the verdict should be carried out as it stands. Every informed person must, I should think, admit that this verdict is solely due to class hatred, prejudice, the inflaming of public opinion by the malicious newspaper fraternity, and a desire on the part of the privileged classes to check the progressive labor movement. The interested parties, of course, deny this, but it is nevertheless true, and I am sure that coming ages will look upon our trial, conviction, and execution as the people of the ninteenth century regard the barbarities of past generations—as the outcome of intolerance and prejudice against advanced ideas. History repeats itself. As the powers that be have at all times thought that they could stem the progressive tide by exterminating a few "kickers," so do the ruling classes of to-day imagine that they can put a stop to the movement of labor emancipation by hanging a few of its advocates. Progress in its victorious march has had to overcome many obstacles which seemed invincible, and many of its apostles have died the death of martyrs. The obstacles which bar the road to progress to-day seem to be invincible, too; but they will be overcome, nevertheless. At all times when the condition of society had become such, that a large portion of the people complained of the existing injustice, the ruling classes have denied the truth of these complaints, and have said that the discontent of the portion of the people in question was due only to the "pernicious influence" of "malicious agitators." To-day, again, some people assert that the "d——d agitators" are the cause of the immense dissatisfaction among the working people! Oh, you people who speak thus, *can* you not, or *will* you not, read the signs of the time? Do you not see that the clouds on the social firmament are thickening? Are you not, for instance, aware that the control of industry and the means of transportation, etc., is constantly concentrating in fewer hands; that the monopolists, i. e., the sharks among the capitalists, swallow the little ones among them; that "trusts," "pools," and other combinations are being formed in order to more thoroughly and systematically fleece the people; that under the present system the development of technic and machinery is from year to year throwing more workingmen on the wayside; that in some parts of this great and fertile land a majority of the farmers are obliged to mortgage their homes in order to satisfy the greed of monstrous corporations; that, in short, the rich are constantly growing richer, and the poor poorer? Yes? And do you not comprehend that all these evils find their origin in the present institution of society which allows one portion of the human race to build fortunes upon the misfortunes of others; to enslave their fellow men? Instead of trying to remedy these evils, and instead of ascertaining just what the cause of the widening dissatisfaction is, the ruling classes, through their mouth-pieces, press, pulpit, etc.—defame and misrepresent the character, teachings, and motives of the advocates of social reconstruction, and use the rifle and the club on them, and, if opportunity is favorable, send them to the gallows and prisons. Will this do any good? As an answer I may as well quote the following words with which Benjamin Franklin closed his satirical essay, "Rules for Reducing a Great Empire to a Small One,' which he dedicated to the English government in 1776. "Suppose all their (the 'kickers') complaints to be inverted, and promoted by a few factious demagogues, whom if you could catch and hang, all would be quiet. Catch and hang a few accordingly ; and the blood of the martyrs shall work miracles in favor of your purpose " (i. e., your own ruin).

So, I say, society may hang a number of disciples of progress who have disinterestedly served the cause of the sons of toil which is the cause of humanity, but their blood will work miracles in bringing about the downfall of modern society, and in hastening the birth of a new era of civilization. Magna est veritas et prevalebet! ADOLPH FISCHER.

A LETTER TO GOVERNOR OGLESBY.

Dear Sir—I, George Engel, citizen of the United States and of Chicago, and condemned to death, learn that thousands of citizens petition you as the highest executive officer of the State of Illinois, to commute my sentence from death to imprisonment. I protest emphatically against this on the following grounds : I am not aware of having violated any laws of this country. In my firm belief in the constitution which the founders of this republic bequeathed to this people and which remains unaltered, I have exercised the right of free speech, free press, free thought and free assemblage, as guaranteed by the constitution, and have criticised the existing condition of society, and succored my fellow-citizens with my advice, which I regard as the right of every honest citizen. The experience which I have had in this country, during the fifteen years that I have lived here, concerning the ballot and the administration of our public functionaries who have become totally corrupt, have eradicated my belief in the existence of equal rights of poor and rich, and the action of the public officers, police and militia have produced the firm belief in me that these conditions cannot last long. In accordance with this belief I have taught and advised. This I

have done in good faith of the rights which are guaranteed by
the constitution, and, not being conscious of my guilt, the "powers that be" may *murder* me, but they cannot *legally punish*
me. I protest against a commutation of my sentence and
demand either liberty or death. I renounce any kind of mercy.

Respectfully, GEORGE ENGEL.

AN OPEN LETTER.

To Mr. R. J. Oglesby, Governor of Illinois: Anent the
fact that the progressive and liberty-loving portion of the American people are endeavoring to prevail upon you to interpose
prerogative in my case, I feel impelled to declare, with my friend
and comrade Parsons, that I demand either liberty or death. If
you are really a servant of the people according to the constitution of the country, then you will, by virtue of your office
unconditionally release me.

Referring to the general and inalienable rights of men. I
have called upon the disinherited and oppressed masses to
oppose the force of their oppressors—exercised by armed
enforcement of infamous laws, enacted in the interest of capital
—with force, in order to attain a dignified and manly existence
by securing the full returns of their labor. This—and only
this—is the "crime" which was proved against me, notwithstanding the employment of perjured testimony on the part of
the State. And this crime is guaranteed not only as a right,
but as a duty, by the American constitution, the representative
of which you are supposed to be in the State of Illinois. But
if you are not the representative of the constitution, like the
great majority of officeholders, a mere tool of the monopolists
or a specific political clique, you will not encroach upon the

thrist for blood displayed by the executioner, because a mere mitigation of the verdict would be cowardice, and a proof that the ruling classes which you represent are themselves abashed at the monstrosity of my condemnation, and consequently, of their own violation of the most sacred rights of the people.

Your decision in that event will not only judge me, but also yourself and those whom you represent. Judge then!

Cook County Jail, 30, 10, '87. LOUIS LINNG.

P. S.—In order to be sure that this letter will come to your official notice, I will send you the original manuscript as a registered letter. L. L.

CHAPTER XII.

FIELDEN PENITENT. HIS LETTER TO THE GOVERNOR. SPIES' LAST LETTER TO HIS EXCELLENCY. WILLING TO DIE FOR HIS COMRADES.

FIELDEN SUES FOR MERCY.

Fielden's letter is as follows:

CHICAGO, Ill., Nov. 5, 1887.—*The Hon. Richard J. Oglesby, Governor State of Illinois*—SIR: I Samuel Fielden, a prisoner under sentence of death, and charged with complicity in the conspiracy to bring about the Haymarket massacre, pray your excellency for relief from the death sentence and respectfully beg your consideration of the following statement of facts:

"I was born in England in humble circumstances, and had little early education. For some years I devoted my life to religious work, being an authorized lay preacher in the Methodist denomination. I came to this country and settled in Chicago. At all times I was obedient to the law and conducted myself as a good citizen. I was a teamster and worked hard for my daily bread. My personal conduct and my domestic life were beyond reproach.

"Some three years or more ago I was deeply stirred by the condition of the working classes, and sought to do what I could for their betterment. I did this honestly, and with no sinister motive. I never sought any personal advantage out of the agitation in which I was engaged. I was gifted, as I was flattered and led to believe, with the faculty of stirring an audience with my words, and it was said that I was eloquent. I began delivering addresses to assemblages of the working classes, and spoke of their wrongs as I saw them. None of my speeches were prepared nor in any sense studied, and often they were born in an hour of intense excitement. It is true that I have said things in such heat that in calmer moments I should not have said. I made violent speeches. I suggested the use of force as a means for righting the wrongs which seemed to me to be apparent.

"I cannot admit that I used all of the words imputed to me by the State, nor can I pretend to remember the actual phrases I did utter. I am conscious, however, as I have said, that I was frequently aroused to a pitch of excitement which made me in a sense irresponsible. I was intoxicated with the applause of my hearers, and the more violent my language the more applause I received. My audience and myself mutually excited each other. I think, however, it is true that, for sensational or other purposes, words were put into my mouth and charged to me which I never uttered; but, whether this be true or not, I say now that I no longer believe it proper that any class of society should attempt to right its own wrongs by violence. I can now see that much that I said under excitement was unwise, and all this I regret. It is not true, however, that I ever consciously attempted to incite any man to the commission of crime. Although I do admit that I belonged to an organization which which was engaged at one time in preparing for a social revolution, I was not engaged in any conspiracy to manufacture or throw bombs. I never owned or carried a revolver in my life and did not fire one at the Haymarket. I had not the slightest idea that the meeting at the Haymarket would be other than a peaceable and orderly one, such as I had often addressed in this city, and was utterly astounded at its bloody outcome, and have always felt keenly the loss of life and suffering there occasioned.

"In view of these facts I respectfully submit that, while I confess with regret the use of extravagant and unjustifiable words, I am not a murderer. I never had any murderous intent, and I humbly pray relief from the murderer's doom. That these statements are true I do again solemnly affirm by every tie that I hold sacred, and I hope that your excellency will give a considerate hearing to the merits of my case, and also to those of my imprisoned companions who have been sentenced with me.

"I remain, very respectfully, S. FIELDEN."

The above letter to the Governor by Samuel Fielden was endorsed by Judge Gary and States Attorney Grinnell.

SPIES' LAST LETTER TO THE GOVERNOR.

"CHICAGO, Ill., Nov. 6.—*Gov. Oglesby, Springfield, Ill.*—SIR: The fact that some of us have appealed to you for justice—under the pardoning prerogative—while others have not, should not enter into consideration in the decision of our case. Some of my friends have asked you for an absolute pardon. They feel the injustice done them so intensely that they cannot conciliate the idea of a commutation of sentence with the consciousness of innocence. The others (among them myself), while possessed of the same feeling of indignation, can perhaps more calmly and dispassionately look upon the matter as it stands. They do not disregard the fact that through a systematic course of lying, perverting, distorting, inventing, slandering, the press has succeeded in creating a sentiment of bitterness and hatred among a great portion of the populace that one man, no matter how powerful, how courageous, and just he be, cannot possibly overcome. They hold that to overcome that sentiment or the influence thereof would almost be a physiological impossibility. Not wishing, therefore, to place your excellency in a still more embarrassing position between the blind fanaticism or a misinformed public on one hand and justice on the other they concluded to submit their case to you unconditionally.

WILLING TO DIE FOR HIS COMRADES.

I implore you not to let this difference of action have any weight with you in determining our fate. During our trial the desire of the prosecutor to slaughter me, and to let my co-defendants off with milder punishment was quite apparent and manifest. It seemed to me then, and a great many of others, that the persecutors would be satisfied with one life—namely, mine. Grinnell, in his argument, intimated this very plainly. I care not to protest my innocence of any crime, and of the one I am accused of in particular. I have done that and leave the rest to the judgment of history. But to you I wish to address myself now as the alleged arch-conspirator (leaving the fact

that I never have belonged to any kind of a conspiracy out of
the question altogether). If a sacrifice of life there must be,
will not my life suffice? The State's attorney of Cook county
asked for no more. Take this, then! Take my life! I offer it
to you so that you may satisfy the fury of a semi-barbaric mob,
and save that of my comrades. I know that every one of my
comrades is as willing to die, and perhaps more so than I am.
It is not for their sake that I make this offer, but in the name of
humanity and progress, in the interest of a peaceable—if possible—development of the social forces that are destined to lift
our race upon a higher and better plane of civilization In the
name of the traditions of our country I beg you to prevent a
seven-fold murder upon men whose only crime is that they are
idealists, that they long for a better future for all If legal
murder there must be, let one, let mine, suffice.

"A. SPIES."

CHAPTER XIII.

**LINGG SUICIDES. DR. BOLTON WITH THE PRISONERS. THEY DECLINE
SPIRITUAL COMFORT. THE LAST NIGHT OF THE DOOMED
MEN. PARSONS SINGS IN HIS CELL. TELE-
GRAMS FOR PARSONS. HIS
LAST LETTER.**

LINGG COMMITS SUICIDE.

His Excellency, the Governor of Illinois, took action in the
anarchists' case on November 10, commuting to imprisonment
for life the sentence of Samuel Fielden and Michael Schwab,
sending the death warrant of the remaining four to Sheriff Matson by his son, Robert Oglesby, who arrived early on the morn-

ing of the 11th of November. Prior to the Governor making known his decision, Louis Lingg anticipating what his fate would be, and in keeping with his threat, had by some process unknown to the keepers, secured a fulminating cap such as is used in exploding dynamite, which he coolly placed in his mouth, and igniting the fuse which protruded from his mouth a short distance, calmly awaited the end. A terrific report sounded in the jail about 9 o'clock on the morning of the day previous to the day set for the execution. The deputies hastened in the direction of the sound of the explosion and beheld clouds of bluish-white smoke curling out from between the bars of the door of Lingg's cell. On entering the cell Lingg was lying upon his face. On turning him over he presented a ghastly sight, the entire lower jaw was blown away, and the features mutilated beyond recognition, only the stump of his tongue was remaining, which fell back into the larynx and made respiration difficult. He died in great agony at 2:45 of the same day. He had eluded the disgrace of the hangman's noose and the ignominy of a public execution.

During the ensuing night the gallows was erected in the north corridor of the jail, and tested by heavy bags of sand to make sure that everything was in working order.

THE CONDEMNED MEN'S LAST NIGHT.

SPIES AND DR. BOLTON.

THE EX-EDITOR OF THE "ARBEITER ZEITUNG" REFUSES THE MINISTER'S SYMPATHY.

Not long after the death watch had been set the Rev. Dr. Bolton, pastor of the First Methodist Episcopal church, called

upon the prisoners. The reverend gentleman visited the whole four unfortunates, and his reception was almost the same in every case.

Spies received him quietly and with a smile. "I have called on you, Mr. Spies," said the clergyman, "to help you to prepare for the awful end which is now but a few short hours away."

Spies smiled again, but shook his head slowly. "There is no use praying for me," he said in a meloncholy tone; "I need them not; you should reserve your prayers for those who need them."

The two men then discussed matters of religion and social economy, and Spies waxed warm in his defense of the doctrines of socialism as it looked to him. The conversation was a long and somewhat rambling one, and finally Mr. Bolton arose, bade Spies adieu, and left him.

When he had gone the latter turned to the two deputies (Quirk and Josephson) who kept watch over him, and with a short laugh exclaimed: "Now, what can you do with men like that? One doesn't like to insult them, and yet one finds it hard to endure their unlooked-for attentions."

Spies then waxed talkative and aired his opinion freely to his death watch, Deputy John B. Hartke. Speaking of the anarchists' trial, he said that its conduct and the finding were without precedence in the history of this country.

"Why, don't you know," said he, "that when the jury brought in the verdict they were all so badly frightened that they trembled, and the judge himself, when he pronounced the sentence, shook like a leaf."

This, he said, looked bad.

"The anarchists had no reason to be afraid, but the judge and the jury had good reason to be afraid."

"I told him," said Deputy Hartke, "that I had heard that Fischer had signed a petition to the Governor asking for mercy, and added that I had heard he had done the same thing."

"That is not true," he responded. "I said in my letter to the Governor that if one was to be murdered, I was the one. That is the kind of a document I signed."

"I'll tell you," he continued, "in five or six years from now the people will see the error of hanging us, if they do not see it sooner."

With this Spies, who had been lying on his back with his hands above his head, removed them and turned on his side with his face to the wall.

The anarchist editor then lay down on the bed, and with his white face upturned, talked continuously with Deputy Hartke about mutual acquaintances and things and events of days gone by. He never referred to to-morrow, and seemed desirious of keeping the thoughts of his approaching execution as far as possible from his mind.

Engel grew a little more serious as the night wore on, and when he came to be more familiar with the death watch (Deputies Bombgarten and Hastige) he talked with them about the cause for which he was about to die. He protested his innocence over and over again, and told the story of the Haymarket riot, and all he knew of it.

The Rev. Mr. Bolton called on Engel as he did on the others, but with the same unsatisfactory result. The wretched Engel dwelt with bitter emphasis upon the fact that it was the informer Waller, who afterward swore his life away, that first informed him of the massacre. "I was drinking beer and playing cards with my neighbors when Waller called and taunted me with not being down in the Haymarket fight," said Engel, as a big lump seemed to rise in his throat," "and he afterward swore my life away, but I die for a just cause." Engel slept none until about 1 o'clock, but at that hour, just as the death watch was being removed, he turned round in his couch and dropped into a light slumber.

FISCHER AND PARSONS.

BOTH REFUSE SPIRITUAL COMFORT AND PARSONS SINGS "ANNIE LAURIE."

Fischer's last night was quietly spent. He talked but little, but was restless. His death watch, Deputies Healy and Shomberg, said though he did not sleep much, he appeared to take the terrible ordeal put upon him with great composure—almost indifference. He, too, coldly repulsed Dr. Bolton's proffered spiritual aid. Though his sleepless eyes stared vacantly at the wall of his cell, he talked but little. No sign of nervousness or fear could be traced on the hard, clear-cut features. He was evidently prepared to meet his fate unflinchingly and to die boldly. "Annie Laurie," sung in a fairly good tenor voice, broke the the silence. It was approaching 12 o'clock. A dread silence overhung all. All along the anarchists' corridor not a sound was to be heard. The absence of any noise might be likened to the stillness of the grave. Criminals were asleep. The indications were that the anarchists were asleep too.

But hardly so. Parsons was awake, and the spirit of his wakeful hours urged him to sing "Annie Laurie." Soldiers in a foreign clime have shed tears at the strains of this song. It is a passport to the emotions the world wide. And almost within the shadow of the gallows tree, when life was to be registered by hours, Parsons' striking up this song seemed certainly suggestive of the fate he felt to be close at hand. There was in his tone a lonesome melancholy as he sung the first stanza, then on the second one his voice wavered and finally broke. He was cast down. The memory of his wife and little ones seemed to rise before him, a sob, full of pathetic despair served as a period to his further recitation. Once stopped singing, Parsons was in tears. He cried within the quietness of his cell, not through fear of his approaching death, so far as his demeanor indicated. Rather it was due to recollection busy with scenes of the man's early life. His boyhood came back to him as he sung that old song. He could not do else than break down.

When Dr. Bolton called upon Parsons he was received with the same courtesy which has always distinguished that erudite anarchist. The condemned man, however, did not seem to take kindly to the proffered ministrations of the clergyman.

"You are welcome, Dr. Bolton," he said; "pray, what can I do for you?"

The reverend visitor explained his mission, and the old cynical expression stole over Parsons' face. "Preachers are all Pharisees," he sneered, "and you know what Jesus Christ's opinion of the Pharisees was. He called them a generation of vipers, and likened them to whited sepulchers. I don't desire to have anything to do with either."

Dr. Bolton remonstrated a little, and finally Parsons appeared to be relenting somewhat.

"Well, well," he said, "I will say that while I do not absolutely refuse your kind attentions, I will impress on you the fact that I did not want you."

A desultory conversation ensued, and the missionary, on leaving, told Parsons that he would pray earnestly for him during the night.

The anarchist's hard gray eye grew moist, and he murmered hoarsely: "Thank you," but added: "Don't forget, though, I didn't send for you."

SINGING THE MARSELLAISE.

PARSONS TALKS FREELY TO THE DEATH WATCH AND SINGS FOR THEM.

Parsons slept little but kept heart marvelously well. He chatted with the guards on the death watch and furnished them each with his autograph in this form:

"Cook County Jail,
"Cell No. 4.
"*A. R. Parsons.*
"Nov. 11, 1887."

With Bailiffs Rooney and Jones he calmly discussed the out look, touched without emotion upon his pending death, and dwelt with satisfaction upon his assurance of his wife's ability to maintain herself. When told by the guards that Spies was deeply affected by the parting with his wife and complained that of all the incidents of the unnerving time, it most deeply moved him; that Fischer, though reckless of himself, bemoaned the destitution of his young and feeble wife, Parsons feebly expressed his sympathy for his companions and rejoiced that he left behind a lion-hearted wife, and children too young to keenly feel bereavement. Then he commented upon social conditions both here and abroad.

"I will sing you a song," he said about 1 o'clock, "a song

born as a battle-cry in France, and now accepted as the hymn of revolution the world over."

In a low voice he then sang a paraphrased translation of "La Marsellaise," which the guards commended as both inspiring and well performed.

TELEGRAMS TO PARSONS.

A COUPLE OF CHEERING MISSIVES RECEIVED THIS MORNING.

Following are copies of the two dispatches received by A. R. Parsons a short time before his execution this morning:

"BOSTON, Nov. 11.—*Albert R. Parsons, Cook County Jail:* Not good-by, but hail brothers. From the gallows-trap the march will be taken up. I will listen for the beating of the drum.   JOSEPHINE TILTON."

"ST. LOUIS, MO., Nov. 11.—*Albert R. Parsons, Prisoner:* Glorious martyr, in the name of social progress bravely meet your fate.   C. R. DAVIS."

To the sender of the first telegram Parsons desired that his red-silk handkerchief be sent.

PARSONS LAST LETTER.

A COPY OF THE DOCUMENT SENT TO A NEW YORK PAPER.

NEW YORK, Nov. 12.—The letter which Parsons wrote yesterday morning was addressed to a resident of this city, and appears in the *Herald* to-day, as follows:

"COUNTY JAIL, Nov. 11, 8 o'clock a. m.—*My Dear Comrades:* The guard has just awakened me I have washed my face and drank a cup of coffee. The doctor asked me if I wanted stimulants. I said no. The dear boys, Engel, Fischer, and Spies, saluted me with firm voices. Please see Sheriff Matson and take charge of my papers and letters. Please have my book on "Anarchism: Its Philosophy and Scientific Basis," put into good shape. There are millions of Americans who will want to read it. Well, my dear old comrade, the hour draws near. Cæsar kept me awake till late last night with the noise, music of hammer and saw erecting his throne, my scaffold—refinement, civilization. Matson, the sheriff, tells me he refused to let Cæsar—the State—secrete my body, and he has just got my wife's address from me to send her my remains. Magnanimous Cæsar! Good-by. Hail the social revolution! Salutations to all. A. R. PARSONS.

CHAPTER XIV.

DISCRIPTION OF THE EXECUTION. THREATNING LETTERS. PITTYING JUSTICE. OUTRAGED LAW VINDICATED. MERCY TO THE GUILTY IS CRUELTY TO THE INNOCENT. THE UNCHANGED EVERLASTING WILL GIVE TO EACH MAN HIS RIGHT. ABUSE OF FREE SPEECH. THE MILLS OF GOD GRIND SLOW BUT EXCEEDING FINE. CAPTAIN BLACK AT THE ANARCHISTS' FUNERAL.

The following description of the execution is copied from the *Daily News:*

August Spies, Adolph Fischer, George Engle, and A. R. Parsons, the four anarchists who were tried a year ago, and found guilty of the murder of Mathias A. Degan in the Haymarket square on May 4, 1886, were to-day hanged in the Cook county jail and paid the penalty of their crime with their lives. The drop fell at 11:53 and the four men died with words of defiance and scorn upon their lips. Parsons' last word was actually strangled in his throat by the hangman's noose. Seldom, if ever, have four men died more gamely and defiantly than the four who were strangled to-day.

When the word passed around, about 11 o'clock, that the final hour had indeed arrived, men's faces grew pale and the hum of excitement passed through the crowd. They were quickly marshaled and marched down in a line to the gallows corridor.

At 10:55 fully two hundred and fifty newspaper men, local politicians, and others, among them the twelve jurors to view the bodies after execution, had passed through the dark passage under the gallows and began seating themselves. The bailiff said a few words to the journalists, begging them to make no rush when the drop fell, but to wait decently and in order.

Parsons was given a cup of coffee a few minutes before the march to the scaffold was begun.

The rattling of chairs, tables and benches continued for several minutes, but by 10:05 there began to fall a hush, and conversation among the crowd sank almost to a whisper. The bare, whitewashed walls formed a painful contrast with the dark-brown gallows, with its four noosed ropes hanging ominously near the floor.

It was exactly 11:50 o'clock when Chief Bailiff Cahill entered the corridor and stood beneath the gallows. He requested in solemn tones that the gentlemen present would remove their hats. Instantly every head was bared. Then the tramp, tramp of many footsteps was heard resounding from the central corridor, and the crowd in front of the gallows knew that the condemned men had begun the march of death. The slow, steady march sounded nearer and nearer. The anarchists were within

a few feet of the scaffold. There was a pause. The condemned men were about to mount the stairway leading to the last platform from which they would ever speak. Step by step, steadily they mounted the stairway, and again there was another slight pause. Every eye was bent upon the metallic angle around which the four wretched victims were expected to make their appearance. A moment later their curiosity was rewarded. With steady, unfaltering step a white-robed figure stepped out from behind the protecting metallic screen and stood upon the drop. It was August Spies. It was evident that his hands were firmly bound behind him underneath his snowy shroud.

He walked with a firm, almost stately tread across the platform and took his stand under the left-hand noose at the corner of the scaffold farthest from the side at which he had entered. Very pale was the expressive face, and a solemn, far-away light shone in his blue eyes. His tawny hair was brushed back in the usual crisp waves from the big white forehead. Nothing could be imagined more melancholy, and at the same time dignified, than the expression which sat upon the face of August Spies at that moment. The chin was covered with a freshly budding beard and partially concealed the expression of the firmly-cut mouth. The lines were a little hardly drawn around the corners, however, and bespoke great internal tension. He stood directly behind the still noose, which reached down almost to his breast, and, having first cast a momentary glance upward at the rope, let his eyes fall upon the 200 faces that were upturned toward him. Never a muscle did he move, however; no sign of flinching or fear could be discerned in the white face—white almost as the shroud which it surmounted.

Spies had scarcely taken his place when he was followed by

Fischer. He, too, was clad in a long white shroud that was gathered in at the ankles. His tall figure towered several inches over that of Spies, and as he stationed himself behind his particular noose his face was very pale, but a faint smile rested upon his lips. Like Spies, the white robe set off to advantage the rather pleasing features of Fischer, and as the man stood there waiting for his last moment his pale face was as calm as if he were asleep, Next came George Engel. There was a ruddy glow upon the rugged countenance of the old anarchist, and when he ranged himself alongside Fischer he raised himself to his full height, while his burly form seemed to expand with the feelings that were within him. Last came Parsons. His face looked actually handsome, though it was very pale. When he stepped upon the gallows he turned partially sideways to the dangling noose and regarded it with a fixed, stony gaze—one of mingled surprise and curiosity. Then he straightened himself under the fourth noose, and, as he did so, he turned his big gray eyes upon the crowd below with such a look of awful reproach and sadness as could not fail to strike the innermost chord of the hardest heart there. It was a look never to be forgotten. There was an expression almost of inspiration on the white, calm face, and the great, stony eyes seemed to burn into men's hearts and ask: "What have I done?"

There they stood upon the scaffold, four white robed figures, with set, stoical faces, to which it would seem no influence could bring a tremor of fear.

And now a bailiff approaches, and, seizing Parsons' robe, passed a leathern strap around his ankles. In a moment they were closely pinioned together. Engel's legs were next strapped together, and when the official approached Fischer, the latter straightened up his tall figure to its full height and placed his ankles close together to facilitate the operation. Spies was the last, but he was the first around whose neck the fatal cord was placed. One of the attendant bailiffs seized the noose in front of Spies and passed it deftly over the doomed man's head. It caught over his right ear, but Spies, with a shake of his head, cast it down around his neck, and then the bailiff tightened it till it touched the warm flesh, and carefully placed the noose beneath the left ear.

When the officer approached Fischer threw back his head and bared his long, muscular throat by the movement.

Fischer's neck was very long and the noose nestled snugly around it. When it was tightened around his windpipe Fischer turned around to Spies and laughingly whispered something in Spies' ear. But the latter either did not hear him or else was too much occupied with other thoughts to pay attention. Engel smiled down at the crowd, and then turning to Deputy Peters, who guarded him, he smiled gratefully toward him and whispered something to the officer that seemed to affect him. It looked at first as if Engel were about to salute his guard with a kiss, but he evidently satisfied himself with some word of peace. Parson's face never moved as the noose dropped over his head, but the same terrible, fixed look was on his face.

And now people were expecting that the speeches for which the four doomed ones craved twenty minutes each this morning would be delivered, but to every one's surprise the officer who had adjusted the noose proceeded to fit on the white cap without delay. It was first placed on Spies' head, completely hiding his head and face. Just before the cap was pulled over Fischer's head Deputy Spears turned his eyes up to meet those of the tall young anarchist. Fischer smiled down on his guard just as pleasantly as Engel did on his, and he seemed to be whispering some words of forgiveness, but it may have been otherwise, as not even the faintest echo reached the men in the corridor below. Engel and Parsons soon donned their white caps after this, and now the four men stood upon the scaffold clad from top to toe in pure white.

All was ready now for the signal to let the drop fall. In the little box at the back of the stage and fastened to the wall the invisible executioner stood with axe poised, ready to cut the cord that held them between earth and heaven. The men had not noticed this but they knew the end was near.

For an instant there was a dead silence, and then a mournful solemn voice sounded from behind the first right-hand mask, and cut the air like a wail of sorrow and warning. Spies was speaking from behind his shroud.

The words seemed to drop into the cold, silent air like pellets of fire. Here is what he said: "It is not meet that I should speak here, where my silence is more terrible than my utterances."

Then a deeper, stronger voice came out with a muffled, mysterious cadence from behind the white pall that hid the face of Fischer. He only spoke eight words: "This is the happiest moment of my life."

But the next voice that catches up the refrain is a different one. It is firm, but the melancholy wail was not in it. It was harsh, loud, exultant. Engel was cheering for anarchy. "Hurrah for anarchy! Hurrah!" were the last words and the last cheer of George Engel.

But now the weird and ghastly scene was brought to a

climax. Parsons alone remained to speak. Out from behind his mask his voice sounded more sad, and there was a more dreary, reproachful tone in it than even in Spies. "May I be allowed to speak? Oh, men of America!" he cried, "may I be allowed the privilege of speech even at the last moment? HARKEN TO THE VOICE OF THE PEOPLE——"

There was a sudden pause. Parsons never spoke a word more. A sharp, creaking noise, a crash, a sickening, cracking sound, and Spies, Parsons, Fischer, and Engel were no more.

When the pulse-beats of all became imperceptible, which was about 12:10 o'clock, the physicians sat down and the bodies swung back and forth, while the deputies stood above them. There was a continual shifting of seats after the physicians left the bodies, and nearly all who could get away wanted to be allowed to do so. The sheriff opened a door at the west side of the building and a great many of the spectators left.

At 12:20 Spies' body was let down and placed in a coffin, while the doctor examined him and found that the neck was not broken. He wore a dark-gray flannel shirt and dark pantaloons, but no coat. His arms were confined by a strap, as were those of all the others.

Fischer was next cut down. His neck was not broken. He wore a blue flannel shirt and gray trousers.

Engel came next. He had a blue flannel shirt and wore a collar. His neck was broken, but the spinal cord was not severed.

Parsons was the last to be taken down. He was clad in a neat black suit, but had only an undershirt on.

When all the bodies had been arranged in the coffins the physicians made another examination, and then the lids were placed on the coffins, and the work was done.

The condemned men directed that their bodies be turned over to their wives, except Spies, who wanted his body given to his mother. Their wishes were respected, and Coroner Hertz has directed that the body of Lingg be given to Mrs. Engel and the Carpenters' Union, in accordance with Lingg's request, so that they may all be buried together.

Since the conviction and condemnation of the anarchists of Haymarket notoriety in 1886, the whole world has stood with breathless anxiety watching for the ultimate, and no other avenue was left open but to inflict the penalty commensurate with their crime. Officers of the law frequently received letters threatning to wreak a summary vengeance upon them providing the sentence was carried out. The condemned maintained a bold and belligerent attitude, while every means to intimidate and thwart justice which the machinations of the nefarious Herr Most could devise, and his minions could hurl life flaming brands broadcast amid a peace-loving and contented people have been resorted to. But pitying justice wept with drooping head o'er the stern necessity which called for the interposition of her iron hand having discarded the scepter for the rod. When the hand of outraged law and justice is raised the blow must fall in order to vindicate the majesty of the law. America has set the foot of the Goddess of Liberty upon the neck of anarchy and crushed the serpent brood.

AFTER THE EXECUTION.

Two hours after the terrible and disagreeable duty of Sheriff Matson had been performed, in the name, and for the peace of the State of Illinois, in the execution of the four condemned anarchists, their bodies had been delivered to their friends, the gallows had been taken down and stowed in its accustomed place, and not one vestige of the awful punishment which had just been inflicted remained to tell that anything out of the ordinary had transpired.

Every good citizen and right-thinking American will join with me in extending to their afflicted widows and orphan children sincere and heart-felt commiseration for the calamity which has befallen them. While the law inflicts punishment for its violation, it does it for the public good. Mercy was not to be considered longer in their case. "Mercy to the guilty is cruelty to the innocent." The great book of law is prefaced with these words. Justice is the unchanged everlasting will to give each man his right. The right to free speech had been accorded to these men, and it had been abused. Under the diabolical teachings of Herr Most, anarchy promised soon to become the ruling power. But they have, we trust, ascertained that America is a poor and barren soil in which to cause anarchy to grow and flourish. They have found that though the mills of God grind slow, yet they grind exceeding fine.

We shall forever be surprised beyond expression at the words made use of at the funeral of the anarchists on Sunday, November 13, by Captain Black, in his oration over the bodies of these outlaws. He was said to have used the following words:

"For the love of truth they died," said the orator. "They fought for a cause, believing themselves in the right, and in the years to come they will be loved and revered."

Captain Black was followed by other speakers who made use of language very expressive and forcible.

T. J. Morgan followed with a speech in which he dwelt on the last words of the men before the drop fell. The immense throng at the grave became excited and frequently interrupted him.

"Let the voice of the people be heard," he cried, in Parson's last words. When he spoke of the majesty of the law a voice cried: "Throttle the law!" When he asked: "Shall we be revenged on Bonfield, Grinnell, Gary, and Oglesby?" voices cried: "Yes, yes! Hang them!" Albert Currlin, formerly of the *Arbeiter Zeitung*, spoke in German and called the laboring men cowards for permitting the "five-fold murder."

CHAPTER XV.

A DESCRIPTION OF HERR MOST'S SANCTUM. A DEN WHERE ANARCHY WAS BEGOTTEN. THE ANARCHIST CHIEF'S MUSEUM OF WEAPONS AND INFERNAL MACHINES. EASY LESSONS IN THE ART OF ASSASSINATION.

NEW YORK, Nov. 4, 1887.

Since Johann Most's release I had often resolved to visit his editorial sanctum and see some of his surroundings, but I never had the opportunity until a few days ago, when I sought William street and paused a moment before 167. This is the place where undiluted anarchy presents itself through the medium of the Freiheit, which has succeeded so well that it has been enlarged to double its former size. On the ground floor a lager-beer saloon is doing a thriving business, and the old saying that Teutonic journalism always manifests an inclination to take up its abode in proximity to a place where honors are paid to King Gambrinus is borne out in this instance, even when the journalists wage war on all other monarchs.

Entering the hallway you will notice, as soon as your eyes

are able to penetrate the darkness, a large red banner on the wall bearing the inscription, "Vive la Commune." A cast-iron letter-box, marked "John Most," attracts one's attention for a moment, and then we ascend two flights of narrow, creaky stairs, and step into a large, dilapidated room, extending over the entire top floor of the building. Here the *Freiheit* is written, put into type, and, after being printed elsewhere, mailed to subscribers. There is hardly a country on the globe which has not the honor of giving shelter to some anarchist subscriber. A perfect deluge of revolutionary pamphlets issues from this forlorn-looking loft.

About a dozen men were engaged in folding and wrapping the latest number of the *Freiheit*. In order to keep up their spirits at this hard work a goodly quantity of the favorite German beverage is consumed, cigars and short pipes emit big clouds of smoke, and a noisy debate is carried on all the time. Every one of these savage-looking specimens of humanity strives to assume an air that suggests his merely waiting for a favorable opportunity to slaughter all monarchs and capitalists on the face of the earth. There are Germans, Frenchmen, Russians, Bohemians, and a Dane in the group. Regular employment is a notion too conservative and utterly foreign to their minds. They are here folding papers to serve the revolutionary cause, and receive no other recompense than the consciousness of having performed their duty.

OVERAWING THE VISITORS.

One of the heroes, who evidently desires to overawe us, takes a small quantity of gun cotton out of his pocket, another produces a sample of dynamite, and each asserts that the stuff he carries is an excellent agent to further the grand idea of universal anarchy. All join in a dispute concerning the most effective methods for blowing up public institutions, and the folding business is meanwhile neglected. The anarchist chief, Herr Most, has been conversing with a good-looking young female anarchist, who came over for the purpose of paying her respects to the great dynamiter; but now his attention is directed to his hot-headed disciples.

"Get through your work," he shouts; "you may babble all you want afterward."

The admonition is heeded only for a few moments. The folders have a theme demanding urgent action. The sentence of the Chicago anarchists has excited the wrath and of every anarchist and frenzied cries of threatened vengeance burst forth from all sides. Herr Most again commands silence, and his announcement that a mass-meeting would be held on Sunday, at which both English and German speakers would be present, is hailed with tumultuous applause. The presence of strangers seems to be totally ignored for the moment. The anarchists fully understand that they are at liberty here to run the revolu tionary machine at their own sweet pleasure, so long as the struggle is confined to the tongue. I conclude to invest 5 cents, and a copy of the *Freiheit* is handed to me. The editor reflects upon the propriety of a national thanksgiving. His language is not choice, but rather painfully harsh. Here is a goodly specimen:

"Our army of the unemployed, probably, will give thanks that the capitalists are so very prosperous. Poor, haggard women will give thanks over their weak tea and dry baker's bread that they have been allowed to lay up wealth for their employers. Factory children, who never see anything but the grim shop walls by daylight, will give thanks that they have been brought into this beautiful world, and hard-working day laborers lucky enough to have any kind of a job will give thanks that the cormorants of society have not taken the last mouthful away from them."

Another article deals with the anti-Chinese movement on the Pacific coast, and urges the white workingmen to expel every greedy monopolist instead of persecuting the poor celestial.

ANARCHISTIC LITERATURE AND WEAPONS.

Before I proceed to inspect the curiously decorated walls my attention is called to an assortment of anarchistic literature spread on a large table. The most extraordinary productions of fever-brained revolutionists from all countries are here exposed for sale. The works of Herr Most occupy the most conspicuous place, and titles like "Gottespect und Religionsenche," "Eigenthumsbestie," and "Elements of Revolutionary Warfare" embelish the title pages. I open the last book at haphazard and read:

"The best of all preparations to be used for poisoning is curari.

"By heating a dagger and then tempering it in oil of oleander, the infliction of a light wound would be sufficient to produce blood-poisoning and death.

"The cheapest and least expensive way is to apply a mixture of red phosphorus and gum arabicum to the dagger, cartridge, etc.

"This precious stuff (dynamite), which is able to blast a mass of solid rock, might also do good service at an assembly of royal or aristocratic personages, or at an entertainment patronized by monopolists."

Herr Most, who had eyed me sharply, asked at last: "Would you like to join our circle, or perhaps it is only a few of your private enemies you contemplate doing up? All necessary information can be had by studying my 'Kriegswissencraft.'" The hint was a broad one, and I thought it the safest plan to spend a dime on the "murder pamphlet," thus propitiating the tiger in his den.

The room might be considered at first glance an armory. There are revolvers of all constructions, daggers, rifles, infernal machines, and a big saber with a rusty scabbard. I could scarcely repress a laugh at this relic of the great French revolution, or some equally remote historic event.

"You make a mistake by laughing," said Most, unsheathing the sword. "You will observe the blade is as sharp as a razor, and," he added with a certain pride, "the point is, by way of experiment, coated with a solution of cyanide of potassium."

The majority of the rifles are breech-loaders, formerly used in the United States army, and bought by Most in large lots at auction for retailing among his followers. On a shelf above the editor's desk a variety of the most dangerous poisons, liquid and solid, are openly exposed. The anarchist chief remarked, with a grim smile, that he seriously contemplated breeding cholera and yellow-fever germs for the purpose of exterminating mankind, rather than suffer the present condition of society to perpetuate itself.

WALL DECORATIONS.

The walls of the room are almost totally covered with pictures, portraits, newspaper headings, etc. In crazy-quilt fashion is arranged Lieske, Shakspere, Hoedel, Rousseau, Karl Marx, Feurbach, Stuart Mill, Thomas Paine, Richard Wagner, Marat, Hans Sachs, St. Simon, LaSalle, Proudhon, Anton Kammerer, Stallmacher, the Irish patriots, Brady, Kelly, Curley, Tynan, Wilson, Gallagher, and Normann a life-size picture of Louise Michel, an excellent photograph of prince Krapotkine, pictures from Puck, Punch, Fleigende Blatter, sketches from George Eber's "Egypt"—a queer collection indeed.

Herr Most takes especial pride in a gibbet traced in red lines on the whitewashed wall and bearing portraits of the following persons: The emperors of Germany, Russia, and Austria, Queen Victoria, President Grevey, King Humbert, King Christian of Denmark and his premier, Estrup; the Shah of Persia; the Sultan, the Emperors of China, Japan, and Brazil, and President Cleveland. As an illustration of the bitter feeling prevailing between the anarchists and socialists was a caricature of Alexander Jonas, the socialist politician, playing a flute to the inspiring tune, "Wait Till the Clouds Roll By."

The German Chancellor, Prince Bismarck, is caricatured a dozen different ways, and blood-thirsty sentiments are written beneath the pictures. A large picture presents the famous Russ-conspirators against Alexander II.; another recalls the trial of Reinsdorf and comrades, charged with high treason; then follow some scenes from the Paris commune in 1871, and next to these sanguinary sketches an elegant fan is suspended, unconscious of its strange surroundings. Anarchistic papers from every quarter of the world are pasted from ceiling to floor, and we learn the existence of obscure journals like Ni Dieu, Ni Maitre, Fackel, Le Cri du Peuple, Alarm, Lucifer, Revolte, La

Question Sociale, the Roumelian periodical Revista Sociale, Il Fascio Operairo, Der Arme Teufel, and Proletaren. Italians who stray into this nest have an opportunity of studying a "Programma Socialista, Anarchico, Revoluzionario del Giuppo Italiano."

Perhaps the master of this queer den will soon view the world once more through prison bars.

COMYNS RAY.

CHAPTER XVI.

BIOGRAPHY OF HERR MOST. HIS PAST CAREER AND EARLY TRAINING. HIS IMPRISONMENT IN THE BASTILE AND RED TOWER FOR PREACHING HIS GOSPEL OF BLOOD. EXTRACTS FROM HIS INFLAMMATORY UTTERANCES. WHET YOUR DAGGERS. LET EVERY PRINCE FIND A BRUTUS BY HIS THRONE.

THE PAST CAREER OF HERR MOST.

That practice has now become obsolete of predicting the future of a child by consulting the aspect of the planet under which it was born at the day and hour of birth. At the advent of Herr Most upon this mundane sphere, who, looking through the horroscope of his future, but could in the interests of humanity, have wished that the feeble spark of life in the frail teniment might have become extinguished, or that it had never existed.

In the city of Augsburg on the River Lech, which is a tributary of the blue rolling Danube in Bavaria in Germany, in the year 1846, and on the 5th day of February Herr Most first saw the light of day. A long period of sickness while yet an infant served to render his features hideous by some malignant disease eating away a portion of his cheek, but his record goes to prove conclusively that he still retained enough to render himself obnoxious to every lover of law and order.

Endowed by nature with procivities to resist all rule and law, gained from an unloving stepmother much harsh treatment. He became apprenticed to a book-binder when a mere lad, and the cruel treatment received at the hands of his employer failed to change the bent of his inclinations. He had a passion for the stage which he gratified by striking an attitude and reciting in tragic style with dramatic effect any occurrence which attracted his attention to the infinite amusement of boys, and pedestrians on the street would stop to listen to his native eloquence and behold his crude dramatic gestures. We find him in Switzerland in 1867, endeavoring to establish anarchy with a zeal worthy of a better cause. We next find him in Vienna where in one of his scathing speeches he characterized Liberalism as a swindle; the priests as deceivers. For this speech he received a jail sentence of four weeks. Shortly after his release, he was again sentenced to five years' imprisonment for high treason. However, after having served six months of the term, through some ministerial change, he was released. A half an hour later he was again on the platform firing hot shot and shell into the ranks of the government with all the force of his burning invective. His ability to sway the masses alarmed the new government, and they took measures to have him banished. He went to Chemnitz where he became popular as an agitator, and successful in establishing his doctrine of anarchy as the gospel of blood, for which he was incarcerated temporarily in the red tower, a very unpopular jail. September 3, 1872, while returning from Mayence, where he had attended a socialistic congress, he was again arrested, and a few days later was sentenced to eight months in prison. In 1874, for some expressions used in favor of the commune of Paris, although a member of Parliament, he was given eighteen months in the German bastile. At the expiration of his sentence he became identified with the Berlin *Free Press*, and for his freedom of speech he was again sentenced to six months in jail, having served his sentence he crossed out of his native land to London where he took charge of the new journal, the *Freiheit*, and while occupying this position he received a pressing invitation to come to Chicago and take charge of the *Arbeiter Zeitung*, which he declined, believing as he did that the era of the mad misrule of anarchy was on the eve of being inaugurated. He visited Paris, and during his stay directed a speech full of burning hatred against the German Emperor, for which he was accorded two years in jail. On his release he hastened to put the channel between him and that hated country. In 1880 he was again in Switzerland, scattering the seeds of anarchy, and forging thunderbolts for his enemies, and many of his publications found their way throughout the length and breadth of Europe.

In one of his effusions he said.

"Science has put in our possession instruments with which beasts of society may be removed. Princes, ministers, statesmen, bishops, prelates and other officials, civil and clerical, journalists and lawyers, representatives of the aristocracy and middle classes, must have their heads broken."

When Alexander II. of Russia was murdered, "Triumph! triumph!" he wrote; "the monster has been executed," etc., and yet this "monster" (?) was the man who had struck the manacles from the feet of Russia's serfs; had lifted millions of a degraded people to citizenship. His outburst on this occasion gained him sixteen months in an English prison. In December of 1882 he was en route for New York, where he met with a most enthusiastic reception.

The anarchists have now eleven regular organs in circulation. Five of these appear in English, five in German, and one in the French language. A few extracts we herein embody will serve to demonstrate the savage nature of these agitators. He says:

"If each member of the anarchist party some fine morning would seek out some hated tyrant and pick a quarrel; if only each man would carry a private supply of some destructive agency in his pocket and would either stab, poison, or with powder, lead, or dynamite do to death our enemies, wherever found, in house, office, bureau, shop, or factory; if that could only be done in fifty places at the same moment; if fires could only be started in fifty different places at the same time; if only special parties detailed for the purpose would cut the telephone and telegraph wires—must not a general panic result? Would not society be wild with fright? And would not the rabble as if by magic be inflamed with revolutionary passion?"

Can anything be more diabolical? But Most's paper, from which I have quoted, is mild compared with the *Rebell*. This sheet is the organ of Peukert. At present both papers vie with each other in disseminating anarchism among the farming population. In 1884 Most said: "To find a way for getting $100,000,000 would do the cause more good than to dash the brains out of ten kings. Gold—money—is wanted.

"Lay hold where and when you can," he continues. "The

less noise you make in laying and carrying out your plans the less danger and the better success. The revolver is good in extreme cases, dynamite in great movements, but, generally speaking, the dagger and poison are the best means of propagation. Yes, tremble, ye canaille, ye bloodsuckers, ye ravishers maidens, murderers, and hangmen, the day of reckoning and revenge is near. The fight has begun along the picket line. A girdle of dynamite encircles the world, not only the *old* but the *new*. The bloody band of tyrants are dancing on the surface of a volcano. There is dynamite in England, France, Germany, Russia, Italy, Spain, New York, and Canada. It will be hot on the day of action, and yet the brood will shudder in the sight of death and gnash their teeth. Set fire to the houses, put poison in all kinds of food, put poisoned nails on the chairs occupied by our enemies, dig mines and fill them with explosives, whet your daggers, load your revolvers, cap them, fill bombs and have them ready. Hurl the priest from the altar; shoot him down! Let each prince find a Brutus by his throne."

The foregoing language is calculated to tend toward subversion of law and justice, and is revolutionary and treasonable in its nature, teachings of this nature from Reinsdorf and Most, are the direct cause of our Haymarket massacre. The authorities are responsible largely for the commission of crime which they may prevent even by resorting to extreme measures in enforcing the law. While we desire peace in all our borders, yet we believe that transgressors of the law should be made to feel that "God reigns, and the government at Washington still lives."

CHAPTER XVII.

BIOGRAPHIES OF SPIES AND THE OTHER SEVEN CONDEMNED MEN. THEIR BIRTHPLACE, EDUCATION AND PRIVATE LIFE. PARSONS' LETTER TO THE "DAILY NEWS" AFTER THE EXPLOSION, WHILE A FUGITIVE FROM JUSTICE.

AUGUST SPIES.

August Vincent Theodore Spies was born in Landeck, Hesse in 1855. His father was a ranger. Spies came to America in 1872, and to Chicago in 1873, where for a number of years he worked as an upholsterer. He first became interested in socialistic theories in 1875, and two years later joined the socialistic labor party, and the Lehr und Wehr verein. He became connected with the *Arbeiter Zeitung* in 1880. He succeeded Paul Grottkau as editor-in-chief in 1884. From that time onward he was looked up to as one of the ablest and most influential anarchist leaders. He was educated by a private tutor during his early boyhood days. He afterward studied at a Polytechnic institute.

ALBERT PARSONS.

Albert R. Parsons was born in Montgomery, Ala., in 1848. His parents died when he was young, and his rearing fell to the lot of his elder brother, W. R. Parsons, who was a general in the Confederate army. In 1855 he removed to Johnson county, Texas, taking Albert with him. The latter received some schooling at Waco, and subsequently became a printer on the Galveston *News*. When the war broke out he ran away from home and became a "powder monkey" in a company of confederate artillery. Subsequently he served successively under the command of his brothers, Richard and William H. Parsons. After the war he edited the *Spectator*, a weekly paper, at Waco. Much to the disgust of his brothers, he became a Republican, and something of a politician. As such he held one or two subordinate federal offices at Austin, and at one time was secretary of the State Senate. Coming to Chicago he worked for a time in various printing offices, and then became a professional labor agitator. He was at one time Master Workman of District Assembly 24, Knights of Labor, and president of the Trades Assembly for three years. In 1879 he was nominated by the Socialistic Labor party as a candidate for their President of the United States, but declined, as he was not then thirty-five years old. In 1883, at Pittsburg, he helped to frame the platform of the International Working People's Association. He was put forward by the socialists as a candidate for city clerk in 1883. He became editor of the *Alarm*, the organ of the "American group" of anarchists in Chicago in 1884, which position he held up to the time of the Haymarket riot in May 1886, but on the morning following the explosion, A. R. Parsons was not found in his accustomed place as editor of the *Alarm*. He had decamped, but many believed he was hiding in Chicago, as on the evening of the 7th of May a letter posted in Chicago at 7:30 was received by the editor of the *Daily News*, which ran thus:

'*Mr. M. E. Stone, Editor Daily News:*

"DEAR SIR—I want to speak a word through you to my fellow-workers, just to let them know that I am still in the land of the living and looking out for their interests.

"And further, give a few hints to some of the fellows who desire to live on anarchists, that may be for their welfare. In the first place, I am watching the papers and also the knowing chaps who give the pointers as to my whereabouts, some of whom will make good subjects for the coroner's inquest one of these days should they persist in their present course. To the public I desire to say that the devil is never so black as you can paint him. I will in due time turn up and answer for myself for anything I may have said or done. I have no regrets for past conduct and no pledges for the future if there is to be nothing but blood and death for the toilers of America. Whenever the public decide to use reason and justice in dealing with the producing class, just at that time will you see me. But, should the decision be to continue the present course of death and slavery just so long will I wage relentless war on all organized force, and all endeavor to find me will be fruitless. Watching my wife and her kind friends is of no use. I am dead to them already. I count my life already sacrificed for daring to stand between tyrants and slaves.

"To show you how well I am kept posted, I know who was sent to LaGrange for me to-day. I was not there. I know who put you on the track of Glasgow, and just where to find him. Just say to that man for me that his day of reckoning will come soon. I read all the papers to-day, and will see the *Times*, *Inter-Ocean*, and Hesing later.

"Now, as to what must be done to satisfy the anarchists is to stop all these demands for blood and show a spirit of reason and a disposition to put down the oppressors of the people, and enforce laws against rich thieves as readily as you do against the poor. Grant every fair demand of labor. Give those poor creatures enough to satisfy their hunger, and I will guarantee a quiet period in which all the great questions of land and wages, and rights can be put in operation without further bloodshed. But if not, I am already sacrificed as a martyr for the cause. I have thousands of brethren who will sell their lives just as dearly as I will mine, and at just as great cost to our enemies.

"I shall wait as long as I think necessary for the public to take warning, and then you decide your own fate.

"It must be LIBERTY for the people or DEATH for CAPITALISTS. I am not choosing more. It is your choice and your last. I love humanity, and therefore die for it. No one can do more. Every drop of my blood shall count an avenger, and woe to America when these are in arms.

"I have not slept, nor shall I sleep until I sleep the sleep of death, or my fellow-men are on the road to LIBERTY.

"A. R. PARSONS."

SAMUEL FIELDEN.

Samuel Fielden was born in Todmorden, Lancashire, England, in 1847, and spent thirteen years of his boyhood working in a cotton mill. In early manhood he became a Methodist minister and Sunday-school superintendent in his native place. In 1868 he came to New York, worked for a few months in a cotton mill, and in the following year came to Chicago. For the greater portion of the time since he has worked as a laborer. He joined the liberal league in 1880, where he met Spies and Parsons. He became a socialist in 1883, and has spent much time as a traveling agitator of the International Working People's association.

We feel sure that Samuel Fielden is to-day serving out a life sentence as the result of forming associations through which he was led to mingle with agitators anarchistic, whose teachings were treasonable. Though not endowed by nature with proclivities whose tendencies were toward violence and bloodshed, yet being full of vanity and of a vacillating nature was led to make speeches of an incendiary and revolutionary character which indentified him with those responsible for the result of the fatal bomb, and doomed him to a life of unrequited toil and of penal servitude.

ADOLPH FISCHER.

Adolph Fischer, who was about thirty years old, came to this country from Germany when a boy, and learned the printer's trade with his brother, who was editor of a German weekly at Nashville, Tenn. For several years Fischer was editor and proprietor of the Little Rock (Ark.) *Staats Zeitung*. This he sold in 1881, after which he worked at his trade in St. Louis and Chicago. After coming to Chicago he became a most rabid anarchist, and often accused Spies and Schwab of being half-hearted, and of not having the courage to express their convictions. He, like Engel, believed they were not radical enough. At one time he, with Engel and Fehling, started *De Anarchist*, a fire-eating weekly, designed to supplant the *Arbeiter Zeitung*.

He entered with all his possible energy into the spirit of socialism and anarchy, so much so, that it became his only theme and the source of happiness to him which he fully expressed in his last words upon the gallows, viz: "This is the happiest moment of my life." If that were the case, what an unendurable life were his, and the prospect of dissolution offered a rest from the self-inflicted torment of continuing to live.

GEORGE ENGEL.

George Engel was born in Cassel, Germany, in 1836. He received a common school education and learned the printer's trade. He came to America in 1873, and a year later to Chicago, where he became a convert to socialism, and later a rabid anarchist, He founded the famous "Northwest group" in 1883.

He spoke English very imperfectly, and with great difficulty, he manifested no desire to make progress in anything except in anarchy. The sinister expression of his countenance indicated a dogged stubborn and cruel nature, full of malice and hatred which led him to use this latest breath in a "hurrah for anarchy" upon the gallows. Such men behold nothing beautiful in nature, nor anything to admire in well organized society, under the mad misrule of anarchy controlled by such an element, society would soon lapse back to the days of primitive barbarism and superstition.

MICHAEL SCHWAB.

Michael Schwab was born near Mannheim, Germany, in 1853, and was educated in a convent. For several years he worked at the book-binding trade in various cities. He came to America in 1879.

He was a co-adjutor with August Spies in connection with the *Arbeiter Zeitung*. He was a pronounced socialist, though of a milder type than Spies, Parsons or Fischer. He was vacillating in his nature, and not calculated for a leader, but capable of being led. Had he chosen for his companions loyal and patriotic associates, he doubtless would have become a trusted citizen and a champion of American institutions instead of a propagator of anarchy which cost him the price of his liberty.

AUTOBIOGRAPHY.

Oscar W. Neebe was born in New York city on the 12th day of July in the year 1850. His parents were German, and in order to give their children an education in German they removed from New York to Germany when Oscar was but a child. His boyhood and school days were spent in Hesse Cassel. But at the age of fourteen years he returned to New York and as he expresses himself, was glad to set foot once more upon the land of the free, where all men were equal regardless of color or nationality, for the war had just closed which had stricken the chains and festering fetters from the limbs of the African slave, which meant the unbarring of the dungeon of the mind, giving them the right to acquire an education which before was denied them, and making them heir to the inalienable rights of citizenship. He says " I saw the sun-browned soldiers of the federal army returning from the South where they had fought for liberty and freedom, and learned to love them as brothers when I heard them say: 'There is now no more slavery.'"

Catching the inspiration of these words of Horace Greely: "Go West young man," he accordingly came to Chicago at the age of sixteen years, but returned to New York again where he learned the trade of tinsmith and cornice-maker. But New York, with all its fascinations, failed to constitute him contented and happy, and in February, 1877, we find him again in Chicago where he commenced work for the Adams and Westlake Manufacturing Company. He states that he was discharged July 1, for daring to champion the working man, and at times was reduced to poverty and almost starvation because of his avowed proclivities as an agitator.

He had become identified with the socialistic agitators in 1877, and the active part and interest manifested by him in the socialists was largely responsible for his lack of success in obtaining and holding a situation. In 1878 he obtained a situation as salesman for the Riversdale Distillery Company, selling their compressed yeast.

His financial embarrassment threw him largely among the agitators of the Labor party, and in 1886, after the Haymarket riot, he was arrested and tried for murder or for complicity in the conspiracy which led to the massacre for which he received a sentence of fifteen years in the penitentiary.

LOUIS LINGG

was only twenty-one years old, and was the youngest of the doomed anarchists. He was born in Baden, Germany, in 1864. He secured a common school education in Germany. He left his native country when very young and went to Switzerland where he remained several years. He came to America in 1885, working at the carpenter trade, at the same time availing himself of every opportunity for the development of his anarchistic proclivities, which seemed to be the heighth of his ambition. He wrote his autobiography after having received the death sentence, which we decline to publish in consequence of its rabid and treasonable type of anarchy, sufficient in itself to prove his complicity in the foul conspiracy. He was one of the most arch plotters of dark and tragic history.

JNO. BONFIELD.

CHAPTER XVIII.

BIOGRAPHICAL RECORD OF JOHN BONFIELD, INSPECTOR AND SECRETARY OF POLICE DEPARTMENT. BIOGRAPHIES OF SHERIFF MATSON, JUDGE GARY, JUDGE GRINELL. TRIBUTE TO CAPTAIN SCHAACK.

BIOGRAPHICAL RECORD

of John Bonfield, Esq., inspector and secretary of Police Department.

He was born in the year 1836, at Bathurst, New Brunswick. His father was a thriving farmer, but in order to give his children the advantages of superior facilities for education, removed to Buffalo, N. Y., in 1842, and in 1844 he came with his family to Chicago.

John Bonfield, after finishing his education, and by his natural talent and shrewdness having obtained a large stock of general knowledge from the ordinary pursuits of life in which he had engaged, became identified with the police force of Chicago in the year 1878 as patrolman. But he was destined to occupy a subordinate position for only a brief period, as in 1879 he was placed upon the staff of detectives.

His true nobility of character, noble bearing, and faithful discharge of his duties won for him the confidence of all, and in 1880 he gained one more step in the golden ladder of fame, being raised to the rank of lieutenant. He was next appointed captain of the Third precint, and in 1885 was made inspector of the entire police force.

Owing to the brave and gallant bearing of Inspector Bonfield in relation to the faithful discharge of his every duty during his past career, (thereby winning the confidence of superior officers relative to his ability,) he was entrusted with the entire command of the detachment who so bravely on the night of May 4, 1886, turned back the tide of anarchy which threatened to sweep like a tidal wave over the fairest heritage upon God's green earth, scattering death and debris all along its terrible track. Truly if brave deeds and noble acts, and honesty of purpose, coupled with patriotism are worthy of note, the name of John Bonfield and the brave officers under his command on that terrible night of the Haymarket massacre, shall live forever upon the brightest page of the historian.

CANUTE R. MATSON

was born in Norway in the year 1843. He emigrated with his parents to America in 1848, and settled in Walworth county, Wisconsin, but removed in a short time to Dane county, Wisconsin, where in 1858 he entered Albion Academy, and as a natural sequence of his insatiate thirst for knowledge he made rapid progress maintaining ever a prominent place at the head of his class. He was a student in Milton College at the opening of the war. The inherent patriotism of a noble nature had been fanned into a flame by the institutions of American freedom, and he at once offered himself as a sacrifice, if need be, in the defense of his adopted country, by enlisting in 1861 in the Union army as a private soldier in Company K, Thirteenth Wisconsin Infantry. In 1862 he was made commissary sergeant, He was raised to lieutenant of Company G., in 1864, and was acting regimental quartermaster at the close of the war in 1865,

C. R. MATSON.

and received his honorable discharge bearing the untarnished reputation of a brave soldier and a noble officer.

He afterward obtained a position in the postoffice where he published the *Postal Record*, an official paper of the department.

In 1868 he was elected clerk of the Police Court. In 1871 he was accorded the power to appoint, and also the supervision of the deputies. In 1875 he was appointed justice of the peace. In 1878 he was admitted to the bar. He ran for sheriff in 1879 and was only defeated by a very small majority in favor of his opponent. He served two years as coroner, being nominated by acclammation when he satisfied all parties of his intent, and ability to perform the duties of his office with credit to himself and honor to those by whose effort he had been placed in so responsible a position.

In 1882 he was again a candidate for the office of sheriff through the importunities of his friends, and was barely defeated by S. F. Hanchett, who in selecting a chief deputy made the wise choice of C. R. Matson, which position he filled to the close of the term, giving entire satisfaction to all parties with whom he came in contact in connection with the discharge of his official duties.

He has obtained all the honorable and responsible positions which he has filled solely upon his merits, and has retained them with the confidence of the public by the efficient and impartial manner in which he has served the people of Cook county.

He was installed in the office of sheriff of Cook county Dec. 6, 1886, enjoying still the confidence of the people. He is a man of great heart, broad and deep sympathies, yet unswerving in the administration of the law as a sacred obligation he owes to the public, and in the years to come history replete with the sayings and doings of the great men of to-day will shed a halo of glory forever upon the name of Canute R. Matson as a brave, true and noble man, and the most prominent Scandinavian leader of the era in which he lived, having left an example worthy of emulation by those who shall come after him.

JOSEPH E. GARY,

the presiding judge at the trial of the anarchists, was born at Potsdam, New York, July 9, 1821, at which place he received a common school education where he also spent his early boyhood days until 1843, when he went to St. Louis, Mo., and read law, opening his first law office at Springfield, Mo. But in 1849 he removed to Las Vegas, N. M., where he learned to write well and speak fluently the Spanish language. He removed to San Francisco, Cal., where he practiced his chosen profession until 1856, when he returned to Chicago and formed a co-partnership with Murray F. Tuley, now Judge Tuley of the bench. He finally became a law partner with E. and A. Van Buren, which continued until 1863, when he was elected to the bench. His judicial mind and clear comprehensive sense of right places him high among his compeers as a celebrity upon the technicalities of law. He is esteemed by all who know him.

JULIUS S. GRINNELL

was born at Massena, St. Lawrence county, New York, in 1842. He is of French-Welsh extraction, but it is not of his illustrious ancestors we wish to speak in this sketch. Suffice it to say that the Grinnell family are among the oldest and best families of the Eastern and New England States. Julius S. Grinnell graduated in the office of the Hon. William C. Brown in Ogdensburg, N.

Y., in 1868. He came to Chicago in 1870 where he commenced to struggle manfully toward the summit of fame. His eloquence and oratory, along with the comprehensive grasp of a most extraordinary mind has made his ascent rapid and sure. His high aims and lofty aspirations have in early life been rewarded. He can exclaim "Eureka," as at the age of forty-six years he has been elected to the bench.

CAPTAIN SCHAACK,

of the Fifth precinct is deserving of great credit, not merely for the assiduity with which he applied himself to the fatiguing duties of unraveling the mysteries of anarchy in secret organization, but also for the tact and shrewdness coupled with the fearless manner in which he discharged the dangerous duties incident to his office during the reign of terror which succeeded the Haymarket tragedy. It is a well known fact that Captain Schaack was one of the most energetic workers, as well as one of the principal factors in ferreting out and dragging to justice the dangerous element of socialism and anarchy in the great conspiracy. Chicago is indebted to Captain Schaack for a large majority of the evidence which resulted in the conviction, condemnation, and execution of these lawless men whose object and aim was to sow the seeds of discord and confusion in the refined and well-organized circles of society. The low-browed class of ignorant men who stood around their leaders and in discordant voices howled their praise, were, under this leadership capable of the wildest onset, or the dark and patient vigil, of him who treasures up in heart of hatred an imaginary wrong. Every step taken by Captain Schaack and his faithful band of tried men was full of dangers. Over fifty bombs had been made and distributed throughout the city. One had fallen with deadly effect, and any moment another might be expected to scatter death and debris among the ranks of faithful officers, who when detailed for service knew not but they were being led as sheep to the slaughter.

In the ages to come when as a record of history this anarchistic conspiracy of 1886 is referred to, the bold acts of noble daring, the skill, bravery and self-sacrificing spirit of Captain Schaack in the suppression of anarchy will be remembered by a grateful people as a monument to immortalize his name.

CHAPTER XIX.

EULOGY TO THE POLICE. BOLDLY THEY FOUGHT AND WELL. CONTRAST BETWEEN CAPITAL AND LABOR. THE ANARCHISTS' FATAL DELUSION. THE UNITED STATES NATIONAL ANTHEM.

EULOGIZING THE POLICE.

What peace-loving citizen of Chicago desiring her commercial prosperity and the perpetuity of American institutions, with all it means of home and protection for free-born American citizens to behold our starry banner still proudly floating from the citadel of the most free country upon God's green earth, but will with me thank God for the blessings of peace secured to us by the prompt and steady action of our brave and noble police on the night of May 4, 1886. When forgetful of their own personal safety in their devotion to the cause of liberty, over the prostrate forms of mangled and dying comrades they charged this treacherous band of alien outlaws, beating down the red hand of anarchy which was reaching out its tentacles to usurp the birthright of this nation bequeathed to it by our ancestors and made sacred to every loyal heart by a baptism of the blood of our sires and grandsires in 1776.

Not one ray of light from one single star upon our grand old flag shall ever tarnish its glory or dim its radiance in the shadow of the crimson flag of anarchy.

With reference to that terrible night who will not with me adopt the following language:

"When can their glory fade?"

It was to us a blood fought victory, and every officer who poured out his life on that eventful night is deserving of a monument in the hearts of a grateful people and a prominent place among the wreath-crowned martyrs in the cause of liberty. Chicago's entire force who respond so promptly to a call, discharging their duty so faithfully, are worthy the name of heroes as justly as those who have spilled rivers of blood upon the ensanguined field of Marathon or Waterloo.

What matters it now to Officer Degan and his slaughtered comrades that "boldly they fought and well." Their widowed wives and orphan children tell the price they paid for the blessings of peace we to-day enjoy.

The maimed and suffering officers we daily behold as the result of that direful night speak plainly of what it cost them in the protection of our blood-bought privileges of 1776.

Verily, a monument of marble should be erected to their memory upon the spot where they fell, bearing the names of that gallant band who so bravely turned back the incoming tide, whose black and seething waters threatened to wreck the foundations of our social, civil and national institutions.

CAPITAL AND LABOR.

Two young men from the same flourishing little town, and bosom friends graduate from the same school, each with aspirations lofty as the pinnacle of fame. Each one chooses an art or craft, or profession. Each man has the same chance to succeed. The avenues of trade and commerce are open alike to all. One of these young men well knowing that there is no royal road to wealth and fame, and that his success depends solely upon his economy and industry, wisely adopts a code of laws by which his life is to be regulated and governed, and his future of success or failure determined. He remembers that his preceptor once remarked to him thus: "Raymond, remember this: If you ever expect to become wealthy, spend each day less than you earn," and he had adopted it. He husbanded each week, and month, and year a portion of his earnings; years pass on and his coffers are filling with that yellow god which sways the destinies of men and empires. He engages in manufacturing enterprises or mercantile pursuits, and his happiness is complete in his palatial home, with a lovely wife and children as a keystone crowning the arch which spans the dark and turbid stream of life.

Let us follow the other young man who started in the race at the same time and under the same auspicious circumstances. He has taken a different course. He has not been idle but a spendthrift, working during the week earning money to spend among his boon companions during Sunday, and is always in debt and trouble as he is spending more than he earns. He has availed himself of the privilege of rejoicing in the days of his youth, walking in the ways of his heart and the sight of his eyes, forgetting that for all these things he will be brought into judgment, as no law of our physical nature or social standing can be violated with impunity, there is no appeal from the self-inflicted punishment of an accusing conscience for extreme prodigality and reckless expenditure in riotous living. To-night he is standing upon the corner of the street shivering under the biting blast which is sifting the early snow of winter amid his prematurely grizzled hair. He is not at peace with himself or the world. He hates himself for being poor and others for being rich. At this juncture the elegantly equipped carriage of his former classmate rolls past. Its owner is now a millionaire by earnest, honest and persevering endeavor. He is a homeless pauper and the self-constituted architect of his own misfortunes, yet he is willing to offer himself as a representative of the terrible contrast between capital and labor.

THE ANARCHIST'S FATAL DELUSION.

Under the fascination of rose-tinted delusion whose fatal mists obscure the mental and moral realm of thought, many become criminals, goaded on by blind infatuation which persevered in becomes a passion all-absorbing in its nature. In the blindness of their infatuation they seek to immortalize their names by a bold and base attempt at the subversion of law and order.

Having by the mad misrule of anarchy rendered themselves amenable to law, and by crime forfeited not only their liberty but their lives, they stubbornly refuse to ask for executive clemency, choosing death in the error of their ways, and in the language of Patrick Henry demanding unconditional "liberty or death." These anarchists under the delusion that they were becoming martyrs, courted death, and from the gallows raised a defiant shout for the perpetuity and progress of anarchy which they fondly hoped would go ringing down the corridors of time, increased by tributaries until anarchy as a mighty torrent should bear away law, order and civilization by the fury of its resistless force, until bombs, dynamite and treason should triumph. Under the sophistry and insidious teachings of the nefarious Herr Most, anarchy developed rapidly in Chicago, and his minions were willing to offer up wives and children, liberty, even life if necessary, in the interest of the cause they had espoused. They raised their voice publicly in denouncing imaginary wrongs and the plaudits of the admiring ignorant lower classes amounted to an inspiration to them which urged them on to openly advocate deeds of violence and blood. Herr Most has stated that the gibbet upon which these anarchist murderers paid the penalty for their crimes will in the ages to come be looked upon with the same veneration that the cross is by the Christian.

Now, that the majesty of the law has been maintained in their execution, their sympathizing followers seek to erect a monument to perpetuate their memory, the most fitting tablet over their grave should be, " Here lies anarchy in her shameful tomb." "Oh! Torquemada, from thy fiery jail," and thou "George Jeffries, from underneath the altar which seeks with Christian charity to hide thy hated bones," with the long line of hideous cruel monsters from the dead, come and compare thy deeds in contrast with thy lesser light and knowledge.

"Come seek thy equals here."

UNITED STATES NATIONAL ANTHEM.

BY W. R. WALLACE.

GOD of the Free! upon Thy breath
    Our Flag is for the Right unrolled,
As broad and brave as when its stars,
    First lit the hallowed time of old.

For Duty still its folds shall fly;
    For Honor still its glories burn,
Where Truth, Religion, Valor, guard
    The patriot's sword and martyr's urn.

No tyrant's impious step is ours;
    No lust of power on nations rolled;
Our Flag—for *friends*, a starry sky,
    For *traitors*, storm in every fold.

O thus we'll keep our Nation's life,
    Nor fear the bolt by despots hurled;
The blood of all the world is here,
    And they who strike us, strike the world.

God of the Free! our Nation bless
    In its strong manhood as its birth;
And make its life a star of hope
    For all the struggling of the Earth.

Then shout beside thine Oak, O North!
    O South! wave answer with thy palm;
And in our Union's heritage
    Together sing the Nation's Psalm!

THE END.

www.ingramcontent.com/pod-product-compliance
Lightning Source LLC
Chambersburg PA
CBHW030018240426
43672CB00007B/1002